Anyone with more money than needed for immediate survival feels the need to find the best, most value-adding investment opportunities for their wealth. Traditional options, such as handing money to a banker in the hopes of getting a return in the form of interest or dividends may, following mature introspection, not provide emotionally, intellectually, or socially satisfactory benefits. Ever larger numbers on a bank statement are just that—they do not contribute in any way to your sense of purpose or set an example for your children. Hoarding money to leave to your children can actually rob them of the opportunity and pleasure of succeeding in life by themselves. Beyond basic financial needs, people have physical, emotional, social, and spiritual needs that wealth cannot fulfill. To satisfy these needs requires a balanced and authentic life.

Anyone with some level of wealth or surplus income can engage in: 1) simple charity or community service; 2) philanthropy; 3) corporate social responsibility; 4) social enterprise. Any of these forms of engagement will create levels of value far beyond the monetary. They can provide satisfaction and happiness, allowing you to nurture something meaningful and sustainable in your sphere of influence. We all have the ability and freedom to choose to change the world, one well-chosen investment or social project at a time. Through our efforts and passion, we can have an impact by creating a serious ripple effect. Giving something meaningful of what you have adds value to your own life and makes you wealthier. The more you give, the wealthier you get and the more valued and valuable you are.

Doing well by doing something good can bring us a wealth of happy memories, gratitude, and a feeling of tantric wholeness, as we become holistically connected to those who may need a little (or a lot of) help to enjoy their lives more.

In this book, the writer draws on his own experience (rather than citing well-known names) to communicate ideas on a human scale and to emphasize that every effort counts. Any positive contribution will ultimately be appreciated, empowering us to improve the world around us. We just need to show up for life, start wherever we choose to, and do something meaningful for our world!

It was a pleasure to read your book. How much you have matured as both a thinker and writer! (As a businessman, you were always at the top!). Written with passion, wit and clarity, *Tantric Impact* is a deeply enriching meditation on money and meaning, a superb guide for the thinking businessman (and others) to what I would call practical spirituality. It should be required reading for all those who are fortunate to have money beyond immediate needs and want to make a difference. The book eminently succeeds in convincing the reader that doing good to others is doing good to yourself, that altruistic empathy and egotistic prudence are not in conflict but complementary to each other.

Sudhir Kakar: Author, psychoanalyst, professor at various universities, including INSEAD, Harvard, and the University of Berlin, acknowledged as one of the 50 greatest thinkers of our time

Only an author that has gone this deep to find the truth about life and business as Toine Knipping, and has his broad experience, can write a book like this. It is a well written work, intended to help in making the world a better place to live. It will help the reader think about fundamental questions that sometimes people either do not analyze at all or they do it in a very simple way. The reader can agree or disagree with its content, but one thing is sure: it is a book worth reading.

Francisco Soberón: Former CEO of Acemex, a Cuban shipping company, former President of the Banco Central de Cuba, Habana, author of various books on financial and shipping-related subjects, frequent public speaker

This book is a truly inspirational collection of advice and values that are in direct contradiction to those of greed, egoism, selfishness and the short-sighted view of the environment that some of our recently elected leaders are putting forth today. It seems to arrive at a crucial moment in history.

Knipping is an inveterate and very successful entrepreneur—a doer. Extremely well read and well-traveled, he calls upon an astonishing range of sources in support of his personally held values and truths of selflessness, generosity, and love and concern for his fellow man and the planet, as well as the animals that struggle to continue to roam the earth. In plain language, he puts his money where his mouth is and he talks the talk and walks the walk. His businesses do as well. He has spent decades involved in enterprises and projects that benefit those in need and fight for sustainability in the environment around them. Mr. Knipping recounts several interesting, formative, humorous, and dangerous episodes that have highlighted his exhilarating journey, in reality a quest.

This book is initially directed at the top 1 percenters, providing advice to those fortunate enough to have the financial resources to be able to effect change and leave a lasting positive impact for generations to come. However, everyone can be inspired by the book, and all who can should read it. We can all do something, no matter how insignificant it may seem, in the face of the dire predictions of the limited time our species has left on earth.

Jon Sheeser: Former banker, top executive at Perrier International, language professor and editor

This book is not only great reading but also an inciting mirror for the reader, as it reveals the origin of the DNA of the writer's many, diverse social responsibility initiatives and programs and shows the reader how every individual, in his own way, can contribute to the very same society that gave him the opportunities to become a person who is in the privileged position to reciprocate.

For those who feel the urge to contribute but lack the time or stamina to initiate their own program, there is always the fallback of donating to one of the writer's programs, which cover people, nature, and wildlife, or have the Amicorp Community Foundation organize and manage a program for them.

All these programs are very concrete, with a focus that every dollar donated supports the program, instead of going toward the costs of the infrastructure of professional organizations.

Floris van der Rhee: Veteran of the fiduciary business at Citco, Equity Trust, TMF, and Amicorp in the Netherlands and the Caribbean

The business of life is the acquisition of memories and at the end it is about the values and legacy that we leave behind that truly maketh man. In *Tantric*

Impact, Toine, an accomplished entrepreneur, humanitarian, and conservationist, once again challenges readers to look at their own personal values, to rethink what they want to leave behind and what is really important. An inspiring and easy reading book full of valuable insights for those who have been blessed with more than they need.

Rudi Viljoen: Life coach, CEO Warriors Academy, and Toltec training

Tantric Impact is different from any book you have ever read before. It makes you think about what you can do that really matters in life, and the different stories motivate you to do something about it. I think you fulfill the purpose of the book—at least I was more motivated than before to do something.

Are Kjensli: Member of the Lillehammer Olympics organizing committee, CEO NHO Logistikk og Transport

A book with a lot of dimensions; a moral appeal on our responsibility to make a difference in this world, and a guide with a lot of concrete and practical handles to do so. The book is also a spiritual consideration of the essence of life. A book with a lot of personal experiences written with passion, enthusiasm, and wisdom.

Hugo Hillenaar: Chief Public Prosecutor, Courts of Appeal, The Netherlands

I read the book twice over. Thanks for sharing and allowing another glimpse into the *Tat Tvam Asi* that you are.

Binu Joseph: Co-worker and Head of Talent Development, Amicorp Group

TANTRIC

IMPACT

Lessons on Promoting Fair and Sustainable Communities

Toine Knipping

BALBOA
PRESS
A DIVISION OF HAY HOUSE

Balboa Press books may be ordered through booksellers or by contacting:

Balboa Press
A Division of Hay House
1663 Liberty Drive
Bloomington, IN 47403
www.balboapress.com
1 (877) 407-4847

Because of the dynamic nature of the Internet, any web addresses or links contained in
this book may have changed since publication and may no longer be valid. The views
expressed in this work are solely those of the author and do not necessarily reflect the
views of the publisher, and the publisher hereby disclaims any responsibility for them.

The author of this book does not dispense medical advice or prescribe the use of any
technique as a form of treatment for physical, emotional, or medical problems without the
advice of a physician, either directly or indirectly. The intent of the author is only to offer
information of a general nature to help you in your quest for emotional and spiritual wellbeing. In the event you use any of the information in this book for yourself, which is your
constitutional right, the author and the publisher assume no responsibility for your actions.

Any people depicted in stock imagery provided by Getty Images are models,
and such images are being used for illustrative purposes only.
Certain stock imagery © Getty Images.

Categories: Impact investments, philosophy, spirituality, psychology, wealth
planning, inheritance planning, death and taxes, HNWI, asset management.

Scripture taken from the King James Version of the Bible.

Scripture quotations marked ASV are taken from American Standard Version (ASV)
Copyright © 1901 by Public Domain

Print information available on the last page.

ISBN: 978-1-5043-9849-7 (sc)
ISBN: 978-1-5043-9850-3 (hc)
ISBN: 978-1-5043-9891-6 (e)

Library of Congress Control Number: 2018902244

Balboa Press rev. date: 02/24/2018

Contents

Dedication

Dedicated to:

Frank Nathan Aldrich
Francisco Soberón Valdés
Charles Jacobs/Gede Aria Charles
Sudhir Kakar

Four great men on whose lives the sun is slowly setting. Four authentic men, merchants of meaning, whom I am privileged to know quite well—who showed up for life and lived it to the fullest, and who, by passionately living their values and convictions, are lighting the path for all of us.

The Bodhipathapradīpa of Atisha (980–1054 CE) makes reference to people of three capacities:

> *Man is to be known in three ways: as inferior, mediocre and excellent.*
> *He who by any means whatsoever provides for the pleasures of*
> *Samsāra*
> *For himself alone, is called an inferior man.*
> *He who turns his back to the pleasures of the world, and abstains*
> *from evil deeds,*
> *But provides only for his own peace, is called a mediocre man.*
> *He who seriously wants to dispel the misery of others,*
> *Because in the stream of his own being he has understood the nature*
> *of misery,*
> *Is an excellent man[1].*

---

[1]   The *Bodhipathapradīpa* of Atisha (980-1054 CE), quoted in Gampopa's (1079-1153 CE) Jewel Ornament of Liberation. Sgam-po-pa (author) Guenther, Herbert V. (trans) (1959, 1986). The Jewel Ornament of Liberation. Boston, Massachusetts, US: Shambhala Publications., Inc. ISBN 1-570-62614-6(pbk.)

The purpose of this book is to entertain you, the reader, and to make you think about subjects of importance to me that might prod you into action. It is not an autobiography or a historical account of projects that I have been involved in. They (and I) merely serve the purpose of illustration. Nor is this a "how to" book on multiplying your assets, or a money-raising instrument, as defined under the laws of any country. This book is about optimizing the value of your investments beyond the one-dimensional monetary realm, and creating something of multi-dimensional value and meaning for you and the people around you. Which assets, projects, dreams, or activities are really worth investing your time and money in?

Nothing that is written here should be mistaken for regulated professional investment or tax advice. I do not claim or aspire to be an investment advisor, an expert in tantric wisdom (I wish!), sustainable development (another wish…), psychology (more wishes), spirituality (etc.), or any other subject. For assistance in any of those fields, you are recommended to seek the services of an expert. I will consider my quest a success if I can convince some of the most lucky/ wealthy 1 percent of the world's inhabitants to use some of their money and influence for the benefit of those who are less well off.

Following the advice in this book will not necessarily imbue your life with meaning or make you happier, although it is the author's conviction that having a sense of purpose and contributing to someone else's happiness will automatically move you significantly closer to achieving both goals. The only person who can ever make you happy is still you! And you will be happy whenever and at the moment when you choose to be. Similarly, the only person who can create meaning in your life is you! Meaning cannot be bought or sold. It is created by each individual for personal use only. My task will be completed when I can challenge you to think about the true value and benefits of investments and the values that matter for life.

When Disney World in Orlando first opened in 1971, Walt Disney had already died. His widow, Lillian, was interviewed on opening day and the interviewer said, "Isn't it a pity that Walt Disney isn't here today to see his dream become reality?" Lillian answered, "Walt saw Disney World more than ten years ago, he just had to build it so that you could see it too."

And that is how it is. If you passionately believe in something and can vividly imagine it being done, it's already halfway there. You just need guts and grit to actually realize it.

The net proceeds from sales of this book will go towards protecting endangered species, especially rhinos, at Shared Universe Ventures.

Every effort has been made to ensure that the information presented here is as complete and accurate as possible, without any claim that this book is a scientific paper.

If you hold a printed version of this book in your hand, remember that trees have sacrificed their lives to help spread the message and advice contained herein. When you are finished, please share this book with a friend or recycle it sensibly.

Neither the publisher nor I accept any responsibility or liability to any person or entity with respect to any loss or damage caused or alleged to have been caused directly or indirectly by any of the information, or by following any of the advice, in this book.

If you do not wish to be bound by the above, you may return this book to me for a full refund.

Toine Knipping
t.knipping@amicorp.com

Acknowledgments

This book got off to a slow start, as the first two drafts ended up being stolen. It happened for no good reason—somehow this book was the only document on two successive laptops that were not backed up elsewhere. I must draw the self-serving conclusion that someone could not wait to read my work; they could not have been after the mere value of two second-hand laptops. The first laptop disappeared during an odd experience in Abuja, Nigeria, and the second one was stolen from my car in Curaçao, in the Caribbean.

I was invited to Abuja to speak at an annual seminar for some 3,000 chartered accountants. It was shortly before the presidential elections, and the theme of the seminar was ethics, corruption, and nepotism. The main opposition candidate (Muhammadu Buhari, who showed up during a forum discussion I was participating in to give a campaign speech) was running on an anti-corruption platform. The 3,000 chartered accountants reached the conclusion that accountants were the only genuinely ethical professionals in Nigeria. As this seminar took place at the height of the Ebola epidemic, each participant was given a tote bag containing a pair of plastic gloves; we were all supposed to put on the gloves before shaking hands, but I never saw anyone wearing them. As it turned out, mine was the only white face in the crowd—I guess foreigners scared of Ebola weren't flying to Nigeria at the time.

When it was my turn to speak, I moved over to the pulpit and made my presentation. When I returned to my chair behind the panel members' table, just 10 meters away, my laptop was gone. Big confusion! For sure, none of the 3,000 ethical chartered accountants could possibly have done this. The wide robes many of them were wearing could never have concealed a simple laptop. It was more likely that someone from a nearby slum had sneaked in from outside, made his way to the front of the hall, crawled invisibly onto the podium, and (unseen by anyone) made off with the laptop. A remarkable feat of stealth! As a consolation prize, I was invited to have dinner with the President. That evening, I donned my best suit and tie and went up to the Presidential Suite.

He introduced himself by saying, "Goodluck," as that was his first name. It sounded funny, and I could not help saying "thank you" before my name, but he had indeed been very lucky in life. Later that evening, I also met his wife; her name was Patience, and wasn't hard to figure out why. His take on poverty was:

We want to lead a country where people will be less greedy. Where people will know that the commonwealth of Nigeria belongs to all Nigerians, where people's wealth depends on the people around you. If you become a rich person and everyone around you is poor, you are very poor.[2]

Dinner turned out to be more informal than I had expected. It was basically just a bunch of guys hanging out on a couch, dressed in FC Barcelona soccer shirts and watching a game, eating chicken legs with their hands from Styrofoam plates. We had a five-minute conversation about whether I could help to structure a proposed business opportunity to make some of their supporters less poor (I couldn't), and then everyone concentrated on the Nigeria–South Africa soccer match, which, if I remember correctly, ended in a draw.

A while later, some scantily-clad ladies with friendly, but not necessarily decent, intentions joined the party, and I decided to sneak out. The next morning, I was presented with a brand-new laptop computer delivered to my room. I

---

[2]   Isha Sesay. "Transcript: CNN interviews Nigerian President Goodluck Jonathon". *CNN*, October 1, 2010.

gave it to charity, as I somehow did not trust it to be clean. I got myself a new laptop and started, under a new title, the third version of this book, which is the one you now have in your hands or on your electronic device.

I want to thank all of the people who contributed to the accumulation of these 100,000 words.

First, my friends and colleagues who, as first readers, read bits and pieces, making sure that my story accurately reflected the truth and had the right tone. These people include Andrew Rae, Are Kjensli, Bill Fisher, Binu Jose, Claudio Lema Pose, Claudio Luqui, Eduardo Balmaseda, Francisco Soberón, Floris van der Rhee, Ganesh Babu Subramanian, Henri Burgers, Hugo Hillenaar, James Hill, Jesper Nelleman, Jorge Carneiro, Kathy Byrne, Marci Vermeulen, María Gabriela Soto, Mignon Wortelboer, Mik Breek, Mimi Chong, Niranjan Satpathy, Peter Golovsky, Rucina Ballinger, Rudi Viljoen, Sue Meng Chan.

I would also like to thank all of the people who worked to improve my command of the English language: Jon Sheeser, of course, as he has done this now for over 25 years, and also Sally Simmons, the editor.

I am grateful to all of the following:

Sudhir and Katha Kakar for providing inspiration and much needed spiritual depth.

Manfred and Elisabet Kets de Vries for encouraging me and coming to visit me in Africa, and Manfred for graciously writing the foreword.

Kiran Kumar and Xander Arts, who have been my trusted friends in everything I've done for more than ten years.

Margaret Sankatsing and Snow Moreland for making all of the practical arrangements—as usual, with little noise and great efficiency.

My daughter Florence, for designing the cover.

And of course, my wife Paula, for being patient while I spent far too many hours staring at my screen or at the ceiling.

There are many stories of spiritual masters embracing the presence of an annoying student in their community. There are even stories about teachers paying an irritating person to live among their students. From an everyday perspective, this can be difficult to comprehend. We generally work hard to avoid the people and things we find annoying, but that prevents them from challenging us to be all that we can.

From a deeper spiritual perspective, it is much more impressive to remain centered and awake when we feel uncomfortable than in an environment where everything is to our liking. No matter how good we are at controlling our circumstances, there will always be many factors and people we cannot control. How we respond to what happens and how we learn from everything around us—from our experiences— determines the quality of our lives to a large degree. The goal of spiritual development is not to learn to control (or to live parasitically within) our environment—this is an ego-driven desire that becomes futile as we approach the end of life. Our internal reality is ours alone to formulate, to guard, and to express. By defining and expressing our beliefs clearly and steadfastly in every circumstance, we become authentic humans, able to express integrity and to give purpose and shape to our values!

As a final acknowledgment, I have found much inspiration in words that the great Indian poet, Rabindranath Tagore, wrote on the actual day of his death, which happened to coincide with his 80th birthday in 1941:

I'm lost in the middle of my birthday. I want my friends, their touch, with the earth's last love. I will take life's final offering. I will take the human's last blessing. Today my sack is empty. I have given completely whatever I had to give. In return if I receive anything—some love, some forgiveness—then I will take it with me when I step on the boat that crosses to the festival of the wordless end.[3]

[3]   Sigi, R. (2006), *Gurudev Rabindranath Tagore—A Biography*, Diamond Books (published 1 October 2006), ISBN 978-81-89182-90-8 Sigi 2006, p. 89.

Foreword

Henry Ford once said, "When everything seems to be going against you, remember that the airplane takes off against the wind, not with it.[4]" This statement could be a good metaphor for Toine's general *modus operandi*. From a young age, he learned how to overcome obstacles; and he also knows how to get things done. He is not someone who sits on his hands. On the contrary— many people may have ideas, but how many decide to do something about it? Aside from his action orientation, Toine is also a reflective practitioner, someone who knows how to balance action and reflection.

I first met Toine in 2009. He had enrolled as a participant in the top-executive seminar, "The Challenge of Leadership" (COL) that I run at INSEAD once a year. I often refer to this workshop, somewhat facetiously, as my "CEO recycling seminar," because this very introspective workshop encourages participants to reinvent themselves and acquire a more holistic attitude to life. I take on two roles in directing this seminar, that of management professor and psychoanalyst. Combining these roles, I try to make participants not only more effective but also more thoughtful executives.

Since senior executives generally do not have the patience to listen to lectures, I designed the program so that the main pedagogical vehicle is the life case study. As senior executives like talking (and are used to doing it), this approach gives them the maximum opportunity to discuss whatever problems they are struggling with. This design makes for a very "real-life," very pragmatic, workshop.

Toine was no exception in having a number of knotty problems to solve. And like many of the other executives in the program, he had quite a few issues on his plate. To start with, he felt that he should be in better physical shape. Many of his colleagues in the program tended to agree.

My first impression of him was that he looked quite stressed out. As time went on (learning more about his m.o.), I discovered that there were ample reasons for his feeling so exhausted. One of the most obvious was the way he

---

[4]   McLellan, Vern. (1988), *Shredded Wit*, p. 166

had organized his company, a design that forced him to criss-cross the globe excessively. Furthermore, Toine (who is a kind person) had a tendency to take over from people less capable than himself. The result was that he had become seriously overextended.

During the year that Toine was my student—encouraged by the other participants—he made a number of "New Year's resolutions." Ambitious as he is, he decided to take better care of his health, to simplify his business, to diversify his interests, and (if that was not enough) to write a book on entrepreneurship. Concerning this last project, he said, "[I] like to combine all the good things in life by helping people to plan their investments in a tax-efficient manner so they can enjoy good wine, good company, good conversations and exotic travel." Obviously, this statement hit very much home.

Toine is not a person who makes New Year's promises lightly. I am pleased to say that he kept his promises. From an "interest diversification" perspective, the vineyard in Argentina, of which Toine became one of the principal initiators, turned out to be a very special project. It became a way to create even greater bonding between the members of the COL class. Thanks to this initiative, a number of the members of the original class of 2009 (plus some newcomers) are now making a great wine on an 85-hectare property in the Uco Valley of Argentina in the Mendoza region, at the foot of the Andes Mountains. And to make the COL wine even more of a community project, the property has also a guesthouse, which adds a tourism element to the project, capitalizing on the region's increasing tourism industry.

This diversification project would be enough to keep most of us busy, but Toine can also repeat Isak Dinesen's famous words, "I have a farm in Africa." In his case, he became the owner of not one, but two farms. The ownership of the first was somewhat serendipitous, an attempt to create a brand of aloe vera products for skin care and health drinks, but the second became a way to combine sustainable development with his interest in wildlife. It's a perfect demonstration of Toine's strong concern for the greater good—the contributions he can make to benefit society and the environment.

Soon after he had finished the COL seminar, Toine did indeed write a book entitled *Mind Your Business*. In this book (published in 2012), Toine shared his entrepreneurial vision (including spiritual and holistic principles) with practical business advice. I wrote a short blurb for the book. Impressed with his search for meaning I noted, "One day your life will flash before your eyes. Make sure that it is worth watching." Given Toine's insights about what it means to be an entrepreneur, and his views about life in general, what he wrote is certainly worth reading. In a very engaging, lucid style, he not only draws the reader into his philosophy of entrepreneurship but also explains how to live a well-rounded, full life. He notes, "Employees work best if they see that not only the company makes money (and pays their salary), but if they feel valued, have the idea that they contribute something positive to the society around them, the world at large and not damage the environment and the future of their children." He emphasized that our first priority if we want to be successful is to be happy with ourselves, not the other way around. He highlights how to do business in an ethical and holistic way and achieve happiness in the process.

Toine produced a book full of wisdom that's to be recommended to anyone interested in acquiring a deeper understanding of the inner theater of the entrepreneur. It mixes pragmatic advice for would-be entrepreneurs with reflections about the way these people can create meaning. Not only does his book provide business advice, Toine also applied Eastern philosophy to his business model, stressing the importance of environmental responsibility, believing that the environment should not be negatively impacted by business. And knowing what I know about Toine, I'm sure that his interest in Hindu and Buddhist culture must have started when he first traveled as a backpacker in Asia on the "hippy trail" in 1979 and 1980.

The publication of this book must have whetted Toine's appetite to continue his journey and to advocate his passionate ideals about sustainable business, corporate social responsibility, and the environment. His philosophy in his new book, *Tantric Impact*, is to help the rich (or as he calls them the "High Net Worth Individuals"—the 1 percenters) reflect on what is the best investment for their money. Apart from giving these people advice on how to structure their wealth, he suggests that High Net Worth Individuals would do well to engage in philanthropy, to be socially responsible, and to be ethical in business. In his words, "Giving wealth to a bank will just return an interest or dividend. Hoarding money to leave to your children can actually rob them of the opportunity and pleasure of succeeding in life by themselves." High Net Worth Individuals should realize that there is another way. You can do well by doing good.

Toine advocates that wealthy people should try to do something worthwhile and sustainable with their money and their skills; they should do something that will improve the world in one way or another for the benefit of all. As he emphasizes, "We're not going to be remembered for how much money we accumulate, how much beer we can drink, the stuff and power we have, or the color and beauty of our skin. Our enduring legacy will be what we do and mean for others, we have to live our epitaph to deserve it." In this new book he articulates various ways of going about this, taking as an example what he is doing in his own organization. He tries to practice what he preaches. He also explains how the people in his organization encourage (and help) their clients to do the same.

To help his readers better understand his philosophy of life, Toine shares with us a number of defining moments that made him the person he is today. He has the courage to be vulnerable, providing many autobiographical insights that give us a sense of what he is all about. The book contains information about his life's journey and how he has become a citizen of the world. In telling us about himself, he reveals that the themes in his inner theater include self-efficacy, a strong need to be independent, a search for a better understanding of the human lifecycle, the challenge of sexuality, the need for authenticity, the pursuit of self-knowledge, the paradox of gratitude, and the search for meaning. These themes come back again and again, providing us with insights into the many cultures that he has been exposed to while working globally. He also shows us his strong biophilic side—his affinity for the natural world.

Toine realizes is that actualizing his world view is not going to be easy. Many people talk about doing good, but looking at the state of the world are exasperated with what's happening around us. There are times, looking at what we're up against, when we may wonder what can really be done. The challenges may seem insurmountable, making us feel helpless. But Toine is not a defeatist. He believes that the world changes according to the way we see it. He subscribes to the view that if we can change the way people look at reality, we can change the world. He also suggests that in change, the little things count. To persuade one person at a time may be the way to go.

To help change our more materialistic attitudes, Toine makes the point that not every return on investment should be a material one. He believes that many other "returns" can be included in this equation. This has led him to ask people, "Have you ever made the calculation of how many people you, in your lifetime so far, have helped, and as a result of your help you actually saved their lives?" But he then goes one step further, saying, "And what about animals? Every day, more species are being, eliminated from our planet forever. ...Our environment is artificially being heated faster than ever before and we are daily poisoning our planet. It is still the only planet that (realistically) will ever be available for my and your children and grandchildren to live on."

These are the kinds of questions raised in this book. As a person of action, Toine illustrates his commitment to induce meaningful change by describing various projects in which he is involved. His projects create meaning and take us to many different parts of the world: Argentina, Chile, Curaçao, South Africa, Cuba, Indonesia, India, Nepal, and Bhutan. We learn about his involvement in activities like the Mapesu Private Game Reserve, aloe farms, Alpasión, the Chile Forestadora Project, and the Bali Community Center project. Describing his own participation, he urges each company, family and individual to adopt a sustainability strategy. People shouldn't be doing the wrong things when they know better.

To Toine, the best way to contribute to our wellbeing is to do good to others. By doing good deeds, we can enhance goodness in the world. According to Toine, our wish for a harmonious world begins and ends with doing good. Also, as he makes clear, doing business and doing good are not mutually exclusive. But it is our responsibility to prove this anew, every day. What's more, thinking good thoughts is not enough. Having others follow our good examples is what really counts—this is the main reason why he decided to write this book. Eventually, what greater pleasure is there than to look back on days spent in usefulness, in doing good to those around us?

Toine's latest book emanates a sense of optimism, an expression of his faith that much can be done when we work together. He has been highly effective in motivating people to join his efforts. It is my strong hope that more people will follow his example. As Mahatma Gandhi said, "The best way to find yourself is to lose yourself in the service of others." Doing good will do us all good.

Manfred F. R. Kets de Vries

Distinguished Clinical Professor of Leadership Development and Organizational Change, INSEAD, France, Singapore and Abu Dhabi

Tantra is a Sanskrit word that, among other things, means to weave, expand, and spread. According to tantric masters, the fabric of life can best provide true and ever-lasting fulfillment when all the threads are woven in accordance with the pattern designed by nature. When we are born, life naturally forms itself around that pattern. As we grow, our ignorance, desire, greed, attachments, cravings, fears, judgments, and false images of others and ourselves tangle and tear the threads, disfiguring the fabric.

Practicing *tantra, sadhana*, reweaves the fabric, and restores the original pattern. Practices like yoga, *pranayama* and Ayurveda are some of the tools that blend perfectly with tantric disciplines. Those practices bring consciousness to every moment of our lives. They help us to live with gratitude, to love with an open heart, to appreciate the subtle, find the ecstasy in the spaces in-between, and to let go of the mundane, embracing more intensity and passion.

Tantra is like a fast track to enlightenment. It is a way of achieving Nirvana within your own lifetime. *Tantra* teaches that lasting pleasure does not come from physical objects and attachments, but from within. It is a discipline that helps the individual to transcend, to overcome the self to achieve understanding, to let go of greed, judgment and craving, the three key vices that make you ruin your own life, and prevent you from reaching enlightenment. The Bhagavad-Gita stated over 2,000 years ago that, "a person is said to have achieved yoga, the union with the self, when the perfectly disciplined mind gets freedom from all desires, and becomes absorbed (satisfied) in the self alone." By using your assets and efforts to benefit the greater good, you strengthen and expand your fabric and repair the impact made by negative experiences and selfish behavior (your own, as well as those of others).

By dissolving the dichotomy between the spiritual and the mundane, we can integrate our daily lives into our spiritual growth. Tantric practices aim to bring about a realization of the truth that nothing exists that is not divine (*nāśivaṃ vidyate kvacit*), bringing freedom from ignorance and fear and the cycle of self-imposed suffering (*saṃsāra*). Every effort made for the benefit of the community as a whole helps us to expand our understanding of our unique place in and control over the positive development of the self as well as the universe.

Even the best communicator cannot expect another person to provide contentment, insight, happiness, or pleasure! Happiness, pleasure, satisfaction—they all happen only and exclusively in our own minds. By definition, they are all caused by ourselves, although outside experiences may help us generate them. My favorite tantric saying declares: "Existence is an orgasm, an eternal orgasm going on and on and on. It is forever and forever an orgasm, an ecstasy." Our existence on earth is a once in a lifetime experience. I intend to enjoy every minute and every year of that existence.

To weave a happy live from many multi-colored and multi- textured threads, we need to try to build a great variety of experiences and to learn from each experience what it can teach us—and then to not resist, but to accept the lessons learned and to keep piling up the experiences, all the while striving to enhance the positive ones!

"If you want to be happy, be."

—Leo Tolstoy

Chapter 1

Wealth and Value

With wealth comes opportunity and responsibility. We can use our wealth to create value and change our world for the better.

Someday, somewhere—anywhere, unfailingly, you'll find yourself, and that, and only that, can be the happiest or bitterest hour of your life.[5]

—Pablo Neruda

I have spent much of my working life in the financial services industry, dealing mostly with corporations that establish international investments or obtain international financing, but also with High Net Worth Individuals (HNWIs), people who make or have more money than needed for their immediate financial needs. Although much of what is written below is directed at HNWIs, I hope that the key concepts will appeal to a broader category of people. You do not need to be a millionaire or exceptionally gifted to add something of real value or meaning to the lives of others. In the first few chapters, I will focus on the "what, why, and how" of making a contribution. In later chapters, I will describe some real-life cases I have been involved with, and will try to explain the many tangible and intangible benefits of adding value and meaning to the lives of others.

Our business specializes in what is called "fiduciary services." This business sector is not widely known. Essentially, it helps individuals and companies structure their assets against the negative influences of death and taxes. As it deals with the two key certainties in life, it is no surprise that it's arguably the oldest business in the world, at least for Christians and other "people of the Book." In Genesis 2:15, Adam is appointed the first trustee of the garden of Eden, which was reputedly located somewhere near Basra in Iraq, at the confluence of five known rivers (global warming flooded the area several thousands of years

---

5   Pablo Neruda (1904-1973)

ago and two of these rivers are now dry). The tasks entrusted to him included taking care of the Garden of Eden, together with his partner, Eve, according to the wishes of God, the settlor and protector: "The Lord God took the man and put him in the Garden of Eden to work it and take care of it." And the Lord God, (in legal terms, the settlor), commanded (written instructions did not yet exist) the man, "You are free to eat from any tree in the garden; but you must not eat from the tree of the knowledge of good and evil, for when you eat from it you will certainly die."

After Adam acted outside the powers granted to him by the settlor, with respect to the trust, by eating from the tree of the knowledge of good and evil, the consequences were swift and the cushy eternal life of being a trustee was replaced with a much harder transient existence. From that point on: "by the sweat of your brow you will eat your food until you return to the ground, since from it you were taken, for dust you are and to dust you will return." With that death penalty verdict, the eternal cycle of working up a sweat to simultaneously make a living and make your life meaningful was established, through generational transition, proper asset management and estate planning, and deciding whether or not to leave a legacy.

Homo sapiens sapiens (the man who thinks, and knows he thinks) is us, the only species on earth with the capacity to think abstractly about the future (as far as we are now able to ascertain). Our frontal brain lobes are further developed than those of any other species. This is a double-sided sword. Being able to look back and think ahead, we can plan for the future (although plants, trees, mopane worms, bees, squirrels, and brown bears also plan for winter), imagine the greatest ideas and dreams, and cooperate effectively with other humans. As Karl Marx said, in *Das Kapital*,

A spider conducts operations that resemble those of a weaver, and a bee puts to shame many an architect in the construction of her cells. But what distinguishes the worst architect from the best of bees is this, that the architect raises his structure in imagination before he erects it in reality.[6]

---

[6]   Marx, Karl. (1867/1887). *Capital: A Critique of Political Economy. Vol. 1, The Process of Production of Capital*. Edited by Frederick Engels. Translated by Samuel Moore and Edward Aveling. Public Domain Books, Kindle Edition (2008-11-19). Originally published as *Das Kapital: Kritik der politischen Ökonomie, vol. 1*.

As a consequence, we can also visualize and plan for our own unavoidable deaths, deciding how to dispose of our assets, what to organize for our relatives, and to whom we should bequeath our work, accomplishments, plans, and dreams.

One of the wealthiest people in the modern world, Warren Buffett, once said, "If you belong to the luckiest, wealthiest 1 percent of the world, you owe it to the other 99 percent to care about their wellbeing." Based on cold numbers, you belong to that 1 percent if (believe it or not) your gross annual income exceeds U.S. $60,000 (this is not a typo). Alternatively, the major private banks estimate that, once debts have been subtracted, an adult requires just U.S. $4,000 in net assets to be within the wealthiest 50 percent of the world's citizens and about U.S. $80,000 to reach the top 10 percent. An amount totaling U.S. $800,000 in assets is also enough to put you in the club of the wealthiest 1 percent of the world's inhabitants.

I assume that many of the readers of this book either belong to or are close to belonging to the luckiest 1 percent of people in the world, either through income or inherited wealth. I direct my comments to them. Many of those who are not fortunate enough to be in this category either cannot read, are too busy surviving to have time to read, or may not be interested in the subject of this book.

Let me start with the very basics:

How does one achieve a top 1 percent income or become wealthy?

This question has a simple answer, as there are really only a few ways:

1) Swing the Wheel of Samsara well and be lucky at birth. Lots of wealth is inherited and kept in families for a few generations (three generations is usually about the maximum, as we will see). People are born into wealthy families or wealthy countries (in Singapore, 17 percent of the population consists of millionaires). They acquire assets that end up being gold mines (sometimes literally) or easily increase in value, as often happens with real estate. If you are reading these words, chances are it's too late to influence where you were born.

2)   Your second option is to marry well and be lucky enough to have a good pre-nuptial agreement, or even to marry on the basis of intestate rules. This requires some effort, but it works for many. Being female and good-looking tremendously increases your chances of succeeding with this approach. In general, however, marrying for friendship, care, and love is a better choice. The correlation between wealth and happiness is a weak one. But the wealthier you are, the smaller is the chance that your suitors, friends, and business partners will only be interested in your sense of humor or humility. Gold diggers come in many disguises.

3)   Winning the lottery or getting lucky in a casino is an often-tried but not very promising way to get rich. The odds are solidly stacked against you. And in reality, people who win big—musicians who have a few top hits or sports champions with a few great seasons—very often end up poorer than they started out. One-time shots at getting rich hardly ever stick and leave one poorer and less satisfied at the end of the roller-coaster ride.

4)   Stealing, cheating, misusing power, corruption, and bribery are often tried, but won't do much for your self-esteem, restful nights, or happiness. Poverty with honor feels better than ill-gotten wealth. As Mother Teresa commented: "Being unwanted, unloved, uncared for, forgotten by everybody, I think that is a much greater hunger, a much greater poverty than the person who has nothing to eat."[7] Now that robbing banks has become more complicated due to all kinds of electronic security and less physical cash, most aspiring bank robbers, the ones who milk clients for fees, are actually employed by banks. German poet and playwright Bertold Brecht said it best: "Bank robbery is an initiative of amateurs. True professionals establish a bank."[8]

5)   The seemingly harder, but definitely surer way to become wealthy is to actually earn money, by reaching a top position in a multinational

---

[7]   The Rotarian: An Internationa Magazine, November 1981, p 10. Mother Teresa during a speech at a Cincinnati seminary.

[8]   "Was ist ein Einbruch in eine Bank gegen die Gründung einer Bank? Was ist die Ermordung eines Mannes gegen die Anstellung eines Mannes?" – Bertolt Brecht, Die Dreigroschenoper, Suhrkamp, 1994, p. 91.

organization, being better at sports or an art than anyone else, being sufficiently entrepreneurial to start and run a successful business or trade, or by investing prudently and wisely. Working hard at something worth doing can also be a source of great satisfaction. Most entrepreneurs keep working hard long after they no longer have to; after all and whatever less fortunate people think, it is not the money that motivates them.

The way in which you get rich makes a lot of difference; realistically speaking, only the entrepreneurs have a fair chance of ever repeating the feat. As a consequence, most wealthy people share the same nightmare-inducing fear: that they might become poor (again).

The fear of being poor is one of the key fears of life, together with the fear of losing the love of your life, friends, or social contacts, and the fear of ill-health, getting old, and death itself.

> *"You can live to be a hundred if you give up all the things that make you want to live to be a hundred."*

> **—Woody Allen**

The fear of poverty and the need to plan for inevitable death is what private bankers and a whole industry of financial advisors feed on. Their mantra is that wealth preservation is the key purpose of investing money (with the help of wealth managers and private bankers).

But is this true? I do not necessarily believe it. Why should it be true?

Money by itself does not make you happy! It can help to satisfy needs at the lower levels of the Maslow pyramid (food, drink, sex, shelter) but not at the higher levels (friendship, self-realization). The Dalai Lama, when asked what surprised him most about humanity, answered:

Man. Because he sacrifices his health in order to make money. Then he sacrifices money to recuperate his health. And then he is so anxious about the future that he does not enjoy the present; the result being that he does not live in the present or the future; he lives as if he is never going to die and then dies having never lived.

In one of the world's very first philosophic books, the Indian epic, *Mahabharata*, written in Sanskrit about 3,000 years ago, the most amazing thing in the world is "man's unfaltering belief in immortality, ignoring the inevitability and omnipresence of death."

Although we are very well aware of the inevitability of death, "the worm at the core of our existence," most of the time we pretend and act like we will live forever, wasting humongous quantities of energy and time on totally irrelevant activities. As we get older, ignoring the approach of death becomes increasingly difficult, especially as we watch our bodies decay, and friends and older family members die. We confront diseases and repeated loss, but live in denial until almost the last moment of life. Death happens to others, not to us!

Although our self will be extinguished, our life energy, experiences and memories once stored in our amygdala, will remain available somewhere or in multiple places in the universe for future use.

Memories are not being stored in our brains like books on library shelves, but must be actively reconstructed from elements scattered throughout the brain. As there is no compelling reason why this information should only be stored within our physical brain, the related energy streams are just as likely to remain accessible as energy waves somewhere in the cloud, and thus one day can potentially be downloaded onto some device, and maybe the i-mind would be an appropriate name for it. Previous life memories and other amazing feats of memory could result from minds downloading information from or hacking into this cloud.

All of the belief systems and religions that we have created promise one type of afterlife or another as a consolation prize. As life is easier to manipulate and bear if we have the prospect of an afterlife, the majority of people believe in an afterlife, in spite of most of the evidence being circumstantial at best. We conveniently forget that we created all of these beliefs and religions ourselves, and have just repeated them often enough to convince ourselves that they are eternal truths. After all, they are written in the Bible, the Quran, or ancient texts. Our imaginary friends, the various Gods, provide true or imaginary consolation. Having these imaginary friends helps us to remain in denial most of the time, as well as motivating us to give life meaning by doing meaningful work (doing something important or bigger than ourselves). We may long for a sense of freedom or impact, or hope to master a skill better than anyone else. These motivators are very important, as worrying about death all the time would be pretty depressing and take the pleasure out of living. We also have an innate need to be important, to feel that we have added something to the universe or at least to one tiny part or a few people. We want to find meaning beyond simply existing and passing our genetic code on to our offspring.

Manfred Kets de Vries says, "Children are our major immortality project, the living messages we send to a time we will not see."[9] We project our own aspirations and achievements onto our children, hoping that they will perpetuate our beliefs and values. Children help us to see death as a transition that we can survive through others' memories. After all, the dead are never dead to us until we have forgotten them. Work, creating successful businesses, erecting buildings and statues, making art, writing books and songs, and scientific work are all in that same category.[10]

When we get closer to the end of our lives, we should be able to look back with integrity and see with satisfaction a life full of accomplishments and meaning. If we can see that we have led a generally happy, balanced, and productive life, shared with friends and family, we can feel content that our mission has been fulfilled. In the Hindu tradition, life has four age-based life stages of about 24 years each, known as *ashramas*. The first three are *Brahmacharya* (student, learning phase, bachelor, growing in knowledge, and skills), *Grihastha* (provider, worker, protector, creator, becoming independent) and *Vanaprastha* (retired, coach, teacher, helping others to become successful), which starts when a person hands over household responsibilities to the next generation, takes on an advisory role, and gradually withdraws from the world.

The last phase, *Sannyasa*, starts from an age of 72–75 and represents a form of renunciation. This stage is traditionally associated with men or women in the last years of their lives. However, some young people purposely choose to skip the provider and retirement stages, renounce worldly and materialistic pursuits, gift away all their material goods, and dedicate their lives to spiritual pursuits (*moksha*) through medication and contemplation.

---

9   Neil Postman, *The Disappearance of Childhood* (New York: Vintage, 19947), p. xi.

10   Kets de Vries, Manfred F.R. Death and the Executive: Encounters with the "Stealth" Motivator. INSEAD, Faculty & Research Working Paper, France: 2014. https://sites. insead.edu/facultyresearch/research/doc.cfm?did=53712

For those people who get older by leading "lives of quiet desperation", and who are going to their graves "with their song unsung," thus failing to reach the stage of *Sannyasa*, John Maynard Keynes proposes eight alternative motivations that can lead individuals to refrain from spending or gifting their money.

These are:

1) To build up a reserve against unforeseen contingencies.

2) To provide for an anticipated future relation between the income and the needs of the individual or his family different from that which exists in the present, as, for example, in relation to old age, family education, or the maintenance of dependents.

3) To enjoy interest and appreciation, i.e. because a larger real consumption at a later date is preferred to a smaller immediate consumption.

4) To enjoy a gradually increasing expenditure, since it gratifies a common instinct to look forward to a gradually improving standard of life rather than the contrary, even though the capacity for enjoyment may be diminishing.

5) To enjoy a sense of independence and the power to do things, though without a clear idea or definite intention of specific action.

6) To secure a *masse de manoeuvre* to carry out speculative or business projects.

7) To bequeath a fortune.

8) To satisfy pure miserliness, i.e. unreasonable but insistent inhibitions against acts of expenditure as such.[11]

In his book, *The General Theory*, Keynes argued that these eight motives might be called the motives of precaution, foresight, calculation, improvement, independence, enterprise, pride, and avarice. His corresponding list of motives for consumption includes enjoyment, short-sightedness, generosity, miscalculation,

---

[11]   http://www.hetwebsite.net/het/texts/keynes/gt/chap09.htm Last viewed June, 2016.

ostentation, and extravagance. From my experience, I would say that most people are drawn to the independence motive.

> *The ideals that have lighted my way, and time after time have given me new courage to face life cheerfully, have been Kindness, Beauty, and Truth. Without the sense of kinship with men of like mind, without the occupation with the objective world, the eternally unattainable in the field of art and scientific endeavors, life would have seemed empty to me. The trite objects of human efforts—possessions, outward success, luxury—have always seemed to me contemptible.*[12]

—Albert Einstein

Money gives wealthy people power over other people and the chance to influence many of the external factors that affect their lives. Strangely enough, money gives you little or no power over your family life or the happiness of your inner circle. On the contrary, it usually contributes to making family life much more complicated.

I think there are only a limited number of things you can do with your money.

1) You can spend it on consumables. This is really easy; there are plenty of temptations. Anyone who has become rich will attest to the fact that the more they have, the more they spend. If they are not careful, the money will one day run out. There are not many people like Warren Buffett, who can make billions and remain living in the same simple house with the same modest habits they started out with. He tries to instill similar values in his children, saying: "I believe in giving my kids enough so they can do anything, but not so much that they can do nothing." People who make a lot of money at a young age (like successful sports people, musicians, or celebrities) often realize too late that once they stop being successful, no real new money will be added to their stack. It turns out to be really difficult to earn money the hard way (by working). And once a comfortable lifestyle has been achieved, it becomes clear that luxury does not really create more happiness or love. On the contrary, people often end up in trouble as

---

12   What I Believe." *Forum and Century* 84 (1930): 193-94. Reprinted as "The World as I see It" in *Ideas and Opinions* 1954). 8-11

a result of having too much money. As early as 1625, Francis Bacon wrote that "money is like manure, it will start to smell unless it is spread around."

2) You can save some of it to spend it on necessities later, like healthcare, a nice house, the education of your children, and other expenditures.

3) You can give it to the government. If you do not plan carefully or structure your wealth well, over time, your money will be taxed until it is all gone. Unfortunately, paying taxes is not something that typically makes people feel great; governments are usually considered hopelessly inefficient and lacking the creativity to spend money on things that add value to the world.

4) You can give it to a church or faith you believe in. This is, for many people, a moral obligation. Muslims are supposed to donate about 2.5 percent of their assets annually as *Zakah*, one of the five pillars of belief, based on the notion that all wealth belongs to Allah and we merely act as his trustees. In Buddhism, giving is one of the ways to improve and purify oneself; for Hindus, *Dhana* (giving) is an important part of your *Dharma* (way, or duty). Unfortunately, most religious organizations are only slightly less wasteful than governments. In many cases, it may be more efficient to bypass these organizations and to make your charitable donations directly to the beneficiaries you want to assist.

5) You can conserve your wealth, bury your talents, put your money in the bank and one day leave it to your kids, quite possibly to their detriment. My two children understand this (I hope). I would never want to deprive them of the wonderful feeling of making money on their own. I don't think you do your kids a favor by leaving them a lot of money, or by letting them think they're home free. But if you decide to hoard your money to give it to your kids, at least give it to them early, so that they can do something great with it early on in their lives. Accumulating wealth through passive investments is great for banks, but not necessarily the best way to preserve wealth or especially value over time.

6) You can invest in another entrepreneurial business, either alone, through a private equity fund, or with a small group of like-minded investors, and make more money. For many people, this is a very stimulating and satisfying activity that sustains them until the end of their days. It makes the amount of money that is available for a useful purpose so much bigger. After all, only relatively wealthy people can afford to be philanthropists.

7) The last thing you can do with your wealth, which is not necessarily all that different from the previous one, is to create something good and sustainable with your money and your skills that will positively impact the world in some way, to benefit all of us. I think it is incumbent on everybody with any amount of wealth to at least think about doing that!

The choices you make may depend on many factors, including how you were brought up, your religion, your caste, social background, and beliefs, as well as your thoughts about how you want to be remembered. When my INSEAD Professor, Manfred Kets de Vries, arrived for the first time at our farmhouse in South Africa, we unexpectedly encountered a black mamba snake in the stairwell. Those snakes move really fast and can kill you if they bite. We found a shovel and a broom and together we ended its life. Afterwards, it was a good moment to discuss the Professor's well-known epitaph question: "How do you want to be remembered? What would you like people to say about you at your funeral? How do you want people to describe you, once you are gone?"

1) Would you like to be remembered as a good person, a caring parent, a thoughtful spouse, a loving sibling, colleague, or friend?

2) Would you like people to say that you made a positive difference in their or other people's lives, that you were a source of encouragement or inspiration, that you helped them, coached them, supported them, made them stronger, or made them laugh and have fun, and showed them how to be happy?

3) Would you like to be remembered as a courageous and righteous person, someone who actually lived his or her values and principles, walked the talk and stayed the course, had a clear sense of justice and

fairness and never let any close relationship down, whatever the cost and the circumstances, but instead was helpful, supportive and a leader?

4)   Would you like to be remembered as someone creative and imaginative, who developed thoughts, science, progress, and promoted practical improvements in the world around us?

What is pretty clear is that we're not going to be remembered for how much money we accumulated, how much beer we could drink, the stuff and power we had, or the color and beauty of our skin. Our enduring legacy will be what we did and meant for others. We have to live our epitaph to deserve it.

In this book, I will concentrate mostly on using money to do well by doing good. However, I will also briefly voice an opinion on using money to preserve wealth and the process of transitioning assets to the next generation.

In the end, it will all come down to what you feel gives you more bang for your buck. I just want you to realize that we have been conditioned to think that return on investment is limited to interest on deposits or dividends and capital growth on risk-taking investments. Those are not the only returns available, and perhaps not even the most desirable!

Not every return on investment is material in nature. That is just one way of looking at value. In reality, there are many values. A slightly more tantric approach to wealth at least differentiates between physical, emotional, spiritual, social, and financial wealth.

As an example of emotional wealth, have you ever tried to calculate how many people you, in your lifetime so far, have helped, and—as a result of that help—how many lives you have actually saved? People who without your help would have died of hunger, malnourishment, preventable diseases, unavailable medical treatment, sexual or other abuse, servitude as child soldiers, inhumane working conditions, or other risks? Have you ever actually ever heard anyone say to you: "thank you for saving my life?"

Have you ever thought about how many people you still can save, starting today, with the contacts, care, skills, and money you have at your disposal? Would that not be a wonderful return on investment?

And what about animals? Every day, more species are being eliminated from our planet forever. You may never hear of them, and they cannot say "thank you for saving my life," but these species are as valuable as our own, and may hold clues to treating diseases, or developing new materials, theories, or solutions. Our environment is artificially being heated faster than ever before, and we are daily poisoning our planet. It is still the only planet that (realistically) will ever be available for my and your children and grandchildren to live on.

I think that a slightly more holistic or tantric view of return on investment would include the following choices:

1) Interest, dividends, and capital gains are **returns on passive investments.** Unfortunately, in times of low economic growth and interest rates, these returns can easily be very small. Moreover, as money by itself has no emotional value, what happiness or wellbeing does the growing number on a bank statement really create? Does either the number or the money really make you feel better, more secure, more satisfied, happier, or more enlightened? And what about inflation or devaluation? How good is your advisor, and how predictable is the market on which you, individually, have no influence at all? Basically, if you think about it, returns on passive investments can produce happiness for a day, and only for yourself.

2) **Spending** money on something nice for yourself that you do not need: a sports car, mansion, trophy wife/toy boy. This also brings happiness for a day and only for your own benefit.

3) The value of doing something good if you make a **donation**, to your children, your friends, your church, or a charity of your choice. This will already feel much better. Charitable donations create short-lived happiness, but being for the benefit of someone else, will make you feel good. If they benefit many others, they will make you feel even better. It has been scientifically tested and proven that those who reported giving more help and support to family, friends, and colleagues—people who really cared—went on to live longer than those who gave less, whereas the amount of help that people reported receiving showed no relationship to longevity. In other words, it is indeed more blessed to give than receive.

4) The value of making a **philanthropic investment** that changes at least one small aspect of the world for the better. This approach creates happiness for much longer than a day, and for more than one other person. In my opinion, it provides a much higher return on investment.

5) **Saving someone's life** is an investment that produces a return for as long as the person saved remains alive. And that return may live on in what that person achieves, invents, creates, and thinks.

6) **Learning and appreciation**. By investing in social enterprise, one gains new insights and receives appreciation from a new range of people, for actions beyond the normal course of business. Helping people to grow by using your own knowledge and experience will enhance everyone's self-esteem.

7) **Friendship**. Bonding with family members, siblings, business associates, co-workers, friends, and neighbors. This may give you an ongoing return on your investments in them.

If you want happiness for an hour, take a nap.
If you want happiness for a day, go fishing.
If you want happiness for a year, inherit a fortune.
If you want happiness for a lifetime, help somebody.

—Chinese proverb

It is important to remember that, in the end, we all have the potential to be exactly what we want to be and to do exactly what we want to do. We may not be able to influence the presidential elections, or to have a relationship with the most beautiful model in the world, but we are always able to organize our own world in such a way that we get the things that really matter, by giving them in abundance. Love, power, respect, care, gratitude, friendship are all emotions we can influence. Former U.S. President Barack Obama once said:

If you only think about yourself—how much money can I make, what can I buy, how nice is my house, what kind of fancy car do I have? —over the long term, I think, you get bored, I think your life becomes diminished. The way to live a full life is to think: what can I do for others?[13]

In this book, we will explore just that. How we can enhance our lives by doing something for a worthy cause? I will draw mainly on my own experiences, not to demonstrate how great they are, but to show that you don't need to be a Warren Buffett or Mother Teresa to have some positive impact on the world. We can all leave our mark; we all can do something—and by throwing a stone into the pond and creating ripples around us, we may inspire others to do the same. Together we can do incredible things. No, together we will do incredible things!

Every man dies—not every man really lives.

—William Ross

---

[13] President Barak Obama, The President's Remarks at Town Hall Meeting and a Question-and-Answer Session in Strasbourg, France. April 3, 2009.

Chapter 2

How to control our wealth and use it well; how to avoid falling into the interconnected traps of greed, consumerism, and tax evasion.

> *"Would you tell me, please, which way I need to go from here?"*
> *"That depends a good deal on where you want to get to," said the Cheshire Cat.*
> *"I don't much care where"—said Alice.*
> *"Then it doesn't matter which way you go," said the Cheshire Cat.*
> *"—so long as I get SOMEWHERE," Alice added as an explanation.*
> *"Oh, you're sure to do that," said the Cheshire Cat, "if you only walk long enough."* [14]

—Lewis Carroll, *Alice in Wonderland*

We certainly have a number of good reasons for preserving our wealth. We are all afraid of losing our money, overspending, and not having a way to recover, especially as we get older. We also see wealth as a part of our social status. It is a fact of life that wealthy people are held in higher regard than poor people. However often we say, "be a man of values, rather than a man of wealth," in the hard light of day, money talks.

There is nothing wrong with having a little something (legally) salted away for a rainy day. But how much is enough?

When I was about eight years old, I contracted with my father, who owned an orchard, to clear the six-hectare orchard of cut wood, following an annual pruning. The job took all of my out-of-school time for over a month and

---

[14]   Carroll, Lewis. *Alice's Adventures in Wonderland*, New York: MacMillan, 1865.

instilled in me a healthy respect for the value of money. I made exactly 25 Guilders (U.S. $12), for a month of back-breaking labor. I understood that I had made a bad deal and from then on, I focused on making money in different, more entrepreneurial ways. Ten years later, at 18, I calculated that, as interest rates were around 8–10 percent per annum, placing U.S. $100,000 in a bank would generate enough interest income for me to live off for life, and that I should have done that by the age of 30. Over the years, as I started making more and more money, I kept setting the bar higher and higher until, one day, I realized what I was doing. Making money may be great fun, but money by itself cannot be a goal in life. It is just a paper fiction that gives you the opportunity to buy the things you really need or want.

Professional financial advisors, like asset managers and private bankers, typically say that anything less than U.S. $10 million will not guarantee you a comfortable life (but don't forget that they are paid on the basis of Assets Under Management, as well as for churning passive investment portfolios). When interest rates are as low as 2 percent, a U.S. $10 million investment in a bond or deposit will give you an annual income of U.S. $200,000 before taxes, still a very comfortable sum of money. If you have some indication of how many years you still have to live, you may want to eat into your capital. So, for example, if you want to be able to spend U.S. $200,000 a year and have 20 more years to live, then U.S. $3,500,000 should do the trick. As you get older, you are likely to travel and spend less, a lot less than that will be enough to ensure a comfortable life. In addition, if one has a pension, stipend, or other recurring income (e.g. real estate rent) or some basics already covered (a house without a mortgage), the amount needed to live a comfortable life rapidly becomes much lower.

Wealthy people are usually advised to structure their investments and put them into a trust, private foundation, investment company, variable life insurance policy, or something similar. Structuring your wealth can have many tax, financial and asset protection benefits. A trust or foundation can help you to reign from your grave, determining who can benefit from your wealth, often for a specific purpose (like education) or at a specific moment (marriage, a certain age). This way you can influence what happens with your money in many jurisdictions for up to 100 years after your death. Of course, nobody has a clue how the world will look like in 100 years, let alone what direction you would want it to move by then, or for what purpose. You won't be around to see any of that.

Irrevocable trusts, shared investment funds, single premium variable life insurance policies, and similar solutions can, if established correctly, protect you against many negative influences from the outside, such as high fees, excessive taxation, greedy partners and siblings, or extortion and blackmail.

As a word of warning, you need to be very careful using "confidentiality" to shield your assets from prying eyes, extortionists, and tax collectors. Nowadays many, if not most, fiduciary asset protection structures are fiscally transparent; investors may unwillingly or unknowingly end up as tax evaders, by "forgetting" to report their income on foreign investments in their home country. The most common reasons people give for promoting or selecting a "confidential" structure are not trusting the government to spend their taxes wisely (however true this may be, it can never be a valid legal reason for evading taxes) or not wanting everyone to know how much wealth they have (without, however, giving up the opulent house, chauffeur-driven Mercedes, or diamond earrings).

Failing to properly reporting your income or not paying adequate tax in the country where you are a tax resident is a criminal offense called tax evasion. In a growing number of countries, anyone who helps you evade taxes is equally punishable by law, and anyone (including your friendly Personal Assistant or the cleaning lady who checks your mail) who reports your tax evasion may be eligible for a reward (in the U.S., for instance, this would amount to a flat 25 percent of the amount you withheld from the tax system).

Money laundering is when you invest someone else's illegal funds. For example, a bank, asset manager, or trust company might help someone who has evaded taxes in one country to invest the proceeds in another. It is also possible to launder your own money, for example by taking money that you acquired by evading taxes long ago, before the period referred to in the Statute of Limitations, and now, when you can no longer be prosecuted for the tax crime itself, using it to make a "clean" investment in a genuine and legitimate transaction. Such personal money laundering is also a crime in most countries.

For centuries, the famous secrecy of Swiss banks created a safe haven for people escaping taxation. Bank secrecy was first developed in the eighteenth century when the Catholic kings of France had to borrow money from Protestant Geneva and Zurich-based bankers. The French government swore the bankers to secrecy and the Swiss codified the habit, as it appeared to make good business sense to do so.

In 1933, one of Hitler's first acts as Chancellor of Germany was to pass a law prohibiting Germans from owning foreign bank accounts, on penalty of death. In return, the Swiss, in 1934, strengthened their bank secrecy laws by creating numbered accounts, attracting lots of deposits, both from corrupt Nazi officials and from wealthy Jewish victims, as well as undeclared assets and money obtained from criminal activities all over the world. There was no humanitarian motive involved; at the time, it was just considered a clever business approach. In both categories, Nazis and Jews, many investors never returned from the vagaries of war. The unfortunate banks were stuck with lots of unclaimed bank accounts. Only many years later were settlements made and some of the money returned to surviving relatives of the Jews and victims of the Nazis.

Over the last few years the pendulum has swung in the other direction. "Don't ask, don't tell" will no longer help either investors or bankers. All passive investments in basically all relevant countries are linked to their Ultimate Beneficial Owners (UBOs) and the income made on those investments is disclosed to the (tax) authorities in the country of tax residency of the investors involved. The OECD has excluded rogue countries (including Yemen, North Korea, Venezuela, Cuba, and Syria). Some countries without a meaningful financial system have not yet bothered (or been forced) to sign up. Between 2009 and 2015, Swiss bank secrecy was dismantled step-by-step and in 2016, a Swiss court ruled that Switzerland should automatically and voluntarily exchange information on assets held and income made on Swiss investment accounts to EU member states.

Even today, many investment advisors promote secrecy or confidentiality as an important aspect of structuring wealth, but you should be extremely careful how you do this. Traditionally, international tax planning experts only looked at solutions that would be legal in the country where the assets were kept, and did not worry much about how these assets would be treated from a tax point of view in the country where the investor was living (as a tax resident), knowing full well that, in practice, that country's tax authorities had little or no chance of finding investments that the investor had "forgotten" to report. Until recently, these advisors answered the age-old question, "Am I my brother's keeper?" with a wholehearted "no." Now, under new international standards, that is no longer the case. Anyone who clings to the old approach will, sooner or later, end up in major legal trouble!

In September 2013, the G-20 met in Saint Petersburg and accepted proposals by the OECD to change the common international approach to taxation and to create Common Reporting Standards (CRS) and rules for Base Erosion and Profit Shifting (BEPS), built on top of older legislation like the EU Savings Directive of 2005 (repealed in 2015) and the 2010 U.S. Foreign Account Tax Compliance Act (FATCA). This legislation was designed to ensure that both corporations and High Net Worth Individuals paid a fair amount of taxes on their worldwide income.

It is remarkable that, despite all the conflict between the U.S., China, the EU, India, Russia, and other powerful nations, it took very little time to work out the principles and detailed guidelines that signatories to the agreements will have to adhere to, at some point between 2017 and 2020, to achieve a meaningful exchange of information. Over 100 countries quite quickly signed up, representing the lion's share of the world economy. This group included (undoubtedly after some major, behind-the-scenes arm wrestling) almost all of the world's key financial centers, including Switzerland, the UK, the Cayman Islands, Bermuda, Luxembourg, Singapore and Hong Kong. The hold-outs, like Panama and the Bahamas, ended up being steamrollered by international organizations. It wasn't worth holding out, because failing to sign the agreements would have damaged their reputations to such an extent that no one would have parked assets in those countries in the long run, since any investments would have attracted suspicion (not to mention the legal and moral dilemmas passed on to the investors' children).

Eventually, once technical difficulties have been ironed out (which will take a while), the world will become very transparent from a financial point of view, just as Western countries are already very transparent internally. Private corporations will have to register all shareholders who own over 10 percent in publicly accessible registers. Tax authorities will electronically log into the accounting systems of companies and exchange information with the tax authorities in other countries to ensure that each country gets its fair share of the total tax to be paid. As an example, consider the 2016 Apple incident. As the country did not update its structure in time, Ireland was forced to collect

U.S. $15 billion from Apple for issuing a tax ruling which breached these principles by including an effective rate of significantly less than 1 percent. Although contractually agreed, it was hardly a fair amount of tax.

High Net Worth Individuals may expect similar incidents to happen. The EU wants to know where its citizens have their assets, and how much passive investment income or capital gains they earn, just like the Chinese, Americans, Russians, Brazilians, and Indians. In every major country, legislation is actively being adjusted to create a much more level playing field. This will allow over a hundred governments around the globe to see where their citizens own assets, businesses, and bank accounts and to receive reports on how much income is being made on those assets, businesses, and accounts. They will do this by forcing all regulated financial institutions to collect and share that information. Amazingly, the U.S., one of the early promoters of the process, has dragged its feet, probably because it has belatedly realized that a significant part of the world's undeclared assets ends up financing oversized U.S. deficits. If the U.S. routinely exchanges information on the income that investors in the U.S. make on their T-bills, investment portfolios, and real estate, many of those investors may choose to re-invest their declared assets closer to home in higher yielding alternatives. This delay has temporarily made the U.S. an attractive place for tax evaders and money launderers, who forget that, according to the 2005 Pasquantino rules, foreign tax evasion is recognized as a criminal offense under U.S. law. My prediction: once a lot of them have swum comfortably into the net, it will be jerked out fast and hard, accompanied by legal confiscatory penalties.

To sum up, hiding your assets is not a good idea, but structuring them well is.

The world's tax systems are converging much more rapidly than we all want to believe and, technically speaking, exchanging tax information is becoming easier and easier. This will therefore happen, as all the large governments of the world will benefit from the exchange (and they do not really care what happens to the poor, small so-called "tax haven countries"). The powerful countries have just renamed what is acceptable in the international (tax) competition game to fit their needs. Trends in tax systems include tendencies towards transparency and substance over form. This means treating all artificial and fake transactions as transparent, or as nonexistent. Going forward, income will mostly end up being taxed where it is actually being generated; in the case of corporate income, that is where the laborers work and the smokestacks stand, rather than where the paperwork is signed, the intellectual property resides or the finance comes from. In the case of passive income, that is where the actual control over the investments takes place. Any Ultimate Beneficial Owner exercising any form of control over how his assets are being invested must expect to be taxed on the resulting income in his country of tax residence, whatever gimmick is applied in structuring.

1) If you do not want to pay a lot of taxes on your investment income, the most common solutions are listed below. Don't try any of these at home, without consulting a specialized firm first:

2) Move to a country where the taxes are low (like Dubai or Singapore) or where there are preferential regimes for people who immigrate for tax purposes (The UK non-domicile regime is world famous, like the Swiss Pauschalbesteuerung, and lots of preferential regimes in countries such as Malta, Portugal, Italy, St Vincent, Curaçao, and Costa Rica. For Americans (subject to worldwide taxation), this will not provide any real benefits. For some others, even a short stint residing in such a country will result in a step up in base and a significant tax saving.

3) Make sure your assets do not generate passive income, so that you are not taxed on passive income. The easiest way to do this is to invest in real operational businesses, and to run real business risks.

4) Organize your life in such a way that you do not own the assets or have de facto control over them. In quite a number of countries, benefits from properly structured irrevocable discretionary trusts, variable life insurance policies, and pension plans are excluded from taxation. Certain types of mutual funds, shared investment schemes, and other structures separate the original investor from ownership and control, achieving a similar result.

5) Donate your assets to relatives living in low-tax jurisdictions or to charitable foundations or trusts that you create, philanthropic third-party organizations, or similar entities. So far, the tax authorities have not found a way to tax you on what you do not own and do not control. Establishing foundations and trusts and actually running them from tax logical places, helps to make investments go a lot further. Many firms specialize in helping with that.

The money you keep under your control for passive investment purposes, as well as the family businesses you wish to preserve intact (organized through a family office or through a range of ad-hoc arrangements) will typically serve any one or a combination of the following goals:

1) Ensure that needy family members get what they need. This includes money set apart for medical emergencies, school and university funds, and for family members with special needs. A patriarch or matriarch may want to support children and grandchildren, as well as other close relatives, loyal employees, lifelong business partners, and significant others.

2) Ensure that subsequent generations have enough to live on. This may seem easy, but, if you do the math, you will soon realize that almost every family runs the risk of ultimately outbreeding the growth of the family business. The simple reason for this is that healthy, well-to-do families can afford to have more children. Over a couple of generations, the number of siblings will explode. However, the growth of the family business is restricted by the needs and opportunities presented by the market. By definition, it cannot grow ad infinitum, or provide unlimited dividends.

3) Ensure that there will be growth and a well-managed effort to spread the risk. As families grow, more people get involved in managing the family jewels. This will invariably lead to a splitting of the assets into pet investments, not all of them necessarily offering a positive rate of return. Family charters, family boards, and investment committees all add diversification, costs, and administrative complexity. Almost nobody listens to the advice of Warren Buffett, who said: "What an investor needs is the ability to correctly evaluate selected businesses. Note that word selected: You don't have to be an expert on every company, or even many. You only have to be able to evaluate companies within your circle of competence. The size of that circle is not very important; knowing its boundaries, however, is vital."[15] He also advises readers to "keep all your eggs in one basket, but watch that basket closely." And my personal favorite: "Diversification is a protection

---

[15] Warren E. Buffett, Chairman of the Board, Letter to the Shareholders of Berkshire Hathaway Inc., February 28, 1997.

against ignorance. It makes very little sense for those who know what they're doing."

4) As the circle of beneficiaries of a family fortune grows, more governance will be needed. Put simply, over time the needs and values of the beneficiaries will start to diversify. Not all family members will be involved in the family business (many may not be interested, qualified, or capable). Not all family members will necessarily be committed to remaining in the same family, or at least the people they marry may not be. As investments become more complicated and widespread, the need will arise for more sophisticated reporting to maintain trust between family members. At the same time, there will be a need to outsource functions to family offices, private bankers, administrators, and valuators. Conflicts will arise, a family charter may need to be developed, and there may be calls for mediation and conflict resolution. New generations, growing up accustomed to wealth and with very different values from previous generations, will need to be coached, trained, or even excluded from the shared wealth. The earlier one starts, the more conflict and chaos later will be avoided.

5) As businesses and investments grow, they almost invariably become global, adding to their complexity and costs. The more broadly international they are, the more professional organization, structuring, and corporate governance they will require.

6) From one generation to the next, feelings may change about the family fortune. The old Bible adage of Luke 12:48: "whomsoever much is given, of him shall much be required[16]" does not resonate with everyone. Children or grandchildren often take care and privilege for granted and never learn to fend for themselves. They burn through the family capital without having the skill, guts, or grit to replace used-up assets.

In most U.S. and European families, it is still "shirtsleeves to shirtsleeves in three generations." Meanwhile, in Japan, the expression is, "Rice paddies to rice paddies in three generations." And the Scottish say, "The father buys, the son builds, the grandchild sells, and his son begs." In China, it's, "Wealth never

---

[16] American Standard Version (ASV)

survives three generations." I am not sure that is necessarily a bad thing. Too much accumulation of wealth will stifle progress and renewal.

> *Your profession is not what brings home your weekly paycheck, your profession is what you're put here on earth to do, with such passion and such intensity that it becomes spiritual in calling.*

> **—Vincent van Gogh**

What will keep your family together when you are no longer here? Assuming that's what you want! If your assets and/or businesses can easily be divided up among family members and siblings, that may be the best way to avoid future strife and conflict. Each of your heirs can decide what to do with his or her piece of the inheritance. Shares in listed companies, real estate, and passive investments are relatively easy to split up (at most a one-time effort and cost to get things organized) and can avoid a lot of future complications, strife, and potential conflict.

However, if you wish to keep the family and its assets together, this is what you need to think about:

1) A **shared family business**, especially if it continues to grow, needs to be well-managed. Almost by definition, the patriarch or matriarch must have been an able business manager in his/her time (or there would be no family business in the first place). Over time, his/her edge may have been blunted. Because of advancing years, he or she may have missed major changes in technology, legislation, or market preferences. His or her children are not by definition his or her best successors. Most businesses are better off as meritocracies, where the best professional managers are involved in management, and family members unqualified to be managers are only shareholders, with no say in how the business should be run. Shared business endeavors are less and less often the best way to keep a family together.

2) **Shared values** are essential for keeping a family together. The founder of the dynasty must have had a clear set of values to have become successful. Quite likely, he or she has projected or even imposed those values on his/her children, but the children have not necessarily

picked up on those values. The people they marry and their children will have little in common with the long-gone days and values of the founder. This means that when decision-time comes, those people will vote for decisions in line with their values, which may be very different from the ones the family founders started out with. Without shared values, there is no family unity. It does not even make sense to force a family to stay together if there are no shared values, as this will inevitably lead to strife and infighting. So, if you wish to keep a family together over a longer period of time, start working on aligning and nurturing values.

3) **Shared activities** are also important. Few members of succeeding generations will be involved in running the family business, but many more may be involved in other family interests, such as an art collection, museum, charity, or any other shared project that both represents the family values and gives family members a chance to work and interact together other than on social occasions. It has been demonstrated over the years that family offices with well-managed joint art collections or charities (think the Rockefellers, the Nobel family, the Guggenheims) have a much, much better reason and likelihood of staying connected and interested in remaining a family.

4) **A (shared) family office** makes a lot of sense for an extended family. It will help greatly in branding the family, uniting the family behind shared goals, developing and maintaining shared values, and managing shared activities. Typically, such a family office will provide services that include: a) managing the relationship with the original family business, circulating financial information, organizing shareholders' meetings, and distributing dividends and information on important business decisions; b) managing private equity investments, which often include pet projects, such as restaurants and other hobby-related activities; c) managing passive investments, contracting one or several professional asset managers, private bankers, trustees, tax advisors, auditors, and other professional service providers, and evaluating their performance; d) managing, documenting, administering, evaluating, and reporting on art collections, family heirlooms and heritage properties, charitable projects and philanthropic investments that can make family members proud and encourage them to participate; e) providing joint professional

services, such as insurance and pension plans. Dealing with family conflicts, mediating, and designing family charters; f) providing a concierge service to organize shared vacations and taking care of real estate, boats, and valuable assets; g) taking care of needy, elderly, and disabled family members and managing study funds; h) anything else that the family defines as a shared interest. These may become costly or unwieldy and may need pruning from time to time.

Which route is the best depends very much on how close the family wants to be, and whether it wants to stay together. The patriarch or matriarch may have very strong feelings about how the family and family business should develop after his/her demise, but in the end, the family will only stay together if its members want to stay together. A patriarch or matriarch is therefore well advised, in the best interests of his/her heirs, to plan in such a way that future generations are never forced to stay together, if they no longer wish to. A thorough planning process may be needed. Courses and help are available. In my case, a combination of professional advice and discussions with other owners of family-owned businesses helped me hack a path. Start early, and make SURE you finish the process. You never know when your planning will need to prove its effectiveness! Life is short!

Doing something as a family is great if you want to be a family, if there is the drive to be and stay together because you share common values, aspirations, and goals. Start working on those shared values and the importance of staying together will develop automatically. If you have no shared values, do not force the next generation to have shared investments.

It is not true that people stop pursuing dreams because they grow old, they grow old because they stop pursuing dreams.

—Gabriel García Márquez

Chapter 3

Everything is intricately connected; even creating a small effect can have a big impact.

I love you without knowing how, or when, or from where. I love you simply, without problems or pride: I love you in this way because I do not know any other way of loving but this, in which there is no I or you, so intimate that your hand upon my chest is my hand, so intimate that when I fall asleep your eyes close.[17]

—Pablo Neruda, *100 Love Sonnets*

In every life, there are defining moments that are etched on the back of your mind and give clear direction where to go. You may call them insights, visions, moments of enlightenment, epiphanies, or whatever.

The earliest one I can remember happened when I was very young. I was only just learning to lift myself onto my own feet at the bars of my crib, and to stand on my own two legs. The crib was outside in my parents' orchard, a fair distance from the farmhouse. My mother was doing the annual spring cleaning and needed me to be out of the way. It was a beautiful crisp day in early spring and I was basically a happy kid of 14 months, enjoying the colors and sounds of spring in the orchard until I saw, in the distance, my mother going in and out of the house with furniture and cleaning equipment. I called for her attention, but she did not hear me, so I called her a bit louder and then as loud as I could. She did not react. Then, all of a sudden, I somehow realized that she actually did hear me, but had just decided to ignore me. Three things happened. First, my legs tightened—from that moment on, I started to be able to stand firm and I learned to walk. Second, I realized that I was caged, and that the crib was preventing me from going where I wanted. Third, my

---

[17]   Neruda, Pablo. *100 Love Sonnets*, Ontario: Exile Editions, 2007.

mother (whom I'd never had anything to complain about) had deliberately left me there to fend for myself. Two important character traits were set at that very moment. Whether you believe it or not, I realized then and there that I would need to take responsibility for myself and be independent, and also that I was strong and could achieve anything I wanted, if I set my mind to it.

A few years later, I went with my father on an early morning walk. It was autumn and the morning mist was slowly lifting from the wet meadows. Ducks were noisily gathering in messy circles above us before starting their long journey to winter in Africa. It was cold, although the morning carried the promise that the warm sun might come out later in the day. My father carried a gun and we patrolled the ditches, looking for ducks, pheasants, and rabbits. Out of nowhere, a large rabbit suddenly crossed our path; with an amazing speed, my father shouldered his gun, cocked it, aimed, and fired. The rabbit somersaulted into the air and dropped into the grass. We slowly walked over and found the animal in its final spasms, its eyes already vacant. After a while, it was completely still. Something welled up in my throat. My father took my hand, something he normally never did, as he wasn't a touchy-feely kind of person, and we silently watched the rabbit for several minutes as if apologizing for having taken its life. I had never felt closer to my father. While we were standing there, I clearly realized how the circle of life worked and how we and the rabbit were united in one universe, in one dance of life where each individual depends on all others for its survival, and all individuals together are actually just one. Only seven or eight years old, I intuitively felt that I understood the workings of the universe. Much later, a fraction of this moment of insight was taught to me in school. And many times since, I have remembered that moment with my father, whenever I felt lost or disconnected. I even remember how long the body of that rabbit remained warm while I carried it home, and how we ate it that Sunday. It was only much later, when he was already gone, that I realized that my father must have learned to shoot so well during the war. Now, I somehow wonder whether he looked at dying people in the same way as we looked at the rabbit that misty morning.

On a very cold winter morning, when it was still dark and everything was covered in snow, I rode on the back of my father's bicycle to the train station. I was eight or nine years old and I was going on my first train journey. We went to the cattle market in 's-Hertogenbosch, a city about an hour and a half away. I was very excited, as I had never been on a train, to a cattle market, or so far from home before. Even today, I can vividly remember the granite steps of the train station and their sprinkling of shiny pieces of embedded mica and other minerals. I remember the layout and details of the train carriage, with its smell of stale tobacco and wet winter coats. I remember the smell of the fresh manure at the cattle market and the weathered faces of the farmers. My father explained how to choose a calf or heifer; together, we handpicked and my father bought 18 heifers, to be delivered by a humongous truck later in the day and raised to maturity at our farm. After the deal was sealed with a lot of clapping, my father and the farmer selling the heifers went to a nearby coffee house to drink a shot of Jenever (Dutch gin) to seal the deal. I knew my father never drank alcohol, but I guess that shot was important for the success of the deal, which in those days represented a fair amount of money. After the seller had gone, we looked each other in the eyes and knew we had completed an important task. We felt good about the deal we had made together. We were farmers and the wellbeing of our family depended on the choices we made. I knew there and then that I would never make a good employee, and that I would need to be independent and free to make my own choices, like my father.

I was with some friends on a vacation trip in the mountains of Austria. I was driving very slowly up a steep road enjoying the view when the motor suddenly stalled and the car stopped and then started rolling backward with increasing speed. The brakes didn't respond well and the steering became very difficult. I started to panic, afraid that we would fall over a cliff. I rounded a sharp curve, which was difficult in reverse with a car that was malfunctioning, and felt our speed increasing. Fortunately, I spotted the entrance to a farm road going steeply up the mountain, and I managed to back the car onto that side track. I lost a lot of speed, hit some bushes, and then finally came to a standstill. The car was basically undamaged and so were we. But at the moment when I was rounding the curve, I was almost certain that we were going to fall over the cliff. I saw two things: my whole life passing by and also the road I still had to travel. Although I have been driving much more carefully since then, I realized at that moment that my life was immaterial in the greater scheme of things. If I died, everything would continue, just as it was, without me being part of it. More importantly, that that was fine. I had a certain role to play in this life; in the future, there would be new challenges, new people and animals to meet, new things to do and challenges to face, and it would all be different but no less fun or valuable than the life I was leading at the time.

I was on a business trip, tired, jet-lagged, and disoriented. I fell asleep in an unpleasant hotel room in Buenos Aires, and in the middle of the night my phone rang. I was angry at myself for not having turned off the ring tone before going to sleep. A friend at the other end of the line told me the story of a poor young woman in Indonesia, who needed a caesarian to save her life and that of her unborn child, but had no money or hospital insurance. I felt I had no choice but to commit and I donated the funds for her operation. I spent the remaining hours before dawn looking at the ceiling and calculating that woman's odds: the many misfortunes and pieces of luck that had ultimately linked her to me at that exact moment. I felt proud of having clearly saved at least one person's life. I also realized, perhaps for the first time, how many lives I was not saving, how many people I was not helping, and how much of my time I was not dedicating to doing something valuable for our wider community.

Each of the five defining moments described above changed my life profoundly. Each was like a moment of total darkness, where a sudden flash of light shined on the path in front of me. Each brief moment of insight gave me the confidence to strengthen my stride and commit to a direction.

If I think long enough, there are quite a few more of those moments. Some made more of an impression on me than others, but together they clarified my life and gave me points of reference as to where to go and what to do.

To make our lives have impact, it is important to focus. We must direct our time and energy to those tasks we have chosen for ourselves. And each and every day, we must think about how we can do them better.

I have chosen the early morning for that. Even when I have no time for meditation (or don't feel like doing it), I spend at least a few moments in front of the mirror, deciding on my key tasks for the day.

Of course, there is work to do: big challenges and small ones. However, a few items always jump to the front as especially important: wishing someone a happy birthday, sending a message of reconciliation to someone I may have been harsh with the previous day, or encouraging someone who seemed to have lost his way. These tasks are important, but there are also the big goals: jobs that need to be done that day, week, month, or year. They must not be pushed aside by important small tasks. The time needs to be split between warm, caring human touches and structural goals to be achieved.

For some stupid reason, in front of that mirror, I often think about a piece of advice I read in "Achtung—Panzer" by Heinz Guderian: "You hit somebody with your fist and not with your fingers spread." It is so easy to lose track or focus by spreading out your efforts; for optimum impact, you have to concentrate most of your energy on the structural key goals you want to reach.

I guess that is why there is some merit in making a "bucket list," a to-do list of must-dos. Trying to make one is a fun exercise, good to do alone, but also as a family (we call it a family charter), and even as a company (where we call it a strategic business plan). You will amaze yourself by seeing how many things you add to the list that you've never made the smallest effort to bring even one step closer to realization.

> *Man lives consciously for himself, but is an unconscious instrument in the attainment of the historic, universal, aims of humanity.*[18]

> **—Leo Tolstoy**

Start by answering for yourself the following questions:

1) What if you were to die tomorrow? Or next week? What would you wish you could do before you die?

2) What would you do if you had unlimited time, money, and resources, and no restraints? What are the restraints anyway?

3) What have you always wanted to do but have not done yet? And why?

4) Are there countries, places, or locations you'd like to visit? People you want to meet?

5) What are your biggest goals and wildest dreams? Why aren't you working on realizing them today?

---

[18] Tolstoy, Leon. *War and Peace*, Istanbul: eKitap Projesi, 2014

6) What achievements do you want to have and be known for? What is holding you back from working on them now? What experiences haven't you had yet? What do you want to feel or experience?

7) Are there any special moments you want to witness, and why?

8) What activities or skills do you want to learn or try out?

9) What are the most important things you can ever do with or for others?

10) What would you like to say to or do with other people? People you love? Family? Friends? Why aren't you saying or doing those things today?

11) What do you want to achieve in the following areas of your life: social activities, love, family, career, business, health, mind, soul, spirit?

12) What would you need to do in order to lead the sort of life that would mean the most to you?

The purpose of this exercise is not to make your days even busier by chasing after all the items on your bucket list at once. If possible, you might try to make your days less busy, so that you have more time to be in the moment and enjoy the only moment that really matters: the here and now.

The goal is to find your own voice, your authentic self. Buddhism, amongst other spiritual paths, has been focusing on this for the past 2,500 years. Airplane seats (in the full upright position, to keep your spine straight) provide the perfect environment for regular meditation.

We all have the tendency to be driven forward by the little voice in our head, the narrator or witness that we often confuse with the self. It is actually not the self, but the ego, a spoiled brat. By definition, the ego is never satisfied, it always wants more. It is constantly comparing itself to others. For what purpose? Comparing never adds any positive value; it just creates envy, jealousy, blaming, want, and greed. All the seven sins and more.

This little voice in our head is never satisfied. It is always judgmental and very repetitive, if left alone. It constantly sees itself as both separate from and at the center of the universe. It is forever complaining about the past, which we cannot change: missing people, past experiences, and forgotten places, while also worrying about the future and obsessing about things that could go wrong, especially dark and worst-case scenarios. Those things could just as easily go well, and we can't do anything about them until they happen. So, thinking once about a likely scenario is more than enough times. Worrying doesn't solve a thing!

It is important to make the effort to realize that the little voice in your head is just another opinion, like the opinion of your partner, friend, business associate, neighbor or anyone else; it is not you. It's an opinion you can agree with or ignore. Treat it as what it is: just one opinion, among so many others.

By accepting every situation for what it is in the moment, you can avoid wasting time blaming people, judging situations, or getting worked up, stressed, or opinionated. Instead, you can move straight on to what is important: dealing with the situation as it actually is, not as you perceive it. We should not react to events by projecting emotions onto others, but respond without any negative emotion. The present moment is not an obstacle that you need to overcome to reach a better future moment; the present is the only moment that matters. It is what it is and everything that is. Accept the present moment for what it is and deal with the here and now without being judgmental or trying to force others to see or do things the way you do. Just this one act of acceptance can take all the stress out of your life and give you full control.

By analyzing the little voice in your head, watching what it says from a distance, and thinking about the values and visions you have collected over your life (including your bucket list of dreams and passions), you may slowly get a picture of your authentic self. What sort of person are you now, as opposed to ten years ago, yesterday, or (in your imagination), the day after tomorrow? What values do you subscribe to, what things do you feel are important? What experiences are you proud of, do you dream about, or would you like to be remembered for? Nobody can answer any of those questions for you, but it is important to think about them and to formulate the answers for yourself, until you arrive at a more-or-less coherent picture.

In Hindu philosophy, there is the concept of *Dharma*, the path you were born to hack from the jungle of experiences. If you deviate too far from that path, you will feel lonely, empty, useless, low on energy, or depressed. If you get closer to that path, "listen to the elephant inside you," and begin to fulfil your mission on earth, you will feel energized, motivated, passionate, and fulfilled.

As you get closer to your authentic self, you will notice that you also think differently about wealth and priorities. Once you get to know yourself better, you will feel much less insecure and need less wealth to create false securities for yourself. You may lose the need to show off, or to impress others with what you own and control. You may even realize that you don't need more than one car, television, or house. You may also want to think about the priorities you set in spending or investing your money. You forever remain responsible for where you came from (your parents and the community that taught you), where you have gone (your children, business, and environment), the people who support you (your society and ecosystem), and the ideas beyond you (the spiritual environment you identify with). Instead of spending your money first on all of your personal needs and wants and then looking at what's left over for others, you may want to think about first showing compassion, humility, and gratitude for where you came from, have gone, and are supported and inspired by, before spending money on personal luxuries. Compassion is the deep connection between ourselves and others. True compassion recognizes that the boundaries we perceive between ourselves and others are just an illusion. When we first begin to practice compassion, this very deep level of understanding may elude us. Have faith that if you start where you are, you will eventually feel your way toward it. We move closer every time we see past ourselves to accommodate concern for others. And, as with any skill, our compassion grows most in the presence of difficulty.

> *The test of our progress is not whether we add more to the abundance of those who have much; it is whether we provide enough for those who have too little.*[19]

—Franklin D. Roosevelt

---

[19]   Second Inaugural Address, January 20, 1937, President Franklin D. Roosevelt.

Chapter 4

Celebrate your body, mind, soul, and spirit to ensure that you have many valuable experiences.

The changes in our life must come from the impossibility to live otherwise than according to the demands of our conscience, not from our mental resolution to try a new form of life.[20]

—Leo Tolstoy

I tend to compare myself with a multi-dimensional engine, and I consciously try to fine-tune that engine for optimal performance. As I grow older, I realize that life is increasingly short, and quality time (rather than more stuff, like money) is what it is made of. To optimize life, I am convinced, we should live our lives to the fullest, and gather a plethora of experiences. I have decided to make sure that, if one day my life flashes in front of me, it is worth watching. My energy, qualities, and skills are the pistons that drive the engine, and it runs best if it runs on all available pistons simultaneously, courageously driven forward with passion and at near-full throttle. I think that the way to make life work was perfectly defined by Antoine de Saint-Exupery, when he wrote, "If you want to build a ship, don't drum up people to collect wood and don't assign them tasks and work, but rather teach them to long for the endless immensity of the sea."[21]

Years of research indicate that what inspires people and makes them feel happy is leading a full life: giving it all that they can, which they will somehow, in some way get back in abundance, and being present in the moment, neither

---

[20]   Leo Tolstoy, 1828-1910

[21]   Antoine de Saint-Exupery (1900–1944). The Wisdom of the Sands, Translated by Stuart Gilbert, Harcourt, Brace, 1950.

regretting anything that happened in the past nor fearing anything that might occur in the future. In other words: to live, to love, to learn, and to leave a legacy.

To live: to experience the good things in life, food, drinks, travel, nature, fresh air, mountain views, sea breezes, desert heat and winter cold, art in all its forms, music, sports, culture, entertainment, time taken to smell roses, il dolce far niente, friends, family, enjoyment, and the full range of human emotions. We were created to reproduce our genetic footprint and make humankind progress and to flourish and continue on for generations to come. If we believe in ourselves, we can make anything happen. When we stop believing or living, we will soon get old and die.

To love: to experience caring for and bonding with others: partners, family members, close friends, our loyal pets, the proud and free animals in nature, and the birds in the sky, good colleagues, friendly neighbors, members of our soccer or cricket teams, members of our congregations, clubs, or political parties, and people who share the same passport, convictions, or passions. Feeling connected to others in many different ways and through many different groups makes us feel secure, useful, and part of a larger purpose. Passions may die but love remains. Bob Marley sees it the other way around: "Truth is, everybody is going to hurt you: you just gotta find the ones worth suffering for."

To learn: to experience something new, to enjoy and grow our human experience, to challenge the perceived limitations of our skills, to move from knowing to understanding what is going on in and around ourselves, to search for meaning and importance—all these things will give us a sense of purpose, of being on a journey that goes forever onward and inward. The drive for knowledge and understanding will push us towards exploring the dark corners of our soul and spread the bright light of our good deeds, even if "wisdom comes to us when it can no longer do any good."[22] (Gabriel García Márquez). And when you reach levels of insight and wisdom, it is important to share them with the next generation, not just to pass on the torch, but also because coaching, teaching, and communicating wisdom is a great way to attain more wisdom and experiences.

To leave a legacy: understanding the inevitability of death and our transient and fragile presence on earth makes us want to hang on, to leave our mark

---

[22] Márquez, Gabriel García. *Love in the Time of Cholera*, translated by Edith Grossman, London: Penguin Books, 2007.

while we can. We want to recognize our own traits in the children we conceive, and our ideas and dreams in the businesses we set up, the books we write, and the values we instill in our employees and the sports team members we coach. As long as we are remembered by name or deed, we feel that some part of us will continue into the future. That is why we write wills and family charters, and construct family offices that will continue to run our businesses the way we used to. It is an attempt to reign from the grave, for years after our bodies decompose. There is nothing wrong with pursuing dreams until the day we die, because we grow old as soon as we stop chasing dreams. But I believe that we should free the next generation to have its own dreams and shape in its own ways.

If we are honest about who we are, we care a lot more about our social and material environment than we want to admit. Thomas Mann wrote almost a hundred years ago in *Buddenbrooks*: "Where shall I be when I am dead? ...I shall be in all those who have ever, do ever, or ever shall say I ...Who, what, how could I be if I were not—if this my external self, my consciousness, did not cut me off from those who are not I? ...soon will that in me which loves you be free and be in and with you – in and with you all. I shall live... Blind, thoughtless, pitiful eruption of the urging will!"[23]

Arthur Schopenhauer adds, "Every man takes the limits of his own field of vision for the limits of the world." He also wrote: "Egoism really consists in man's restricting all reality to his own person, in that he imagines he lives in this alone, and not in others. Death teaches him something better, since it abolishes this person, so that man's true nature, that is his will, will henceforth live only in other individuals."[24]

This insight suggests that there really is no self to lose at death. What we usually consider the self is really the same in all people and animals, at all times and everywhere. There is no need to cling to anything, because it will be dispersed over all creation.

In the age of Thomas Mann and Arthur Schopenhauer, there was no way to scientifically prove their ideas. However, in the last ten years, quantum physics has shown that these statements are materially correct. The experiences we

---

[23] Thomas Mann, *Buddenbrooks: Verfall einer Famalie, x*, Ch.

[24] Arthur Schopenhauer, 1788-1860 (W-II, 507)

create can be separated in manifestations of what we sense: the body, mind, soul, and spirit.

Body: The body is the vehicle in which we live and travel all our lives, without which we cannot lead a conscious life, and which (once our last breath becomes air) becomes nothing more than a rotting carcass. While alive, the body is a community of millions and millions of cells that cooperate to ensure that it functions, with all of the body's experience and history imprinted in each cell.

Mind: The mind is the accumulation of all of the experiences and knowledge of the generations before us, what we learn during our lives, and the experiences we collect during our lifetimes, consciously and unconsciously. While we are transient beings, we are aware of what we consciously know, are, and do.

Soul: The soul is, as Jung says, the archetype of life, embedded in the details of ordinary, everyday experience. With the spirit, we try to transcend our humanity; with the soul, we try to enter into our humanity fully and to realize it completely. Motivated by spiritual ambition, a person may imitate the old saints and go into the desert or the forest to be cleansed or to discover a higher level of consciousness. Full of soul, a person might endure the highs and lows of family life, marriage, and work, motivated by a compassionate and big heart. The soul is what makes us deal in a meaningful and imaginative way with the present and our daily lives.

Spirit: In general terms, we can see the spirit as being focused on transcending the limits of our personal, time-bound, concrete lives. The spirit is fascinated by the future, wants to know the meaning of everything, and would like to stretch, if not break altogether, the laws of nature through technology or spirituality. It is full of ideals and ambition: a necessary, rewarding, and inspiring aspect of human life. It is the driving force that makes us look beyond ourselves.

If we combine the two approaches, the result is a matrix that is something like the very simple chart below. Of course, this is just a concept and an oversimplification. Each of us will complete this chart using slightly different preferences and accents.

But that is not the point.

	Body	Mind	Soul	Spirit
To live	Eat healthily, exercise, enjoy life, build experiences	Read, travel, explore, be inquisitive	Create something, add value to our lives and those of others	Help others, invest in progress, improve the world
To love	Sex, tenderness	Share ideas, debate, invent	Be kind, sharing, protective	Help others to grow and connect
To learn	Exercise, conditioning, discipline, yoga	Study, investigate, experiment, and understand	Optimize our world, coach others, work on solving problems	Understand the bigger picture and share it
To leave a legacy	Have children, teach others, build businesses and structures	Write books, express thoughts and ideas	Philanthropy, charity, promote sustainable development	Transfer values, ideals, and spirituality, protect our nature, connect with the source

Which projects or activities you place in each of the squares is not really important. What is important is to have at least something in as many squares as possible. Squares that remain empty will sooner or later feel empty and make us yearn for fulfilment. The size of the items in each box is not relevant; it is the intensity that counts. One person may get as much satisfaction from babysitting the neighbor's children as another person does from organizing an elderly home, inventing a useful device, or eradicating a disease worldwide. The point is to use what you have and do what you can do fulfil your capabilities. When you've given something your best, you've achieved the right level of intensity. Doing things halfway (or even 99 percent) will never satisfy you. If you hide your light under a bushel, sooner or later you will feel that you are not making the most of life. Aim to boldly go where no man has gone before, in every aspect of your life!

What am I in the eyes of most people—a non-entity, an eccentric, or an unpleasant person—somebody who has no position in society and will never have; in short, the lowest of the low. All right, then—even if that were absolutely true, then I should one day like to show by my work what such an eccentric, such a nobody, has in his heart.[25]

—Vincent van Gogh

Part of being human is the search for an individual identity. Bound to this strong need to establish a unique persona is an equally intense desire for acceptance. When we find our individual tribes, both needs are satisfied. The members of our tribe are people who accept us as we are, without reservation, and who gladly accompany us on our evolutionary journeys. Among them, we feel free to be our imperfect selves, to engage unabashedly in the activities we enjoy, and to express our vulnerabilities by relying on our tribe for support. We feel comfortable investing our time and energy in the members of our tribe, and are equally comfortable allowing them to invest their resources in our development.

Spending a lot of time pursuing material interests, empty relationships, and mundane entertainment leaves a lot of boxes open. Sooner or later, people will begin to feel that they lack connection, meaning, and a social fabric.

Using your power, influence, money, experience, and time to improve at least one aspect of the world will tick many boxes at the same time. I try to look at my matrix once in a while, especially when I feel some dissatisfaction or emptiness. Invariably, one or several of the boxes will pop up as not being full enough. I may be neglecting my health or my friends, or not challenging my mind by learning something new. I may not be planning well enough for my kids' future. Merely identifying such issues will not solve them, but it represents a big step toward determining what I can do to make my life fuller.

And one by one the nights between our separated cities are joined to the night that unites us.[26]

—Pablo Neruda

---

[25] Van Gogh, Vincent. 1914. *The Letters of Vincent van Gogh*. Edited by Ronald de Leeuw, Mark Roskill, Arnold J. Pomerans. London: Penguin Classics, 1997.

[26] Pablo Neruda, *"Ode and Borgeonings," The Captain's Verse, 1952.*

Chapter 5

Various degrees of involvement: choosing whether to do it yourself, get professional help, or outsource a dream

> *I am the sum total of everything that went before me, of all I have been, seen, done, of everything done-to-me. I am everyone everything whose being-in-the-world affected or was affected by mine. I am anything that happens after I'm gone which would not have happened if I had not come.[27]*

> **—Salman Rushdie, *Midnight's Children***

Here we will look at the differences and similarities between:

- Charity, examples in Chapters 8, 17

- Community service, examples in Chapters 10, 17

- Philanthropy, examples in Chapters 8, 11

- Corporate social responsibility, examples in Chapters 8, 16

- Impact Investing, examples in Chapters 12, 13

- Sustainable development, examples in Chapters 15, 16, 18

- Social enterprise/responsible business, examples in Chapters 8, 9, 14

as they represent various gradations, or intensities of impact, produced by each dollar invested.

---

[27] Rushdie, Salman. *Midnight's Children*, London: Vintage. (1981)

When deciding which lofty goal or good purpose to support, protect, or promote, you must also think about the format, or method of doing it. There are many different ways to structure your charitable donations, your contributions to philanthropy, your corporate social responsibility, and your responsible businesses. There is no ideal form; everything depends on your preferences, dreams, and ambitions. That leaves endless space for creativity and courage. I would like to add, as a reminder, the following observation by Michelangelo: "The greater danger for most of us lies not in setting our aim too high and falling short; but in setting our aim too low, and achieving our mark."

Remember your dreams, however deeply hidden they may be. Stand up and fight for them! Deep inside, you already understand the purpose of your life, and how to add value through your own efforts. Your soul has always known, even if your mind is too busy, forgets, or at times suppresses what you really want. Only one thing can make your dreams impossible and that is the fear of failure.

I distinguish below between the following ways of making a difference:

1: Charity:

Charitable giving is the act of altruistically giving money, goods, or time to the unfortunate, either directly or by means of a **charitable trust** or other worthy cause. Charitable giving as a religious act or duty is the same; it often referred to as almsgiving. Many religions and advocates of charity agree that "No person was ever honored for what he received. Honor has been the reward for what he gave." Charitable giving does not really improve the world; it merely relieves the personal situation of someone or some group that has been less fortunate at some point in time. It is no less important to the individual who receives the help. Sometimes (for example, during a natural disaster or failed harvests) charity may be the only short-term solution available.

> *My mother told me that life isn't always about pleasing yourself and that sometimes you have to do things for the sole benefit of another human being. I completely agreed with her, but reminded her that that was what blow jobs were for.*[28]

—Chelsea Handler,
My Horizontal Life: A Collection of One-Night Stands

How much giving is enough? According to Saint Paul, "whoever sows sparingly will also reap sparingly, and whoever sows bountifully will also reap bountifully." Still, small donations can make big differences. Common causes of death and suffering in poor countries often have relatively inexpensive solutions. For instance, a U.S. $10 mosquito net can protect a child from catching malaria during the night. Inoculations are typically not very expensive and save many lives. Unfortunately, as big organizations are often involved, there are many overhead costs associated with putting this type of solution into practice. The UN has estimated that about $1,000 can save a human life. I am convinced many lives can be saved or greatly relieved for a lot less.

I sympathize with Michael Bloomberg, who said: "If you want to do something for your children and show how much you love them, the single best thing—by far—is to support organizations that will create a better world for them and their children."[29]

We all enjoy at least one luxury we can do without. If we calculate the value of that luxury over the course of a week or a year, and set the value of that luxury against the cost of saving a person's life, I am pretty sure we would all conclude that we could do without at least one luxury in our lives. If so, we should allocate that money to a good cause and actually save those lives.

This is the easiest way: do a good thing and don't look back. Zero overhead, zero administration, plain and simple. Look around and you will discover a multitude of worthy one-time causes and needy individuals in no time. However, you will have limited impact and your efforts will relieve hardship rather than causing a permanent change. Even limited impact is better than

---

[28]   Handler, Chelsea. *My Horizontal Life: A Collection of One-night Stands*, New York: Bloomsbury, 2005.

[29]   https://givingpledge.org/Pledger.aspx?id=172

no impact, as Mother Teresa explained: "It's not how much we give but how much love we put into giving."

If you want to give **more systematically to charity** and approach issues in a sustainable way, then give money or goods to a reputable charitable organization. There are many. You can pick any category, by location in the world, or religious or moral background. There are many needs to fill, and for each type of need, private or governmental organizations exist. Charities see and deal with needs but do not really address the causes of those needs. That is why we often search for a more systemic approach.

Give **one-time contractual donations** to a reputable charitable organization and agree upfront on the goal or purpose that you want the money to be used for. Of course, the larger your donation, the more willing an organization will be to accommodate your specific wishes. If you donate enough money to a university or hospital, they will name a new wing after you. If you donate a few billions to the Bill and Melinda Gates Foundation, you can decide how the next mega project will be run. Winston Churchill once said, "We make a living by what we get, but we make a life by what we give."

You can contract with a professional organization, such as ours, to manage your structured longer-term donations to that charity. This way, you will only have to worry about deciding on a strategy and setting the goals—a professional organization will make the payments, carry out regular checks, send you regular reports, and measure the efficiency of your endeavors. The slogan adopted by Sue Desmond-Hellmann, the CEO of the Bill and Melinda Gates Foundation, which is the largest philanthropic organization in the world, is as follows: "The world will not get better by itself. We must set big goals and hold ourselves accountable every step of the way."[30]

In Asia, more and more wealthy families follow the rule of thumb of Hong Kong entrepreneur Li Ka-Shing. Li Ka-Shing considers the Li Ka Shing Foundation to be his third son and has pledged to donate one-third of his assets to support philanthropic projects. He has called on other wealthy Asian entrepreneurs to do the same, hoping to alter the traditional pattern of passing on wealth through lineage.

---

[30]   https://givingpledge.org/Pledger.aspx?id=172

2: Community service:

You can achieve many of the same goals through community service, donating your time instead of money on an ongoing basis.

3: Philanthropy:

Philanthropy literally means the love of humanity, in the sense of caring, nourishing, developing, and enhancing what it means to be human. This approach calls on the benefactor to identify and exercise his or her values, and on the beneficiary to receive and benefit from the service or goods received. In other words, it is the practice of giving money and time to help make life better for other people.

An often-used definition of philanthropy is "private initiatives, for public good, focusing on the quality of life," which combines the original humanistic tradition with a more social scientific aspect. This definition contrasts philanthropy with business initiatives, which are private initiatives for the private good, focusing on material gain, and with government efforts, which are public initiatives for the public good, focusing on the provision of public services. Philanthropy goes beyond satisfying your ego. As George Soros has said, "I'm not doing my philanthropic work out of any kind of guilt. I'm doing it because I can afford to do it, and because I believe in it."[31]

Philanthropy is different from charity; not all charity is philanthropy and vice versa, although there is a degree of overlap in practice. One commonly cited difference is that charity aims to relieve the pain caused by a particular social problem, while philanthropy attempts to address the root cause of the problem—the difference between the proverbial gift of bread to a hungry person, versus teaching such people how to grow, harvest, and grind grain.

To become a philanthropist, you will first need money and/or time, as those are the essential ingredients of any philanthropic undertaking. It makes no difference whether the person we help is a neighbor's child right next door, or an anonymous person or cause in a faraway country. The moral point of view requires us to look beyond the interests of our own society. Previously, this

---

[31]   David Brancaccio interviews George Soros, September 12, 2003. http://www.pbs.org/now/transcript/transcript_soros.html last viewed 7.5.2016.

may rarely have been possible; nowadays, it is quite feasible. The world is at our fingertips. As Robert Kennedy said,

Let no one be discouraged by the belief that there is nothing one person can do against the enormous array of the world's ills, misery, ignorance, and violence. Few will have the greatness to bend history, but each of us can work to change a small portion of events. And in the total of all those acts will be written the history of a generation.[32]

I believe that, from a moral point of view, preventing the starvation of millions of people outside our society is at least as pressing as upholding values and norms within. Spending money on unnecessary consumption (including government spending on endless weaponry and unnecessary expressions of consumption, wealth and power) diverts time and resources that could be used in a much better way, for the benefit of all.

Many philanthropists think that future generations should be valued as highly as people who currently exist. They therefore focus on reducing existential risks to humanity. Others believe that the interests of non-human species should be accorded the same moral weight as those of humans; they can work to prevent the suffering of animals, such as those raised in factory farms. Different cultures have differing views about the potential beneficiaries of philanthropy; in Western cultures, the beneficiaries are part of a smaller or larger group of brothers; in Indian cultures, the circle of sympathy may extend to all living beings, human or otherwise.

Along with some other philanthropists, I believe that we ought to prevent something bad from happening, if it is in our power to achieve this without sacrificing anything of comparable moral importance. Anyone with an annual income of above U.S. $60,000 (Purchase Power Parity) belongs to the 1 percent of the world's richest people. Such people are in a position to donate a portion of their income to effective charities, or any comparable alternative, since doing so will not force them to give up purchases essential to their own lives.

---

[32]   Robert F. Kennedy, speaking at the University of Cape Town, "Day of Affirmation" South Africa, June 6, 1966.

4: Corporate Social Responsibility:

Corporate Social Responsibility (CSR), a modern term for responsible or ethical business, is a form of corporate self-regulation or self-restriction integrated into the standard business model. Set standards ensure that a company actively complies with the spirit of the law, ethical standards, and national or international norms in many areas, including environmental impact and natural resources. Often, a company's implementation of CSR goes beyond compliance, engaging in actions that further some social good, beyond the interests of the company or anything required by law. The aim is to increase long-term profits, employee engagement, and shareholder trust through positive public relations and high ethical standards, while reducing business and legal risks by taking responsibility for corporate actions. CSR strategies encourage companies to make a positive impact on the environment and stakeholders, including consumers, employees, investors, communities, and others.

In our business, we have translated this into four key objectives, dedicating a fixed percentage of revenue to CSR projects. We also evaluate our employees on the basis of their adherence to these objectives:

Profit: We want to make sure that, as a business, we are solidly profitable, so that we can ensure the long-term continuity of our enterprise, guaranteeing job security to our employees and continuity of services to our clients and suppliers.

Passion: We want to stimulate our employees to get the best out of themselves and their jobs every day, regardless of how mundane those jobs may be. By providing ongoing training and making everyone both accountable and committed, we encourage employees to feel passionate about their jobs, and to enjoy their time, colleagues, and productivity at work.

People: We are part of a local as well as a global community. We want to be good corporate citizens and to help all of our offices to contribute positively to their communities by adopting ethical business practices, being polite and humble, and consistently meeting their obligations.

Planet: We want our environmental footprint to be no larger than needed. We must not waste raw materials, travel more than necessary, waste time or effort, or endanger nature. Where our business does have a negative impact (for example, by producing CO2 while flying) we offset this activity with a counter-activity (planting trees that produce oxygen).

Many commercial enterprises have a number of social objectives, but their commitment to these objectives is at least partly motivated by ultimately hoping to make the enterprise more financially valuable. That is fine, as long as the corporate social responsibility aspect is genuine. As Vladimir Putin, a fervent promoter, put it in one of his New Year's speeches:

We need business to understand its social responsibility, that the main task and objective for a business is not to generate extra income and to become rich and transfer the money abroad, but to look and evaluate what a businessman has done for the country, for the people, on whose account he or she has become so rich.[33]

We should therefore object to the Seven Social Sins:

- Wealth without work

- Pleasure without conscience

- Knowledge without character

- Commerce without morality

- Science without humanity

- Worship without sacrifice

- Politics without principle[34]

5: Impact investments:

Impact investments are real monetary investments made to companies, organizations, and funds to generate social and environmental impact as well as a financial return. Impact investments can be directed toward many different types of businesses, in both emerging and developed markets, and

---

[33] Vladimir Putin, The Declaration of Strategic Partnership between India and Russia signed in October 2000

[34] Mohandas Karamchand Gandhi published in his weekly newspaper Young India on October 22, 1925. The Collected Works of Mahatma Gandhi (electronic edition), Vol. 33, pp. 133-134. ISBN 8123007353, ISBN 9788123007359 OCLC 655798065

can target a range of returns from below market to market rate, depending upon circumstances and goals.

The growing impact investment market provides capital to address some of the world's most pressing challenges in sectors that include sustainable agriculture, clean and nonpolluting technology, microfinance, and affordable and accessible basic services such as housing, healthcare, and education.

What are some of the **core characteristics of impact investments**?

1) First, there has to be a form of intent to have a positive social or environmental impact through planned investments.

2) There must be the expectation of a proper return on investment; otherwise, the investment is either a philanthropic effort, a donation, or some form of corporate social responsibility. Impact investments are expected to generate a reasonable financial return on capital or, at a minimum, a return of capital. Impact investments target financial returns that range from below market to risk-adjusted market rate, and can be made across all asset classes. Most frequently, they focus on venture capital and private equity.

3) The investor must be committed to measuring and reporting on the social and environmental performance and progress of underlying investments, and ensuring transparency and accountability, while educating others about the practice of impact investing and building the field. How to do this will vary, depending on an investor's specific objectives. The choice of what to measure usually reflects the investor's intentions.

Why impact investing? Impact investing challenges the traditional view that social and environmental issues should be addressed only through philanthropic donations, while market investments focus exclusively on achieving financial returns. The impact investing market offers diverse and viable opportunities for investors to advance social and environmental solutions through investments that also produce financial returns. Many impact investments have been very successful.

Institutional investors and family offices can leverage significantly larger assets to advance their core social and/or environmental goals, while maintaining or growing their overall endowment.

Impact investment has attracted a wide variety of investors, both individual and institutional, including financial institutions, pension funds, private foundations, development finance institutions, family offices, fund managers and individual investors. It also attracts some of the better and more conscious talents in the market. Manfred Kets de Vries once said that "the prime challenge of organizational leadership is to create places to work that give people meaning, where they can feel truly alive and perform at their very best."

6: Social enterprise:

Social enterprises are different from normal businesses because their commitment to impact is central to their business missions. Some may not offer any benefits to their investors, apart from ultimately furthering their capacity to realize social and environmental goals, although there is huge variation in the forms and activities of social enterprises. Such businesses apply commercial strategies to maximize improvements in human and environmental wellbeing. Sometimes this includes maximizing social impact alongside reasonable profits for external shareholders. A good example of a social enterprise is Muhammad Yunus' Grameen Bank, a micro-credit business that makes reasonable returns for its investors, while helping thousands of micro-lenders to become self-employed or to start small businesses in emerging markets.

As he received his well-earned Nobel Peace Prize, Yunus was introduced with the following words:

Muhammad Yunus has shown himself to be a leader who has managed to translate visions into practical action for the benefit of millions of people, not only in Bangladesh, but also in many other countries. Loans to poor people without any financial security had appeared to be an impossible idea. From modest beginnings three decades ago, Yunus has, first and foremost through Grameen Bank, developed micro-credit into an ever more important instrument in the struggle against poverty.[35]

---

[35] Nobel Peace Prize Committee, Oslo October 13, 2006

Chapter 6

How to organize and shape your project

How you can have the desired impact and use professional help to maximize it.

> *Any good that I can do or any kindness that I can show to any human being, let me do it now. Let me not defer or neglect it, for I shall not pass this way again.*

> **—Mohandas Gandhi**

How did we choose to do this for ourselves?

Within our own company, we agreed many years ago to share some of what we had with less fortunate people in our society. We wanted to do this, not because we had to, or because we felt compelled to, but because we realized that we were extraordinarily lucky. We did it just because we could!

Not only do we employ healthy, socially capable and generally highly intelligent people, but most of them make an above-average monthly wage. More than 25 percent of our employees belong to the lucky 1 percent of the world, with an annual gross income in excess of U.S. $60,000! In addition, we focus our efforts on parts of the world where business is concentrated, the money market centers, where money is made. As a bonus, we get to know and work with the most interesting and successful individuals in those markets.

As a company, we have chosen a number of philanthropic and corporate social responsibility projects to work on. Having decided that charity and donations belong more in the personal sphere of the individual, we opted to focus on sustainable development. The projects we have chosen are somewhat random, in the sense that we could have chosen other projects, and maybe even more deserving ones. The important thing is that we started somewhere. Over the years, we have seen our efforts slowly starting to bloom.

Our first step was to empower and encourage our own employees by helping them understand how fortunate they were to be healthy and intelligent, with well-paid jobs. Now, all of our 30+ offices are making an effort to engage in some form of corporate social responsibility. I think that is great progress. Fortunately, most of our colleagues have chosen to get involved just because they can—and because they genuinely want to contribute. In addition, corporate social responsibility is part of each employee's measured performance. There are monetary and emotional rewards for results, as well as recognition and celebration ceremonies. However, any contribution is strictly voluntarily.

Our next step was to engage our clients. Given that we are in the trust business, all of our clients are, by definition, more fortunate than most people. Most of our clients work in international trade or investments or are HNWIs with money to invest. No one who is not a millionaire or well on his way to getting there should be our client. Many of our clients are very busy making money and do not take the time to think about making meaning, or analyzing which investments give the greatest returns. Psychological studies have shown, time and again, that the highest returns (in personal happiness) come from relationships, from the satisfaction of doing something with and for others.

We want to make people think. We hope to entice the people around us to start helping others in the here and now. We are all wealthy. Some us have a lot of money; others have a lot of skills. Some of us have tea, sympathy, and time to spend—but we all have something we can give.

In our company, we decided to establish a separate foundation to channel our corporate social responsibility ideas and activities. The Amicorp Community Foundation (ACF) was created in 2001 and is run by our employees. It is not a charitable foundation, as we consider charity the personal responsibility of each individual. Development is the realm where we can collectively hone our skills. Our community foundation was created as an instrument to channel our creative focus and energies towards environmental and community actions. We know that it isn't possible to change the world overnight, but we will make a difference, one sure step at a time, through meaningful accomplishments in the societies where we operate!

We believe in stimulating our employees to reach their full potential as human beings and we hope to engage employees as well as clients (typically wealthy individuals or successful businesses), to engage with our projects. To prime the well for those endeavors, we have pledged to allocate 1 percent of our gross revenues for corporate social responsibility projects.

Of course, we need to make money to pay good salaries, reimburse our suppliers, and make a healthy profit to invest in future growth. However, it is equally important to develop the potential of our employees by inspiring them to become passionate about our business, to work on their skills and talents, and to use them to build an ever-better company. As a company does not exist in isolation, we also want to make a positive contribution to the communities in which we operate and find opportunities. We aim to add value, act as a positive example, generate energy, and spark creative ideas—all this while minimizing our negative impact on the natural environment and polluting as little as possible.

We encourage our employees to embrace high ethical standards and community involvement. We want to support and inspire our environment by sharing knowledge and expertise, and by providing manpower, financial support, materials, and other facilities to the less privileged around us.

The foundation works on the principle that we all are responsible for leaving this world a better place than we found it. Some of our time is spent on the welfare of local communities, not because we feel obliged to give something back, but because it is our duty to use our talents and skills to benefit our entire community in sustainable ways. Serving others makes us better people, enriching our minds, bodies, and spirits, and helping us lead fuller lives. Each individual's contribution to social and environmental causes has become an important component of our annual appraisals and employee performance evaluations.

The history of mankind is full of people who, through seemingly small symbolic acts, make a significant difference. Gautama Buddha is one example. Originally one of many Sadhus, he achieved a state of enlightenment and has become an inspiration to an ever-expanding group of followers, nearly two thousand years after his death. Mohandas Gandhi, whose non-violent struggle was full of simple acts, such as drawing his own salt from the sea and weaving his own cotton, achieved full independence for India, creating the foundations for the democratic and diverse society we know today. It takes only one Bill Gates to eradicate polio worldwide. A single person can invent a ground-breaking medicine or make a major improvement in people's lives. Seemingly small actions can mushroom into major structural changes. If one person stops throwing trash into the street, he may inspire two more people to do the same. Soon all of our roads could be clean (this might be a great initiative in India, for instance). With our foundation, we aim, within realistic limits, to create meaningful examples that make people think and inspire them to do their bit.

Our mission is: *To build environmental consciousness and to help underprivileged people around the world build lives above the poverty line by offering them sustainable ways to achieve a better life through self-sufficiency.*

This is our vision: *To ensure that we leave this planet cleaner and more socially just for our children, our clients' children and generations to come, and to create inspiring opportunities for the less fortunate among us to develop their self-esteem and grow to their fullest potential.*

What began as an idea became a serious reality in our offices around the world. Active in about thirty countries, the foundation continues to gain momentum as our employees invest time, effort, passion, and resources in uplifting the communities they live and work in. As a company, we celebrated our 15th and 20th anniversaries—not with the glitz and glamour of parties and bonuses—but by joining hands with the people of Curaçao, Bali, India and other countries, to help them achieve more self-sufficiency.

Most of our employees volunteer their time to build awareness and support initiatives that bring self-sufficiency to the underprivileged and heighten environmental consciousness. We are aided in most of our projects by the support and involvement of like-minded partners (often clients) in the communities where we operate.

Colleagues around the world have participated in creative and sports events to raise money. The runners, swimmers, cyclists, and mustache growers have all drawn attention to important causes, ranging from cancer awareness to saving tigers, and from healthy living to protecting endangered animal species.

All of the projects we support must have an element of sustainability. We must teach people how to fish instead of giving them fish, and teach them how to plow and plant grain instead of giving them bread. In addition to a number of flagship projects, many of our offices run smaller local projects, so that all employees have the opportunity to develop caring, giving, and sharing in their own environments. Where we can raise money for our larger projects, we do so. We also fund scholarships to enable deserving children to pursue an education, and to provide books, school supplies, educational materials, and vocational skills training to enable people to find good jobs. We support coaching, reading, and library facilities, access to sophisticated computer infrastructures, and other activities to improve individuals' self-esteem through education and community involvement.

As an organization, we are aware that we impact the environment directly through business air travel and the consumption of resources such as water, paper, and electricity. To compensate, we have planted trees to offset the CO_2 we produce, and have worked hard to achieve our dream of leaving this planet cleaner and more socially just than we found it.

How do we use our experience to help others?

The skills we have developed over many years of corporate social responsibility projects we also offer to friends, clients, and business partners. They include a suite of services, as well as encouragement and advice. We try to run our corporate social responsibility services as efficiently as possible, so that our clients' money can be used for their chosen projects, as opposed to overhead, administration, and internal discussions and reporting. We work as closely as possible with our partners to define the scope and parameters of their CSR or charity project; we are also very open and transparent when allocating funds for the intended purpose. By engaging in constant dialogue, we aim to share any difficulties we encounter along the way, and to offer experience and solutions.

> *Most of your obstacles would melt away if, instead of cowering before them or procrastinating about dealing with them, you made up your mind to walk boldly through them. Nothing in life is to be feared. It is only to be understood. When you dare to face the things that scare you, you open the door to freedom and success. Don't be afraid to take the steps you need to take to make those positive changes in your life. To fight*

your fears, you must act. Your fears increase when you wait, put off, or postpone. If you understood your situation enough, you would never be afraid. The attainment of your dreams is but a determined action away. Successful people take action.[36]

—Rudi Viljoen

Decide to establish your own organization or to outsource the management of your charity, philanthropy or corporate social responsibility:

You can include charity goals in your own **Private Office** strategy or join a multi-family shared office that represents the type of goals and values to wish to pursue. In this way, you increase the professionalism of your approach and exercise more control, while sharing the costs of the vehicle with other purposes and/or other families.

You can create a personal **Charitable Organization**. If you plan to conduct long-term projects, have very specific dreams, or want things done in a particular way, while staying involved in carrying out the strategy, this may be a very good approach.

What assistance can we offer?

1) As an organization, we now offer support, experience, and tools for those who need encouragement or a helping hand, and those who just don't have the time or the team to do it themselves.

2) We help you, the sponsor, select a meaningful project that will meet your and your family's needs and interests. We also have many projects already in place, or on some back-burner, waiting for someone to blow life (or at least money) into them.

3) We can structure the project in your own name, your family's name, or silently—as part of a "do well but don't look back" initiative. We design projects to accommodate various legal, administrative, and reporting requirements.

---

[36] Rudi Viljoen: Life coach, CEO Warriors Academy, and Toltec training

4) We can help to administer or manage any corporate social responsibility project for you by providing directors, doing the accounts, putting into place various controls to ensure that no money gets wasted, applying for permits and licenses, and making sure that all involved parties are paid on time.

5) We can help you deal with complexity, corruption, nepotism and obstacles. Having many local business contacts spread over many countries, we have the knowledge and connections to ensure that we get value for money and correctly apply the law.

6) We can provide corporate governance, measure progress and success, and send regular reports to family members explaining what is being done and spent: regular oversight, regular validation, audits, and annual reports.

Social Responsibility Impact:

There is a direct link between CSR and increased profitability. In addition, the market expects companies to address product liability risks, the environmental impact of their facilities, and the health, safety, and wellbeing of their employees. Numerous studies of CSR, corporate ethics, and social sponsorship suggest that there is a link between social initiatives and improved financial performance. Other studies have demonstrated a link between social initiatives and positive affective, cognitive, and behavioral consumer responses.

From a strategic business perspective, a business benefits from CSR because it promotes positive consumer product and brand evaluations, choice, and brand recommendations. Through a variety of theoretical lenses, academic studies have demonstrated that CSR plays a role in consumer behavior and has a spill-over or halo effect on consumer judgments, such as the evaluation of new products. A halo effect is the positive bias associated with one measure spilling over onto another measure.

There is strong evidence that many consumers value CSR. An increasing number of companies incorporate CSR into their marketing strategies to exploit its appeal to key segments of the market. We need only look at the rapid growth of socially responsible companies to see the importance of CSR in marketing.

1) **Focus on outcomes.** The number of work hours served, dollars contributed, and employees engaged are important when assessing a company's level of commitment to a cause. To understand the value of those investments, however, it is essential to examine the CSR project outcomes—how a project changes the lives of community stakeholders, volunteers, and beneficiaries and helps to create a better planet. Whatever types of investments you are making, think about what would constitute a successful outcome and how to measure that outcome. For example, if your employees are volunteering at a homeless shelter, focus on the number of meals served rather than the hours donated. If you're switching to LED lighting, report on how much energy you're saving rather than the number of lights you're replacing.

2) **Learn from others.** One of the best ways to improve your impact measurement is by learning from others. Review the CSR reports of companies that have used measurement to improve the impact of their programs.

3) **Listen to your stakeholders.** Through conversation, small focus groups, or even social media polling to collect qualitative survey data, you can learn what's important to your stakeholders. These include your employees, members of the local community, suppliers, customers, and nonprofit partners. By taking the time to understand their motivations, goals, and needs, the programs you develop can be crafted to best serve those interests, and to generate the greatest value for all participants. You can also be smarter about the metrics, data and stories you choose to report by taking into consideration what your stakeholders value most.

4) **Don't undervalue stories.** So often, companies fall into the trap of thinking that impact can only be communicated through numbers, such as percentages, hours, dollars, increases, and decreases. Sometimes impact can't be quantified—and that's okay. Stories and qualitative observations are just as important as data when it comes to communicating your impact. The way a worker's entire life transforms when he or she is paid a fair wage is incredibly powerful—and it's something that can best be communicated through his or her own

personal story. Your audiences want to hear those sorts of stories and people who have been personally affected will want to share them.

5) **Measure, refine, and tweak—then measure again.** Programs that have the most impact on their communities, participants, and businesses don't look at measurement as a one-time endeavor. It's an integral part of their programs. Find out what works so that you can do more of it. Find out what doesn't work so that you can intervene, tweak, and improve.

The final step in evaluating non-profit performance is to check the design and outcomes of non-profit impact measurement.

As a reminder, the six steps involve measuring charities, philanthropic projects, and CRS initiatives against specific standards for non-profit performance arranged in the following categories: (1) leadership, (2) financial management, (3) financial sustainability, (4) leverage, (5) strategy, and (6) impact.

How to evaluate the impact of what we do:

Here are eight standards divided into two categories for evaluating the impact of a philanthropic or corporate social responsibility project:

Impact measurement design

1) The scope of the project's vision is realistic and measurable.

2) The project has a scorecard to track Key Performance Indicators (KPIs).

3) The process for tracking outcomes is standardized and reliable.

4) Programs are cut or adjusted based on impact measurement data.

Quality of outcomes

5) Results are outcomes that last, not just annual activities or one-time events.

6) Statistics about the project's beneficiaries are compared to baselines, benchmarks, or averages to determine whether the project is solving the problem it was intended to solve.

7) Recent, preferably independent, evaluations are used to verify the CSR's reported outcomes.

8) The organization surveys beneficiaries to solicit their views on program quality and effectiveness.

At the end of the day, any evaluation of a CSR program remains slightly arbitrary. However, these eight standards will tell you whether an organization is both managing toward outcomes and achieving meaningful outcomes.

Here's how these standards can be useful.

How to measure impact:

To measure impact appropriately, an organization must have a clear vision of the outcome it is working toward (standard 1 above). This is why the organization's vision (or main organizational goal) must be realistic and measurable.

If an organization has a realistic and measurable goal in place, then leaders can create an organizational scorecard to track key performance indicators (KPI). A scorecard with the right KPIs tells an organization whether it is progressing toward its ultimate goal. Of course, KPIs go beyond measuring impact to include many operational activities that strengthen the organization's operations and help to achieve success. However, KPIs related to program impact should be included and analyzed quarterly or monthly.

There should be a standardized and reliable method for collecting data related to program impact and reviewing it among other KPIs. Standards 2 and 3 above are essential for good impact measurement design. When a charity has program impact data in a set of KPIs, senior leaders can make informed adjustments to guide the organization toward greater impact. As standard 4 indicates, programs should be cut or adjusted based on data from the impact measurement system.

Quality of outcomes:

If an organization measures the impact of its programs systematically, it will communicate its outcomes at some point, either in an annual report or in the "results" section of the corporate social responsibility project. How do we judge the information presented here? We can do this by using standard 5, above. The results should include lasting outcomes, not just annual activities or one-time events. Outcomes should focus on long-term results from ongoing activities. How have beneficiaries defied the odds or continued to achieve success six months or even three years after the program?

The fact that 80 percent of HIV-infected people are still alive three years after starting to drink aloe vera juice is only a great outcome if you know that the benchmark figure is below 50 percent.

Having benchmarks, base lines, or averages is essential for determining whether a program is making a significant difference (standard 6).

The seventh standard for evaluating the outcomes of a CSR project's impact measures is independent verification. It can otherwise be difficult to judge whether a CSR project's set of outcomes or internal method for collecting data accurately represents the results of its programs.

Sometimes the impact that a CSR project seeks may not provide the best service for its intended beneficiaries. For this reason, any organization more committed to making a positive impact on its beneficiaries than to serving its own ends will periodically survey the people it serves. This is why we use direct feedback (standard 8) to verify the quality and effectiveness of the project.

Execute and evaluate:

Currently, only 20 percent of serious donors or impact investors carry out any kind of substantive research into the effectiveness of their philanthropic or CSR projects. The eight standards above can help you make the best possible use of your limited time and funds.

At the end of an evaluation, we can draw conclusions and tweak the goals or conditions of any program.

Without constant evaluation, we will undoubtedly (and recurrently) fall into traps involving inefficiencies, high administrative costs, nepotism, corruption, and other similar issues. Here is a recommendation from the 1965 diary of Che Guevarra, then commanding a group of Cuban and Congolese *guerrilleros* in the Congo (just before going to Bolivia):

Help should never be unconditional. If we do not set conditions, we run the risk our support converts into the opposite, into extravagant vacations for Freedom Fighters, who will sacrifice and sell their villages and delay the revolutionary development. There is no cheaper way of disruption than to pull out some millions at a conference table. The conflict and corruption resulting from dividing the money will create more unrest and harmful conflict than any army on the battlefield.

Although most CSR or charitable projects are run under very different circumstances, it is true that, whenever you provide help, you will be obliged to establish certain conditions to ensure that the money is used for the right purpose, and does not merely benefit a small group of corrupt people!

Chapter 7

How to maximize the impact of your investments

Do something right because it is the right thing to do!

If what you have done yesterday still looks big to you, you haven't done much today.

—Mikhail Gorbachev

Money is a by-product of happiness and success, not a goal in itself, as many financially successful people can attest. You cannot eat money and you cannot take it with you when you die. Money can buy you nice things, but none of life's real essentials: fresh air, a peaceful environment, esteem, happiness, self-realization, and satisfaction. It will not help you accomplish important life tasks, such as making friends, building a loving family, or maintaining a healthy lifestyle. Money does not help you figure out how to love somebody, or be famous, rich, or poor. Money does not help you walk away from someone you don't love any longer. There is nothing you can buy that will tell you what is going on in someone else's mind. You cannot write a check to prevent someone from dying. Everything you need to know is determined by fate and circumstance; you cannot buy real life experience.

At school, nobody ever taught us how to light a cigarette in a storm of rain, nor how a fire could be made with wet wood—nor that it is best to stick a bayonet in the belly because there it doesn't get jammed, as it does in the ribs.[37]

—Erich Maria Remarque, *All Quiet on the Western Front*

---

[37] *101 Best Ways to Get Ahead: Solid Gold Advice from 101 of the World's Most Successful People* (2004) by Michael E. Angier and Sarah Pond, p. 30

Piling up money should not be a goal in life. It is just a tool—a golden coffin will not add anything to your funeral. Money is no more than a means to use during your life to create some happiness around you. Money only has value when it is spent or given away—just as friendship is expressed when it is given, and cannot be bought. Similarly, authority can be commanded but not given; respect can be earned but not bought; love can be given but not demanded. By focusing too much on money, we tend to forget what life is all about. You cannot ride a bicycle by focusing on the pedals. You need to look at the horizon while your legs do their work. People who think money is important either never make much money (in the end, greed, a lack of generosity, and win-lose or scarcity thinking don't tend to pay off) or they do come into a lot of money and then realize that it doesn't make them happy, having been obtained at the expense of more important things in life, such as family, friendship, and love. If you reflect on and follow the simple truths in this book, earning money will become effortless and simple. At the same time, money will lose its importance, as you realize how many things are much more important than money.

If it is bad that people suffer and die because they lack food, shelter, or medical care—and if it is in your power to prevent something so bad from happening (and you won't sacrifice anything important by acting), then isn't it wrong not to intervene?

By donating money to aid agencies or dedicating time to community service, you can prevent or eliminate suffering without sacrificing anything nearly as important. If you do nothing to alleviate the suffering of others, you are missing out on doing something good. It seems obvious that an adult ought to save a child from drowning unless, by doing so, he or she would be risking something as valuable as the child's life, such as his or her own life. Yet, as many as 27,000 children die from poverty every day. They could be easily and cheaply helped through existing charities and currently available resources, as well as by you.

In his book, *Man's Search for Meaning*, Viktor Frankl writes: "Man is a being whose main concern consists in fulfilling a meaning and in actualizing values, rather than in the mere gratification and satisfaction of drives and instincts." His central argument is as follows, "Everything can be taken from a man but... the last of the human freedoms—to choose your attitude in any given set of circumstances, to choose your own way."[38]

---

[38]   Frankl, Viktor E. *Man's Search for Meaning*, Austria: Beacon Press (English), 1959.

You can think of your career or business as a carrier for meaning and a path that provides direction, structure, and meaning in life. In this approach, the values that give an (entrepreneurial) career meaning are constructed or chosen based on free will.

According to Friedrich Nietzsche, "The noble kind of man experiences himself as determining values. He does not need approval; he judges that 'what is harmful to me is harmful in itself'"[39] and decides for himself whether his efforts are value-creating. In this sense, an entrepreneur does not accept a given state or practice but creatively gives birth to innovation by producing meaning. Ways to achieve this include the following:

1) Increasing the quality of life (e.g. by introducing a more usable computer device);

2) Righting a wrong (e.g. through the introduction of a garbage recycling system); and

3) Preventing the demise of something good (as in the case of a slow food restaurant being replaced by a fast food dump).

So, what are the values that produce meaning? All instrumental values or goods can be neglected; they are only stop-overs on the way toward causes of motivation and finality: the intrinsic values. Only if these values resonate with you as an entrepreneur or HNWI, and only if you can align those values with what you do in life, can you create a situation where you can and will pursue them.

The modern businessperson, HNWI, or entrepreneur is at the top of the human food chain in terms of power and wealth. His or her basic monetary wealth is, of course, fundamental because it satisfies the more primitive needs—for food, drink, sex, and safety—the lower reaches of Maslow's pyramid of human needs. However, when it comes to higher-level human needs, such as love/belonging, esteem, and self-actualization, wealth is just an effect, like happiness, but with a distinct origin.

---

[39] Nietzsche, Friedrich. *Beyond Good and Evil*, translated by Walter Kaufmann, New York: Vintage, 1989, pg260

Power is another hugely motivating factor. As Friedrich Nietzsche writes: "Anything which is a living and not a dying body... will have to be an incarnate will to power, it will strive to grow, spread, seize, become predominant—not from any morality or immorality but because it is living and because life simply is will to power... Exploitation... belongs to the essence of what lives, as a basic organic function; it is a consequence of the will to power, which is after all the will to life."[40]

The struggle for power can be found in any larger corporation, political institution, or even sports club. In all of those places, you can see people working to identify and realize political opportunities in order to gain political power and promote themselves; even many (possibly most) political entrepreneurs also understand and feel motivated to promote justice in society.

The latter may be the main motivation of the social entrepreneur, a phenomenon which has received more and more attention in the last 20 years. A more recent altruistic figure is the green entrepreneur, who creates ventures for which the dominant objective is the promotion of sustainability.

Our culture increasingly nurtures the kind of entrepreneur who relates more to his or her work than to money. He or she wants to model a sound and exciting life-art-work as he/she is motivated by multiple drivers. And more and more those drivers include altruistic motives. More and more investors and entrepreneurs want to use their money and power to have a positive impact on society.

Impact investing refers to investments made into companies, organizations, and funds with the intention of generating a measurable, beneficial social or environmental impact alongside a financial return. Impact investments can be made in both emerging and developed markets. Impact investing tends to have roots in either social or environmental issues, and has been contrasted with microfinance.

How to have the most impact:

---

[40] Nietzsche, Friedrich. *Beyond Good and Evil*, United Kingdom: Cambridge University Press, 2002.

There are many different ways to make sure you have the most impact with your investments. Here are just a few of them.

1) Invest in areas or technologies that have a kind of a multiplier effect, as they are part of, or themselves create, a breakthrough. Recent examples include electric cars, new polio medicines, 3D printing, and more effective legislation.

2) Invest in exemplary solutions that make money, like high yield foodstuffs (saving many millions of lives), micro-financing, social housing, or elderly homes. Elon Musk of Tesla Motors deliberately does not patent his electric car-related inventions, to encourage as many car makers as possible to apply these technologies or improve on them, bringing his goal of less polluting transport closer.

3) Invest in the areas that reach the most people. These can include investments in new clean water technology, new medicines for epidemics, and solutions that make life easier for the growing number of elderly people.

4) Invest in areas where you can convince many people to support you, like endangered wildlife protection, safety on the streets, and climate change solutions.

5) Invest in education. If you have youth, you have the future. Educational initiatives, when done well, multiply results. In many ways, education is the most powerful weapon you can use to change the world.

6) Invest in sanitation.

To educate is to give man the keys to the world, which are independence and love, and to give him strength to journey on his own, light of step, a spontaneous and free being.[41]

— José Martí

---

[41] Martí, Jose 1853-95. Prospects: The quarterly review of comparative education (Paris, UNESCO: International Bureau of Education), vol. XXIV, no. ½, 1994, p.107-19.

7)   Invest in healthcare. As Brad Pitt has said: "Let us be the ones who say we do not accept that a child dies every three seconds simply because he does not have the drugs you and I have. Let us be the ones to say we are not satisfied that your place of birth determines your right for life. Let us be outraged, let us be loud, let us be bold."[42]

8)   Invest in nature or nature conservation.

9)   Invest in areas that are politically just. These days, efforts to create more fiscal responsibility (fair taxation) and more efficient government (without waste or corruption) are gaining momentum. You can also invest in problematic political areas and change them from the inside. Think of the individuals who challenge and try to transform corrupt governments (India, Brazil) and organizations, like FIFA, from the inside out. Think of the people who changed the economic system in China, or who created the international organizations that help to maintain peace and economic stability in the world.

10) Invest in friendship.

To explore these ideas further, I have used some of my own key projects to create a matrix. This has allowed me to review the impact each project has had on me, and to identify what matters most to me—identifying the types of action that have made the most impact on my own small circle of influence.

As an illustration, a selection of my more impactful activities looks like this:

1)   Teaching credit and risk to bankers in Cuba. I did this for a while to help set up the first commercial bank in post-revolutionary Cuba. I drew on previous experience as a teacher in an American bank.

2)   Promoting foreign investments in Cuba. As one of my core activities, my aim in focusing on Cuba was to help investments come in at a difficult moment in its history.

---

[42]   Brad Pitt statement at the Hyde Park Live Aid Concert United Kingdom, 2005.

3) Researching the potential for Nepal as an offshore financial center, at the request of USAID. Here, I was trying to instill pride and dignity in a country that was used to foreign pressure.

4) Sponsoring arts, music, and theatre training for children in Curaçao and on Bali. Although this was not my core interest, I aimed to help others achieve their social responsibility goals.

5) Sponsoring an orphanage in Bangalore, India. A very rewarding project; it ultimately turned out kids with better job prospects than our own employees.

6) Writing a book on sustainable ways of doing business: Mind Your Business. This was one of the most rewarding things I'd ever done in my life.

7) Helping develop new tax planning solutions as business products for Curaçao. As I had lived there for 15 years, I wanted add something of substance to the business community.

8) Creating a tourism project in Bali, around the Yeh Mampeh waterfall. Even a few jobs can set an example. This small project changed the mood, helping people to develop self-respect and self-reliance.

9) Tuma Mi Man, a daycare center for employees and disadvantaged children in Curaçao. Here, I was building on what people in the office wanted to do to make their mark on the community.

10) Organizing the Kamar Mandi Project in Bali. Sanitation is a major step towards self-respect. Self-respect is a big step towards being able to take care of oneself.

11) Desa Les Community Center, a practical training facility for people hoping to build careers in the hotel business, and to earn more than minimum wage.

12) CO2 project in Chile. If we can make something work for ourselves, one day we will make it work for one client, then one hundred, and then one thousand.

13) Creating health drinks and natural supplements in South Africa. This project involved building an income-supporting business to promote health and combat anti-immune diseases.

14) Helping to create the Mapesu Private Game Reserve, which protects endangered species: one species at a time; even small numbers matter. In the end, every effort is an example that triggers more people to participate.

15) Making with wonderful friends a great Malbec wine in Valle de Uco, Mendoza, Argentina.

Apart from these philanthropic and CSR projects, there were smaller efforts that did not meet my sustainability or durability tests, and were therefore classified as charity: a) sending children from poor families to high school or university; b) feeding people who have no income with monthly distributions of rice; c) providing English and computer classes to kids in emerging markets; d) training children to play the gamelan and/or to dance in traditional Balinese performances; e) maintaining artificial limbs for handicapped people; f) maintaining a car that could double as a makeshift ambulance for a remote village and paying the associated doctors' bills; paying for even one Caesarian every three months saved one if not two lives a quarter. I think that is huge!

What sort of emotional impact did these philanthropic and corporate social responsibility projects have on me?

1) They created an intellectual or emotional challenge for myself and others who worked with me. New challenges made me grow.

2) They helped me to bond with my colleagues and business partners, and strengthened other relationships, making people think. It makes me proud that many of our employees have changed the way they deal with nature, limited resources, and caring for fellow citizens. This is spreading the word.

3) They helped me to bond with my children, family, and friends and to make them think. I feel proud that my children are growing up to be responsible, caring citizens. There are few things that we can do together that have real meaning, but this is certainly one.

4) They passed on to my children important experiences and values.

5) They added value to or resolved a human need or cause. Small actions can trigger big reactions from others, including governments.

6) They added value, promoted self-esteem, and encouraged self-sustainability in disadvantaged communities.

7) They helped to change public opinion, setting an example and creating a multiplier effect that others would copy or follow. Remember the story of the talents in the Bible? A small project can have a major secondary effect.

8) They were all so much fun—more exciting than making passive investments. When was the last time you laughed your head off with your asset manager or private banker?

If I place the activities and the feelings they aroused in a matrix, it looks something like this:

PROJECT / IMPACT

What are the different feelings / impact these philanthropic and corporate social responsibility projects have on me?	intellectual / emotional challenge	Professional bonding	Personal bonding	Leaving behind something of value	Actions trigger reaction & solutions	Personal value	Positive effect / secondary effects	Enjoyability
	1	2	3	4	5	6	7	8
1 Teaching credit in Cuba	●				●			●
2 Promoting foreign investment in Cuba							●	●
3 Research Nepal as financial center					●	●		●
4 Sponsor the arts in Curaçao					●		●	●
5 Sponsor orphanage in India			●		●	●		●
6 Writing *Mind your Business*	●	●					●	●
7 Developed new tax planning in Curaçao		●			●			●
8 Creating tourism project in Bali			●		●	●		●
9 Tuma Mi Man daycenter created		●			●	●	●	●
10 Kamar Mandi Project created and completed		●			●	●	●	●
11 Desa Les Community Center project	●	●			●	●	●	●
12 CO2 Offsett project in Chile	●	●		●	●		●	●
13 Creation of aloe vera health products	●		●	●		●	●	●
14 Creating an South African Conservancy	●	●	●	●	●	●	●	●
15 Alpasión winery, lodge and vineyard	●	●	●	●				●

When I analyze the results, I can draw the following conclusions from my own experiences. You may find these useful when evaluating the potential impact that a project could have on you:

1) The more involved I am, the more fun I have, and the more satisfaction I derive from a project. On the graph, the more boxes are ticked, the more intense my involvement was.

2) For me, a purely charitable donation does not have the same positive impact as a development project geared towards a sustainable goal.

3) Projects I undertake with others create more satisfaction than those I carry out alone, especially when I can be involved with one of my children, a group of friends, or a team of dedicated and passionate colleagues.

4) The amount of money I invest, or earn has little or no impact on the level of satisfaction I derive from a project.

5) For me, it is best to not start out with too rigid or clear an idea of what to do; the people I involve along the way may have better ideas. In addition, people feel most involved and committed when they can help to shape the project as well as the decision-making process.

6) Good investments may take many years to develop, and lots of effort to achieve. I need only a little inspiration and lots and lots of dedication and perseverance, guts, and grit.

7) To keep everyone progressing in the same direction, I need to clearly define one vision of the project and guard it. Otherwise, it is easy to float on the events of the day and loose direction.

8) Emerging markets add many layers of challenges on top of the normal ones associated with investing. There is not much you can do about that. Without such complexities, those countries would be developed, rather than still emerging. I have decided to accept what I cannot change and to keep pushing, day after day, for the things I can change.

9)   I have decided not to be put off by graft, inefficiency, and corruption. Those problems are the reason many communities or countries need help to begin with. They will take generations to eradicate. I refuse to give in to them, and I expose them when I can, even if it means sending people to jail.

10) I have decided not to be put off by greedy individuals or negative experiences. Poorer countries, almost by definition, have more lawlessness and cheating. If you have enough money to make any sort of investment, you will attract the attention of people willing to do whatever it takes to feed their families, whether it is ethical or not. Their survival may depend on whatever legitimate or illegitimate opportunities I present.

11) As there is rarely a direct link between effort and result, it is important to choose my battles carefully. Otherwise, I may end up spending extraordinary amounts of money and time, without many practical results to show for it. If people around me are benefitting from the effort, rather than the result, they may not tell me honestly when I am throwing good money after bad. Staff and overhead anywhere, if not pruned regularly, will continue to mushroom.

12) I am not afraid to ask for help. Many, many times, help has come from unexpected sources. I try to be transparent, vulnerable, and open to advice, suggestions, and a helping hand.

13) I stay away from any project for which success depends on the approval, permission, or the ongoing cooperation of higher powers. In these situations, an investment can become very frustrating. I do not have the money or influence to play in the major leagues.

14) I always expect to spend twice the money and four times the time I initially considered realistic.

15) I try not to plan too far ahead and don't procrastinate. I just get started, knowing that events will unfold in unexpected ways. Not all surprises are negative. There are always many people who want to contribute in positive ways. Once people see how an investment will benefit their families or communities, they will demonstrate exceptional gratitude.

16) I always know when I am doing the right thing, because it feels right and I feel good about that. I try not to compromise, or to let anyone stop or undermine me. I believe in just showing up for life, and letting it unfold in rewarding ways.

17) Almost any project I am involved in creates more fun than I could have had by putting the money in the bank.

In the remaining chapters of this book, I will describe some charitable, philanthropic, and CSR projects, as well as some examples of impact investments and social enterprises drawn from my personal experience, to provide context and show how many elements are involved in any one investment. For people who have worked hard all their lives to create a business and gather assets, impact investment may be a good way to shift toward doing something good for the community, while continuing to rely on their experience and innate monetary instincts.

In the end, this is about being true to yourself. Being authentic and putting what you think, say, and do on the line. It's about genuineness and authenticity. These words are hard to say and, for many of us, even harder to be. We waste so much time keeping up appearances, being tough, and projecting power and status, even though (as Eleanor Roosevelt said), "You wouldn't worry so much about what others think of you if you realized how seldom they do."

The hallmarks below illustrate what it means to be authentic.

First, authentic people are aware of their thoughts and feelings, and they behave in ways that reflect those feelings. They don't see any need to put on an act to impress or control others. They accept their vulnerabilities as well as their strengths, and they know that accepting something isn't necessarily the same as liking it. Do you know something else? Because they accept themselves for who they are, they accept other people, too.

Authentic people don't laugh at jokes they don't think are funny. They don't change their identities, like chameleons, depending on whom they are with or where they are. If you want to grow as an authentic person, take time to really get to know yourself. If you're not completely happy with what you find, don't worry too much. Work on accepting yourself for who you are, right here and right now. Work on being truly authentic.

If you are a parent, let your kids know that, even though you may not always like what they do, you love them for who they are—just the way they are! As Barack Obama commented,

I actually think, when you're young, ambitions are somewhat common— you want to prove yourself. It may grow out of different life experiences. You may want to prove that you are worthy of the admiration of the demanding father. You may want to prove that you are worthy of the love of an absent father.[43]

Sometimes, we all hide behind masks in order to get through the day. Although it is a kind of survival mechanism, the mask actually betrays the good-hearted human being the world deserves to know.

We need to be honest with ourselves. That alarm in our minds that goes off when we are faking it or being phony is our conscience reminding us that we are undermining who we really are. We are denying our true selves because we think we are less than we should be. If we continue to deny our true selves, our mind adapts and the phony self we portray becomes the true self. And that's OK, if the character we portray is who we really want to be. Our minds are that powerful.

If we genuinely dislike our own character or behavior, then we can always take action to change it. If need be, we can find individuals who have the qualities we want, and go from admiration to assimilation, until we have internalized what and who we truly want to be.

We do not need to become anyone other than who we are. We have the freedom to choose positive, contributive change when we want to improve ourselves.

The individual has always had to struggle to keep from being overwhelmed by the tribe. To be your own man is hard business. If you try it, you will be lonely often, and sometimes frightened. But no price is too high to pay for the privilege of owning yourself.[44]

—Rudyard Kipling

---

[43]   Goodwin, Doris Kerns and Obama, Barack. "Panorama – The ultimate exit interview." *The Independent.* September 25th, 2016. Web. September 2, 2016.

[44]   Orel, Harold. 1983. Kipling: *Interview and Recollections,* London: The Macmillan Press, 1983.

Chapter 8

A corporate social enterprise project and a social enterprise, funded and created from within a commercial organization

> *I believe that the purpose of life is to be happy. From the moment of birth every human being wants happiness and does not want suffering. Neither social conditioning nor education, nor ideology affects this. From the very core of our being, we simply desire contentment. I do not know whether the universe, with its countless galaxies, stars and planets has a deeper meaning or not, but at the very least, it's clear that we humans who live on this earth face the task of making a happy life for ourselves. Therefore, it is important to discover what will bring about the greatest degree of happiness.* [45]

—His holiness the 14th Dalai Lama of Tibet

Many, if not most of us, believe that the purpose of our lives is to be or become happy. As social beings, we achieve this by promoting the wellbeing and happiness of others. Whether we live in Europe, Bali, or Africa – three continents, and whether we are rich or poor, sooner or later we realize that the more we make others happy, the greater our own sense of wellbeing becomes. By developing our innate love and compassion for others, we discover inner tranquility and peace. Cultivating a close, warm-hearted feeling for others automatically puts our own minds at ease. Although Ralph Waldo Emerson reasoned differently, he basically reached the same conclusion when he said: "The purpose of life is not to be happy. It is to be useful, to be honorable, to be compassionate, to have it make some difference that you have lived and lived well." [46] In the

---

[45] Dalai Lama XIV. Vancouver, BC, Canada, 26 September 2009 (By The Dalai Lama, Special to The Vancouver Sun)

[46] Ralph Waldo Emerson (1803-1882). *Words of Wisdom*

words of Gautama Buddha, "Your purpose in life is to find your purpose and give your whole heart and soul to it."[47]

In this chapter, I reflect on my experiences with one of our most rewarding corporate social responsibility projects, the Kamar Mandi Project in Bali. I love to remember and celebrate the hard work of the people involved. Most of all, I hope to inspire others to think about supporting some worthy cause or helping fellow human beings in need. In this way, you will be contributing to a more balanced and fair society.

I first visited Bali on a one-year gap year adventure in 1980, when a friend and I hitchhiked and rode buses for a whole year, from the Netherlands via India to Bali, the Island of the Gods, as it calls itself. In retrospect, this trip was my personal interpretation *avant la lettre* of the "Eat, Pray, Love" cult, which, in recent years, has engulfed Bali and persuaded single women of all ages to bicycle around the island trying to find themselves, while hoping to be run over and to end up in a wildly romantic love affair.

Northern Bali has been frequented by Dutch seafarers since 1597, when Houtman's first ships reached present-day Singaraja searching for spices. After the 1840s, northern Bali was effectively a colony. The area south of Buleleng, behind Mount Agung, was not colonized by the Dutch until 1907, after a war in which most of the Balinese nobility died in ritual suicide. In a series of charges, called *puputan*, the members of various Balinese royal families attacked the machine guns of the Royal Dutch Indies Army with ritual daggers and bows and arrows. Independence came with the Japanese surrender in 1945.

At the time of my first visit, the island was a lot less crowded, built-up, and full of tourists. It immediately made a huge impression on me. In 1980, electricity was just coming to Ubud and the villages north of it. Most houses were still made of mud, with roofs of *alang alang* grass. Everywhere, you could see people enjoying a life of contentment, filled with customs (adat), culture and ceremonies, strong family and clan ties, and people with good health in a bountiful environment.

---

[47] Kannings, Ann. *Gautama Buddha: Life & Words (Volume 2)*, Paperback – CreateSpace Independent Publishing Platform: February 27, 2015

> *The difference between false memories and true ones is the same as for jewels: it is always the false ones that look the most real, the most brilliant.*[48]

—Salvador Dalí

I love the food, the *Babi Pangang*, and the *Ikan Bumbu Bali*, and I once exported two traditional *Soto Ayam* carts to our restaurant in the Caribbean, to be used to serve traditional Indonesian foods and remind me of the great tastes of Bali.

I can spend hours looking at *sawahs* on the *desa* mountainsides, the intricate ways that water flows from one level to the next, creating optimum conditions for growing rice. I love the colorful villages with their *penyors*, tall bamboo poles beautifully decorated with woven young coconut leaves, cakes, fruits, and flowers, a must-have decoration in every Balinese household.

A Balinese *desa* (village), like Desa Les, the center of our activities in Bali, is typically host to a set of three village temples, each related to one focal aspect of the village's symbolic life: its origins are honored at Pura Puseh (the navel temple) located near the mountain, where the gods and founders of the village are worshipped; the territory itself is celebrated at the Pura Desa, located in the center of the village, where meetings of the village assembly and fertility rituals are held; the temple of death (Pura Dalem), near the burial place, is where offerings are made and ceremonies conducted to help the dead and honor the forces of death and the netherworld. Besides these village temples, there is also a temple for each sub-division of the village, and the various temples of the local clans and sub-clans, each of which has its own calendar of festivals.

Apart from weddings, funerals, and other ceremonies marking the phases of life, I enjoy the regular festivals, with their colorful processions, many small offerings, and rituals. Although poor, the women are beautiful and gracious and the men, proud and elegant. I especially love the Galungan Festival, which is the most important Balinese feast and festival, held throughout the island to coincide with the *wuku* year. It is believed that, during this ten-day period, all of the Balinese gods will descend to earth for the festivities. *Barongs* prance from temple to temple and village to village, celebrating *Galungan* with the

---

[48] Dalí, Salvador. *The Secret Life of Salvador Dali*, Translated by Haakon m. Chevalier, New York: Dover Publications, 1942

gods. To the Balinese, *Galungan* is the most important festival, as it symbolizes the victory of *Dharma*, or Virtue, over *Adharma*, or all that is Evil.

The last day is the climax of the ten-day *Galungan*, and it brings the celebration period to a close. *Kuningan* is a day for prayer. A special ritual ceremony is held for the spirits of the Balinese ancestors.

Bali also celebrates a New Year festival referred to as *Nyepi*. *Nyepi* falls on the day after the new moon on the ninth month, a new year that is celebrated in total silence and seclusion! On the day of *Nyepi*, there is no activity whatsoever. Roads all over Bali are empty of any traffic and nobody leaves the house. There is no traffic at all on the roads; even the airport is closed for the day. No amusements are held that day; no fires may be lit, in observance of the religious *Nyepi* guidelines. *Nyepi* Eve, however, is a vision of contrasts, as villagers all over the island light torches and parade giant effigies called *ogoh-ogoh* through the streets.

All of these festivals and traditions are beautifully integrated into the modern world. Thousands of people use their scooters to drive to the temple. The spiritual leaders of a village have as much practical influence as the worldly ones. There are plenty of apps that predict which auspicious days are good for a ceremony, or for planting rice or signing a deal. I attended the mystical, traditional wedding of a member of one of the Balinese royal families, with pomp and ceremony, *gamelan* music, famous dancers and clowns, beautiful food and lots of traditions. When I asked how the couple had met, the answer was "through a dating site."

The person who drew me to Bali was Charles Jacobs. We met (having mutual friends through our university fraternity) for the first time in the late 1970s. Now Charles has been living in Desa Les, Bali, for well over 20 years. A professor in sociology, he retired at the ripe old age of 49 and moved to Indonesia. After living for a while in Sumatra and Java, he finally settled in Desa Les. Over the course of the years, he has sold all his earthly belongings to help people in the village. Now he lives in a very modest house and uses his government pension to pay the tuition fees of village kids and to hand out rice to the very poor.

Over the years, Charles has become a local hero. Not only did he fully integrate into the local community, he learned the Balinese language, became a Hindu, shared all his possessions with the local community, and used his knowledge, experience, and influence to attract funding and development to the village. Over time he has organized the construction of two schools, a doctor's post, a dental practice, a community center, and many other projects.

Neighboring villages are jealous, as Les has more. Les has Charles, who is guiding the Desa Adat and Kepala Desa in organizing and finding funding to improve the local infrastructure.

Charles is by far the most selfless person I have ever met. At 80, walking with two ski poles, he is still very active, trying every day to organize one kind of project or funding or another, for the benefit of the community. He is constantly thinking about ways to raise the self-esteem of the villagers, and he always lets others take the honors. Les can indeed consider itself very lucky to have a person like Charles in their midst.

Late in the evenings, members of suffering families come to his porch to seek relief from one kind of personal hardship or another. Sometimes he can help, sometimes he can't. Although Charles has chosen this village and his position there, his life is not always easy. In the mornings, there is rice to be distributed to some of the poorest people in the village. Throughout the day, people are always walking in and out looking for basic medicines to treat minor diseases.

Once in a while, there is an urgent request for funding becomes someone needs a major operation at the hospital. At that moment, a life-and-death question arises. Unless someone can pay for the operation, the villager may die of appendicitis or in childbirth. There is a children's education fund that allocates educational opportunities to village children with enough stamina and potential to complete a proper education and apply for a well-paid job. Hard decisions must be made, as there's not enough money to meet all needs.

Charles will stay in Desa Les until his death. Having become a Hindu, as he could not be buried as a Christian in a traditional Hindu village. On his conversion, he was given the noble name of *Gede Aria* Charles. You can see how much he is appreciated, just walking around the village. Everyone greets him with respect and values his endeavors. Several families vied for the honor of having him buried in their family grave, when the time comes.

Balinese culture is based on age-old Hindu, Buddhist, and animist beliefs and traditions. The Hindu element of *moksha* (or *mukhti*) prevails. *Moksha* is a Sanskrit word that means something between emancipation, liberation, and release. At the same time, it connotes freedom from samsara, the eternal cycle of strife, death, and rebirth, or, to use more palatable psychological language, freedom, self-realization, and self-knowledge.

In Hindu traditions, *moksha* is a central concept, included as one of the four aspects and goals of human life. The other three goals are: *dharma*, to lead a virtuous, proper, moral life; *artha*, to secure material prosperity, income, a stable livelihood; and *kama*, to pursue pleasure, sensuality, emotional fulfillment, and *dolce far niente*. Together, these four aims of life are called *Purusartha* in Hinduism.

In the Balinese philosophy and way of life, *Dharma* and its opposite *Adharma* (chaos, disorder, and disharmony) dominate thinking. Life is a constant struggle to live and act correctly, to fulfill your secular and religious duties, to live with grace and honor, to observe family, village, and regional customs, and much more.

The idea of balance is central to the Balinese philosophy and way of life. Nature and Man meet and complement each other. Good (Right), and Evil (Bad, Wrong) as ethical concepts or moral standards have no counterpart in Hindu Dharma Bali.

Balance is more important, because nothing belongs only to one property.

Every new project therefore begins and ends with a ceremony to inform or appease the Gods and to create or restore the balance.

Over the years, several of our joint projects have come to fruition. I first became involved in a few small projects while helping Charles set up a gamelan orchestra and dance classes in the village.

Later, as projects grew and became more meaningful and expensive, our Amicorp Community Foundation (ACF) became involved, focusing on projects that could make a real difference and be sustainable.

When I first visited Charles, he immediately took me to the Yeh Mampeh waterfall. It is the only named tourist attraction in the village, and allegedly the highest waterfall in Bali. For years, the signboards in Desa Les described it as the "higgest" waterfall in Bali.

It is a magical walk along the river to reach the small but thundering waterfall and it's fun to stand under the strong torrent, or to just take a bath, alongside local people, in the cool waters below it. Heavy rains and flooding had destroyed the simple mud path leading to the waterfall. In the course of that day, Charles convinced me to invest in upgrading and partially paving the footpath to the waterfall so that tourists could easily reach the site.

We sponsored a volunteer, Sebastiaan van der Veer, who went to Bali and spent half a year working on a major improvement to the footpath, stabilizing the banks of the stream through the village, creating leaflets to distribute in several strategic places, designing a website, putting out waste bins, and employing and training a few people to act as tour guides and keep the footpath clear. Although the waterfall is too far off the beaten track to become a major attraction, the trickle of tourists who visit creates some income for the community as well as jobs for the five or six guides who accompany visitors to the waterfall.

Unfortunately, the footpath was damaged several times, when the annual rains brought excessive amounts of water. We ended up sponsoring the construction of a wider road with a big parking lot, much closer to the waterfall, which made it more accessible to tourists and local bathers alike. Tourists spent money in the village on guides, food, and drinks. At some stage, we may set up a nice little lunch restaurant near the parking lot, where students at the community center we are working to build can hone their skills, while more sustainable income is generated. At every step of the way, we must consult with the Gods guarding the village to avoid disharmony. The residents of Les have strong convictions about that.

During the construction of the road and parking lot, a debate arose over whether a cluster of trees should remain or be removed. Several of the workers argued that those particular trees were sacred and had to stay. The foreman of the construction company argued the trees should go, getting very angry, which is unusual in Bali. While arguing, he had a heart attack and died right there under the contested trees. For the villagers, it was very clear who had intervened in the conflict and why. They interpreted this incident as a clear directive that the trees must stay—and they are still there.

Over the years, I have traveled to Desa Les many times. I know very well the long and winding road from Denpasar, via Ubud, to Kintamani—over the rim of the Gunung Batur. I know many of its inhabitants and some of its problems.

We tried to develop ideas that would create local employment, but that turned out to be quite a challenge, as the village is unsuitable for agriculture, beyond small-scale cattle and pig breeding, and too far from towns and ports to attract industry. In order to develop services, villagers will need to acquire more advanced computer skills (one of the longer-term objectives of our planned community center).

A brainstorming project with the Kepala Desa (the mayor, or village manager) to assess needs and shortages in the village identified the overwhelming need for *kamar mandis* (bathrooms that combine a squat toilet with a large water tank for both flushing and bathing, walled in with a roof and individual septic tank).

In Bali, it is quite common for homes to not have in-house bathrooms; it is a traditional Balinese belief that the *kamar mandi* should not be under the same roof as the living quarters (a belief that once was held worldwide). People in the poorer communities in Bali, like Desa Les, relieved themselves in the open, creating a breeding ground for diseases. The UN calculates that more than 160,000 people in Indonesia die every year of infectious diseases related to open defecation.

We established criteria to select families who would be eligible under the project. They needed to be poor, willing to contribute labor (digging the sceptic tank hole and carrying building materials up the mountain) and generally well-behaved. About 100 families were selected, with the help of the Kepala Desa, to become the owners of traditional Indonesian toilets or *kamar mandis*. One *kamar mandi* takes three people about two weeks to build; after a few months, one could see *kamar mandis* popping up all over the village. By the time the 100 *kamar mandis* were finished, we already had a new list of eligible people. Over the course of some three years, we constructed 727 *kamar mandis*.

Why did we want to create this corporate social responsibility program?

The short answer is: because we could! The longer answer touches on the aspects listed below.

The value(s) of corporate social responsibility:

1) As a company, we believe in the quadruple bottom line: we want to make profits to support our business and all the people related to it; we want to stimulate passion in our employees, so that they will develop themselves to their fullest potential and be productive members of society;

we want to reduce our impact on the planet, by offsetting any pollution or environmental harm we cause, for example, by planting trees to offset our CO2 production; and finally, we want to support the people around us. The four objectives of our company are like the four *Purusarthas* in Hinduism; our community foundation is built on the same principles.

2) For all of us to reach our full potential, we need to develop all of our talents and skills, not just work-related skills. Different levels of effort result in different results, rewards, and levels of satisfaction.

3) Our company services a pool of wealthy individuals, as well as businesses investing in international ventures or conducting international trade. We provide services to families, family offices, and corporate entities that invest some of their wealth in impact investment, sustainable corporate social responsibility initiatives, charity, and trans-generational transfers of wealth, including estate planning.

4) "whomsoever much is given, of him shall much be required" (Luke 12:48). We try to apply this principle within our company. Most of us are gifted and talented people in good health, with excellent educations. We are fortunate to have the opportunity to work in an interesting cross-border business that makes money. We are the lucky few. Our clients need international structuring of their wealth and income; they too are privileged and lucky. If death and taxes are among your top worries, you have a blessed life. We therefore try to persuade people to imbue their lives with meaning by sharing part of their wealth (either funding or skills) with people who have been less fortunate in life, or born in the wrong place at the wrong time. With both the Kamar Mandi Project and the Desa Les Community Center, we have been able to mobilize some of our clients and contacts to contribute.

5) Our Director of Sustainable Development is responsible for making sure that, over time, all of our corporate social responsibility projects become self-sustaining. The community of Desa Les now takes care of the new *kamar mandis*. All of the users have been trained in maintaining the facility and its septic tank; they know what to do if a toilet overflows. The *kamar mandis* therefore have the best possible chance of being properly used for the full duration of their economic

life. In the case of the Desa Les Community Center project, we will create or locate sources of regular income, so that within a maximum period of ten years, the center will become economically sustainable through product sales, courses, activities, and ongoing third-party contributions. We will continue to work to train local employees of the project and to push them in that direction. We must prepare the villagers for independence rather than dependency, so that the project will ultimately become a sustainable business, rather than forever depending on donations, like a charity project.

6)   The feedback received by our corporate social responsibility projects in Bali and elsewhere has been overwhelming. Not only have the beneficiaries of the various ventures been heartwarmingly grateful, but we have also received lots of positive feedback from employees, vendors, and suppliers, as well as from clients who have participated in one venture or another. Receiving so much gratitude is much more satisfying than receiving a dividend.

7)   Becoming deeply involved with another culture helps you understand diversity; such exchanges teach compassion and understanding. For us, the corporate social responsibility projects are a great excuse to occasionally visit Bali and enjoy the country up-close and personally. I strongly believe that, as long as you can travel and marvel at new adventures, you are still alive.

Why did we choose Bali, and why Desa Les?

There are many people in need all over the world. There is no point looking for the neediest person. There will always be a more deserving cause or a needier family to be found. You could spend a lifetime looking for deserving individuals when the people around us in places like Desa Les need our help here and now. Desa Les is one of the poorest communities in all of Bali, although there are poorer places in other Indonesian islands and other parts of the world. There are very limited opportunities for people looking for work; unemployment is high and there are few investments. Many, if not most, of the young people have to move to Denpasar to find low-skilled jobs. As the Les villagers live a traditional life, working people must return to Les often to participate in the village's temple festivals and family celebrations. This leaves little time or money for diversions or building additional skills.

The inhabitants of the poorer *dusuns* are malnourished. Health and dental care are rudimentary. More than once, I was unexpectedly asked to help someone who needed emergency medical care and had no money to pay for it. Of course, nobody can carry the weight of all the world on his shoulders. There are times when knowing that your contribution could make the difference between life and death for an individual, or survival or disaster for a family, makes it hard to be involved. Nevertheless, someone needs to do it.

We chose this village because it was there. My friend, Charles Jacobs, lives in this community and could provide local information. He gave us the confidence to become involved, and kept us connected and well-informed.

For me, it would be very frustrating to contribute to a good cause and know that a lot of my money was going to be wasted, either on unnecessary administration and overhead, or on inefficiency, corruption, and nepotism.

All three are rampant in Bali, as in many other places. We have no illusions that we can eradicate any of these practices, and we don't blame the villagers in Desa Les. They reflect their country's current level of development; it takes each and every society a lot of time, effort, and luck to outgrow such practices. There are many people in the charity business who live very well, drive around in large air-conditioned cars, and do small amounts of good work, for which they are appreciated and very well compensated. They often approach us, and some of them are very persuasive in selling their services. But Charles lives in the village and he tirelessly and selflessly promotes our project. He has never received a penny himself, although I (not the foundation) gifted him a motor bike to travel around the dusuns, check on the progress of the construction, and determine, dusun by dusun, who needed a kamar mandi.

When working on the Kamar Mandi Project, we calculated and recalculated the price and quantities of materials many times; we asked around for quotes from all suppliers in this and neighboring communities, and made decisions based on durability, quality and price.

Yes, we could have built cheaper *kamar mandis*, but they would not have been carefully plastered to look fresh and clean. They would not have been made from quality materials, to last 30 years. As the community has few jobs, we could have paid our workers unreasonably low wages for their honest work. A significant part of the cost of building *kamar mandis* is the cost of transporting materials up the mountain (back-breaking manual labor) and the time involved for construction. Gede Wardiasa, the contractor, is a local builder and all of the laborers come from the village. They are all proud to be part of this important project.

Toine with Gede Wardiasa

From day one, we made it clear to everyone that, as a foundation linked to an international financial corporation, we would pay no bribes, money to facilitate processes, or commissions to middlemen. Initially, this caused some delays and inefficiencies. However, once the word was out that we had refused to follow normal practices in Bali, which in the West would be seen as corrupt or nepotistic, the community realized that the project was still worthwhile, even if no side-pockets were filled.

Nowadays, we often hear about people "giving back." In the case of Desa Les, there is no giving back; the people never had much to start with that could be taken from them, let alone taken and then given back. As the land is dry, on the steep slopes of the Gunung Batur volcano, the village was never successful with agriculture. It is too far from the main population centers and ports to be a good place for manufacturing.

Do I personally feel a need to do something in Bali because I am Dutch and past Dutch colonialism weighs heavily on my shoulders? Well, having grown up in the Netherlands, Indonesia was never far away—350 years of colonial rule made Indonesia, with its spices, colors, music, and lifestyle, very much part of my cultural background. Do I feel guilty for the misuse, exploitation, and cruelty of an earlier generation? Not in the least. I am responsible for what I do in the present with the skills and assets I have, but not for anyone else or any other time.

We are blessed to have a meaningful business that helps people to invest or trade internationally. We have highly educated employees, most of whom are in good health. We build experiences, have fun, and earn money. We know that we are privileged to be able to lead this life.

We are therefore in a good starting position to do something for others. And we believe that what we do through our community foundation enriches our lives even further.

We are all born with multiple talents and many, often unused, skills. The more we bring out of our skills and use our talents, the more we will feel useful and happy, as valued contributors to our community. As Albert Einstein said,

"Without deep reflection, one knows from daily life that one exists for other people."[49]

Warren Buffett wanted to impart a sense of social responsibility to his son, and so he gave him three billion dollars with the explicit instruction to spend it all within 40 years on meaningful development projects for the one billion people in the world who lack basic food security. The son, Howard Buffett, traveled around the world and initiated over 40 agricultural projects, creating real change in farming communities. In his book *40 Chances*, some of these projects are described. In our lives, we all have about 40 harvests—about 40 chances to do better at whatever we are doing, to improve the way we work, to improve our harvest.

Most of us lead busy lives. It is easy to have great intentions and noble thoughts and then let them be snowed under by day-to-day realities and business.

Through our community foundation, we are trying to create a framework that makes it easier for families with wealth, surplus assets, and/or skills to contribute positively to a community in need.

I like this observation by Steve Jobs, a Buddhist and a university drop-out, who caused his adoptive father great grief. This is part of a commencement address he made in 2005 at Stanford University:

No one wants to die. Even people who want to go to heaven don't want to die to get there. And yet death is the destination we all share. No one has ever escaped it. And that is as it should be, because Death is very likely the single best invention of Life. It is Life's change agent. It clears out the old to make way for the new. Right now, the new is you, but someday not too long from now, you will gradually become the old and be cleared away. Sorry to be so dramatic, but it is quite true.

Your time is limited, so don't waste it living someone else's life. Don't be trapped by dogma—which is living with the results of other people's thinking. Don't let the noise of others' opinions drown out your own inner voice. And most important,

---

[49] The World As I See It," An essay originally published in "Forum and Century," vol. 84, pp. 193-194, the thirteenth in the *Forum* series, *Living Philosophies*. Included also in Living Philosophies (pp. 3-7), New York: Simon and Schuster, 1931.

have the courage to follow your heart and intuition. They somehow already know what you truly want to become. Everything else is secondary.[50]

Who is going to make our dreams come true, if we don't do it ourselves? Who will make your life meaningful, if not you?

Over a period of three years, we built 727 *kamar mandis* in Desa Les, overcoming all obstacles and coping with all difficulties. Many of the beneficiaries themselves helped by carrying materials and digging holes for the sceptic tanks. The local community is proud of what has been achieved. It has come out of the experience richer, with an enormous boost in self-esteem.

When we arrived in the village to finalize the project on May 5, 2016, the community hall was filled with gamelan music, traditional Balinese dancing, and moving speeches, followed by the sacrifice of a babi guling, or roasted pig. The celebration attracted much attention, even from Balinese TV. The community could feel proud that, in the face of hardship, it was able to create a sense of belonging, a true community, and a spirit of sharing.

This community more than compensated for what it lacked in material wealth through human warmth and caring. Apparently, the Gods looked favorably on the event; the music was enchanting and the dances were graceful. Most people laughed when Charles attempted to teach the gathered community to say "thank you" (dankjewel) in Dutch. The evening went off without a glitch, apart from a brief power failure that lasted exactly the length of the speech of one of the dignitaries, the Kepala Desa. Again, some people commented, it was a sign from the Gods. But it is not always clear which sign means what.

Always upwards and onwards. The day after we completed the Kamar Mandi Project, a small procession of people went to the nearby Pura Dalem temple to tell the goddess there we were starting a new venture and to ask her for blessings for a successful journey. The priest also prayed in the name of, and for, our foundation—so we are now known in the Balinese heavenly realms!

In Desa Les, each piece of land has its own small shrine, which is called the *pepuun* and houses the spirits that protect the site. When a new owner arrives to occupy the land, there is a ceremony that involves gathering one or two

---

[50]   Steve Jobs. 2005 commencement address to Stanford graduates.

rocks from the land and placing them in a shrine. As our land already had a *pepuun* left over from the previous owner, we first had to move the spirits (one male, one female) to a new location. This meant we had to build a new shrine (which took five days and two men to complete). The *pemangku*, or priest, picked the auspicious day of the New Moon of May. He asked the Gods for permission to move the original rocks, and then installed the new shrine, with an abundance of offerings, so permission was smoothly granted.

We erected a little shrine for Dewi Sri (the goddess of rice production and fertility) and Vishnu (the Hindu God, responsible for protecting and maintaining our creations). There were more offerings of flowers and rice, and another pig sacrificed its life, to mark the beginning of a new adventure.

That new adventure was the construction of the Desa Les Community Center, where we intend to create training facilities for young people, enabling them to learn skills beyond those of a manual laborer, and to find jobs. We are collaborating with great hotels, like the W Hotel in Seminyak, and local top restaurants, such as Locavore and Mozaic in Ubud to create a type of hotel school, where people can learn skills related to the hospitality business. We aim to teach accounting, housekeeping, computer skills, creative cooking, working with local plants in a permaculture garden, growing fresh herbs and vegetables, planning a business, and managing a hotel.

The Desa Les Community Center, managed for now by Rucina Ballinger, has the potential to become a game-changer for people in Northern Bali. It will allow young people to learn useful skills, not too far from home, and to later use those skills to earn good salaries that will benefit their families and the community as a whole. The community will increase in self-esteem, the motor of all human progress.

One day, Sue Meng Chan and I spoke to Yuli, one of many home-bound seamstresses in the village, and a beneficiary of the Kamar Mandi Project. She was sewing beads on clothing elements that were collected once a week by a gentleman from another village. Later, they would be assembled, ending up in high-end branded shoes. As is the case with many designer goods, the real secret is what people who create the intricate embroidery and needle work actually earn. In 4–6 hours of work, Yuli can finish sewing one pair of shoes and earn about U.S. \$0.18. If she works hard, she can complete up to three pairs of shoes in a day. She averages U.S. \$14 a month. She is in her thirties and her eyes are already starting to give out, as the work requires a lot of precision and concentration. She cannot move to Denpasar, as she belongs in the village, with her children, husband, and family members. If we cannot find more rewarding work for her, she may wish to train to work in a hotel or restaurant, which would bring in a significantly higher daily income.

The objectives of the Desa Les Community Center:

1) We will give people without much money or training the opportunity to develop skills that will enable them to make money within walking or biking distance of home, while still being able to take care of their families and meet other obligations.

2) We will offer training that reflects the job opportunities for which there is demand in Bali (for example, hotel management). We will offer training, not just in "hard" skills, like manning a hotel reception desk, accounting, computer skills, or catering, but also some soft skills like being on time, being clean, service-minded, assertive, and clear in communications. The primary goal is to increase self-esteem.

3) We will show farmers that some crops (certain herbs and vegetables) either grow better or make more money than the traditional commodities. Some are tastier, healthier, or can be grown without fertilizer. The permaculture garden will provide an example and teaching opportunity for farmers in the region.

4) We are providing a center where people can hold meetings, teach skills, and organize entertainment. There is nothing comparable in the region. As the center will focus a lot of attention on Desa Les and

its needs, appearing on Balinese and international TV programs, it may open up other opportunities for the community.

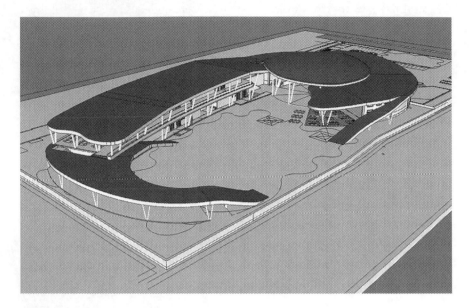

The Desa Les Community Center is designed to become a social enterprise. After a maximum of ten years, the project should have achieved a level of income sufficient to cover its expenses and make it sustainable, without any need for further subsidies or donations.

A social enterprise is a business:

1)   Created and designed to address a social problem.

2)   Self-sustainable, financially and otherwise; profits are reinvested in the business (or used to start other social businesses), with the aim of increasing social impact by expanding the company's reach, improving its products or services, or in other ways subsidizing its social mission.

The prime aim of a social enterprise is not to maximize profits, although generating profits will help it to grow and expand the reach of the business. The ownership of the project will be transferred once the project has become self-sustainable and the community is capable of managing it for the benefit of the community.

As Mohammad Yunus has said, "A charity dollar has only one life; a social business dollar can be invested over and over again."[51]

Philosophically, a social enterprise exploits what Mohammad Yunus calls the two basic human motives: selfishness and selflessness. Selfishly, people seek profit through business; at the same time, people selflessly perform philanthropic services, establishing churches, mosques, synagogues, art museums, public parks, health clinics, and community centers. The profits made by a social business are less important than its beneficial impact on society.

The Desa Les Community Center plans to generate income and cover its expenses through the following income streams:

1) The tuition fees of between 200 and 300 students a year (insofar as they are able to pay for tuition) or deferred payments from former students, once they have landed good jobs.

2) Selling meals in an on-site specialty restaurant to visitors and tourists. These meals will be prepared by the school's students and chefs. The restaurant will be open six days a week, and for special occasions and festivities.

3) Selling produce from the permaculture garden and fish pond.

4) Organizing special training activities and promotional events.

5) Attracting long-term sponsors and using the center for promotional activities and events, such as TV cooking shows.

It is going to be an exciting journey, although it may not always be easy. We have the land, now we just have to construct the building, create the permaculture garden, and hire teachers and maintenance staff. In addition, we will need to set up administration and reporting, and secure funding for both the initial stage and the ongoing training programs. I look forward to organizing my first concert ever—that will be a nice new milestone! I always derive a lot of energy from trying to do new things. As Pablo Picasso once said, "I am always doing that which I cannot do, in order that I may learn how to do it."

---

[51]   Prof. Muhammad Yunus, Nobel Peace Prize Laureate, Chairman of Yunus Social Business

We are trying to entice well-to-do families, companies embarking on a corporate social responsibility project, people who want to invest and make a positive impact through their contacts, skills, or ideas, and people who have time and two hands—just about anyone—to think about contacting us to discuss how they can participate, learn how to be part of an amazing journey that is just about to start, or to embark with us on a different journey altogether. In the end, it does not matter which fellow human beings we touch and share our good fortune with, as long as we do what we can! We can all do much more than we realize, and we release much more of our individual capacity by doing ALL we can!

> *He owned a whole world full of memories, of lovely moments relived and happy recollections. I'm not saying he was happy or that he didn't suffer. He suffered very much, but he did not despair; he still drew nourishment from what he had been given. But the sadness never left him. Happiness needs more than memories of the past to feed on; it also needs dreams of the future.*

—Jorge Amado

Chapter 9

A social enterprise creating stable jobs, sustainable incomes, and healthy products.

And there came also Nicodemus, which at the first came to Jesus by night, and brought a mixture of myrrh and aloes, about a hundred-pound weight. Then took they the body of Jesus, and wound it in linen clothes with the spices, as the manner of the Jews is to bury.[52]

—John 19:39-40

Aloe Barbadensis Miller (aloe vera) is quite a special plant. It belongs to one of the ten most effective medicinal plant families on earth. Mixed with myrrh and cinnamon, it has provided, since the 15th century BC or even earlier, an effective treatment for people who are suffering from large superficial wounds, traumatic shock, severe dehydration, loss of body fluids, and blood clotting. The mixture purifies the blood, widens the veins, filters out pollutants from the blood, re-hydrates the body, restores the rhythm of the heart, heals the skin, and reduces the effects of trauma, allowing the victim to regain consciousness and heal quickly.

I had never heard of aloe vera, other than as a sunscreen ingredient, until one evening in 1997, when I was sitting on a bar stool in a bar called Zambezi in Curaçao (in the Caribbean), next to a Colombian agricultural scientist. Luis Marin turned out to be one of the founders of Ecocity Curaçao, a struggling small plantation. Aloe vera, originally imported from West Africa, had been grown in Curaçao for centuries to treat bruises, burns, and upset stomachs and intestines. Once, more than a century ago, it had been one of the island's major exports.

---

[52]   King James Version (KJV)

In the course of several sessions on that bar stool, I learned about the many maladies that aloe can cure, and its beneficial influence on the skin, stomach, and intestines. The story intrigued me: perhaps the farmer deep inside me was trying to come out. Then, one day, our son Quinten, for a high school science project, deliberately exposed himself to a serious sunburn and treated one half of his back with aloe vera. The effect on his skin was astounding. Since then, we never have underestimated the curative powers of aloe vera, although we were seriously reprimanded by the school. One of our older friends began to drink shots of concentrated aloe juice religiously each day. It appeared to significantly reduce circulation problems in his legs. In addition, his hair grew partly back and he even found a new girlfriend.

A while later, the start-up aloe vera company was in deep financial trouble and our close friend, Mervyn Malan, who ran the Ostrich Farm and African-style restaurant next door to the aloe vera farm on Curaçao, asked me to help him develop a legal structure and find a consortium of investors to take over ownership and control of the ailing farm.

As we were unable to raise the full amount needed to finance the acquisition and upgrading, we and a friend made the final investment and thus became involved in a long journey with the aloe vera plantation. It is a journey that has taken many rewarding as well as painful twists.

> *"Only he can understand what a farm is, what a country is, who shall have sacrificed part of himself to his farm or country, fought to save it, struggled to make it beautiful. Only then will the love of farm or country fill his heart."*[53]

> **—Antoine de Saint-Exupéry**

Although Curaçao is a place where aloe vera has been cultivated for centuries, it is not necessarily the ideal place to grow it. In many places, the water is scarce or too brackish, and when it finally rains, there can be too much, causing plants to start rotting in the field. As we wanted to keep the farm fully organic, we also had to constantly battle insects, fungi and the like and find enough

---

[53]   Saint-Exupéry, de Antoine. Flight to Arras, translated by Lew Galantière, New York: Harcourt, 1986.

organic fertilizer, which on an island with few animals to produce the natural stuff, can at times be a challenge.

We were lucky to obtain a grant from the Dutch government to develop a production facility and train production staff on Curaçao, and we built a processing plant in around 2002. We dealt with many hiccups while building a factory so far from the centers where machines and equipment are actually produced. In our case, the pre-fab construction came from South Africa; most of our equipment was sourced from the wine industry in Spain, and a few machines were tailor-made in the Netherlands. Of course, all of our staff had to be trained from scratch, as there was and is no factory of a similar capacity or quality within a very large radius.

After many adjustments, the production process was fine-tuned to extract the maximum quantity of aloverose from the plants and to produce the highest possible quality aloe vera juice and gel. After several attempts to create wine from aloe vera (after all, it is a plant with high sugar levels; in Afrikaans, the name is alowijn), we had to abandon that idea, as the typical bitterness of aloe vera always remains, to some extent, in its extracts. Nevertheless, we had fun trying.

The team in Curaçao grew over time to some 25 Dutch, South African, Haitian, and Colombian employees, most of whom stayed on board for a good many years. The person in charge was Piet Viljoen, a South African biochemist, who worked on optimizing the cultivation and processing of aloe vera for many years; in 2011, he moved to the South African plantation in Limpopo.

A strong local market presence was created during these years, with several sale points in tourist areas and a distribution network all over the island that later covered the Caribbean and the Netherlands. Curaloe slowly but surely became a household brand.

In 2007, Mervyn Malan, who was still running the plantation and factory in Curaçao, announced that, after 17 years away from the "old Transvaal," he had become kind of homesick and wanted to return to his native South Africa to start another aloe vera plantation.

We took a joint vacation to the Transvaal, by then renamed Limpopo, to look at small farms in that part of South Africa, north of the Soutpansberge, which is permanently protected from occasional frosts (one night of frost will kill aloe vera plants). Although my wife and I had visited South Africa several times before, we fell in love with the country. Or, to be more exact, we fell in love with one particular farm—at 1,200 hectares, much too large for our aloe production purposes— where one night we saw a group of giraffes with their companion birds foraging in the dying light of an African sunset, as we sat enjoying sundowners.

We were sold—my wife Paula and I decided to co-invest in the African business as well. From then on, we could borrow the promising first words of *Out of Africa:* we had a farm in Africa…

We looked at the investment as a way to get to know the country and its culture, enjoy the wildlife, help out a good friend, and become involved from the sidelines in a more back-to-basics and grass-roots business than financial services. Together, we bought the beautiful twelve-hundred-hectare Iphofolo farm, which had lots of game, including different types of antelopes, wildebeest, giraffes, and zebras. We built a vacation home there, and our friend began planting aloe vera and developing the plan and processing the permits to build a processing plant.

Then disaster struck. Mervyn Malan died in a car accident one Friday night after work, close to the farm. We had to choose between abandoning the project and writing off most of our (for us) significant investment and complaining about our bad luck—or continuing with the project ourselves. My wife and I opted for the latter and bought Mervyn's share of the property from his widow. We picked up the pieces of the project (as Mervyn had been a farmer, of course nothing was well-organized or written down), and we learned how to be aloe vera farmers.

We also learned how to manage a game farm, build a factory, and deal with South African red tape and confirmative action, conservative and skeptical neighbors, a totally different culture—and the list goes on. We moved our daughter to boarding school in Haenertsburg, South Africa (some 200 kilometers from the farm), and somehow managed to juggle our lives outside South Africa while living 425 kilometers from an international airport and 100 kilometers from the nearest decent supermarket or restaurant.

About two years later, we celebrated the official opening of our brand-new factory and, shortly thereafter, the launch of our first health drinks and body care products. Cosmetics came later. At the opening ceremony, we organized a big braai with a sheep on the spit roast, invited the local farmers and organized a hoompah band. I gave a speech in which I quoted the following passage from former president Nelson Mandela's inauguration speech (actually written by Marianne Williamson):

> *Our deepest fear is not that we are inadequate. Our deepest fear is that we are powerful beyond measure. It is our light, not our darkness, that most frightens us. We ask ourselves, who am I to be brilliant, gorgeous, talented, fabulous? Actually, who are you not to be? You are a child of God: your playing small doesn't serve the world. There is nothing enlightened about shrinking so that other people won't feel insecure around you. We were born to make manifest the glory of God that is within us. It's not just in some of us; it's in everyone. And as we let our light shine, we unconsciously give other people permission to do the same. As we are liberated from our own fear, our presence automatically liberates others.[54]*

—Nelson Mandela

---

[54]   Williamson, Marianne. *Our Deepest Fear*, from *A Return to Love*, New York: HarperCollins, 1992.

The reactions were mixed. Although in that part of the Transvaal (nowadays northern Limpopo), Mandela is still seen by some as a terrorist, the local farmers began working with us; they respected our perseverance, commitment, and love for nature and the land. I think it is when such decisions cross your path that men are separated from boys, and entrepreneurs from mere dreamers.

So why is this agricultural social enterprise project so important to us?

The values of this social enterprise:

1) The project originally started as an effort to help a friend—as good a reason as any. However, it would never have worked if we, as a family, had not had a deep affinity with agriculture and enjoyed living off the land.

2) We saw the farm as an excellent opportunity to get to know another country, South Africa. When you invest and work somewhere, you develop deeper contacts and experiences than you ever could on vacation.

3) We did not know much about HIV or aloe vera. Now we do. Our investment introduced us to a world that turned out to be fascinating and meaningful. We learned about the various qualities of plants, our food, and the minerals, climate, and forces around us. We have become much more conscious of what we eat and drink. Our people developed products that really benefit users.

4) It is great to work in and connect with nature. Having lived in big cities most of our lives, we had lost our connection to the soil and the seasons, the iron discipline needed to deal with natural cycles, and knowing when to plant, prune, and harvest. The experience showed us how relative and relevant our influence can be on our environment.

5) So far, this project has created close to 100 permanent jobs. We are proud to have made this contribution in areas with such high unemployment.

6) We have developed different types of training for the people who work on our two aloe projects. This enables our employees to become more

qualified and confident in their jobs, and also more qualified for other good employment opportunities. We train and coach unqualified people to become foremen, supervisors, and machine operators. Over time, they take on more senior-level tasks and responsibilities. It is very rewarding to see people, who come in without skills, but with the right attitude, quickly acquiring those skills, learning, and becoming self-confident and self-reliant. We guarantee equal opportunities for men and women, equal pay for people who do the same work, and promote black people wherever we can. We reject child labor and verbal and physical abuse. These things may seem obvious, but they are new to this part of South Africa. It is inspiring to see the pride on people's faces when they get their first bank accounts and ATM cards, finally gaining the freedom to support faraway family members, qualify for cell phone accounts, and buy small luxuries on installment.

7) We have always paid less well-qualified staff members at least 10–15 percent above minimum wage, to ensure that we can choose the best candidates from a huge pool, and to make them feel valued and valuable. Many employers in South Africa misuse the high unemployment situation and pay below minimum wage, as employees have no choice but to accept. Under the current political constellation, investments and new jobs in South Africa are extremely scarce.

8) To house all employees at the farm, we had to restore and build a lot of housing from scratch, and teach the residents to take care of it. Many of our new recruits had never seen or used a flush toilet or electric stove before. We also created a soccer field, as there isn't much to do in the vast emptiness of Northern Limpopo. One Christmas season, a client contributed to the project by donating a container full of brand-new furniture, toys, clothing, and furnishings for our workers.

9) When it comes to efficiently converting CO_2 into oxygen, 20 Aloe plants are equal to one tree. With over half a million aloe vera plants, our plantations actually cleanse the earth of hundreds of tons of CO_2 every year!

10) Many people in South Africa (and elsewhere) have no access to HIV-related medicines. At least some of these are now helped with our

products (which do not cure HIV, but at least provide relief and stop symptoms from getting worse).

If we run our farm well, it will have a positive impact on the surrounding area. Several of the neighboring farmers have upgraded their employee facilities, increased salaries, and slightly adjusted their attitude toward the people who work for them. These are important developments in badly governed South Africa, where unrest is breeding just below the surface.

None of our little triumphs came easy. We faced corruption, extortion, racism, a nasty mass strike, many threats and accusations, an armed robbery, recurring theft, systematic poaching, and many attempts to overcharge or trick us. On the farm, we had to deal with plant and human diseases, bottle fights, knife fights, sodomy with our goats, employees being attacked and killed by snakes, and frequent deaths from HIV or comparable diseases.

In spite of these serious and less serious inconveniences and setbacks, it was great to be in nature; the aloe vera plantation in South Africa, known as African Caribbean Aloe Products Private slowly worked its way towards success.

Our employees come from all over South Africa, as well as from Zimbabwe, Zambia, and other neighboring countries. Some arrived at the height of the

Zimbabwe food crisis with nothing more than the clothes they were wearing; for a long time, they were among our most loyal and knowledgeable workers, until the authorities evicted them for not having proper immigration papers.

Our son Quinten and his girlfriend built a luxury tented camp for overnight guests (Iphofolo Game Farm), where visitors, ornithologists, and hunters can stay to enjoy the quiet of nature at the back of the aloe vera plantation.

A small shop and restaurant allow our visitors, who always come from far away, to purchase our end products and get some healthy South African food before making the long trip back to civilization.

Aloe vera is a relatively easy plant to cultivate. It grows all over the world in desert conditions, where the climate is never wet or frosty. Some 80 percent of aloe vera production takes place in the U.S., Mexico, and the Caribbean, while over 80 percent of its users live in East and Southeast Asia. The demand for aloe vera products, forever known to have curative and antiseptic uses, has grown exponentially. Historically, one could find sunscreens, many cosmetics, and a few health drinks containing aloe vera. Nowadays, there is aloe vera in most disinfectant and bacteria-free products, from tampons, toilet paper, razor blades, contact lens fluid, diapers and toilet paper to health tonics and medicines.

At the farm, we keep a scrapbook of letters and testimonials from people whose lives have been drastically changed by using our aloe vera juices or gels. It always makes me feel proud when I leaf through this book.

Many people who have tested positive for HIV have little or no access to the expensive synthetic drugs available to people in wealthier countries. Some have shown remarkable progress by drinking a shot of concentrated aloe vera juice each day. Similar effects have been noticed in people with other auto-immune diseases, such as diabetes.

Our involvement with the aloe vera farms has deeply changed our lives. We now live much closer to nature, we are much more aware of the importance of lifestyle on our health, and we developed a deep respect for nature's pharmacy. We are what we eat. Food does not grow in supermarkets—that goes without saying. Instead of stuffing our bodies with processed food and chemicals to deal with imbalances, a healthy dose of aloe vera can do wonders, curing certain ailments and helping us appreciate how delicate and precious life is. We live in our bodies and need to keep them healthy, sane, and clean; aloe vera can help us do that.

Soon, we plan to add a line of fully organic cosmetic products, not just produced from organically grown plants, but made into high quality cosmetics through a fully organic process; this is a better, more natural approach that can also benefit users. Fully organic products will help the plantation keep growing in a high quality and competitive market segment. Ultimately, healthy recurring profits will create a sustainable life for a growing group of local people.

> *Four vegetables are indispensable for the wellbeing of man: wheat, grapes, olives, and aloe. The first nourishes him, the second he refreshes the spirit, the third brings him harmony and the fourth cures him.*

> **—Christopher Columbus (1451–1506).**

Chapter 10

Israel – the kibbutz!

The charity or community services you want to support must align with your values.

Courage is being scared to death... and saddling up anyway.[55]

—John Wayne

When, as a kid, I heard about the 1967 Six Day War and the 1973 Yom Kippur War, my heart went out to Israel. Not only did I admire the eternal fight of David against Goliath, but I also had a lot of sympathy for those hardworking and idealistic pioneers, singing and dancing, reviving Ivrit, the age-old Hebrew language, and converting the desert into a flowering orchard. I spoke to several people who had gone to Israel as volunteers, to work on a *kibbutz*.

In 1978, I reached a milestone in my studies and saw my chance. It was my first airplane trip and my first outside Western Europe. I felt good because I was going to do something altruistic, a form of community service, as well as having an adventure. This purpose would prevent my trip from becoming an empty and ultimately boring pleasure—a bit like the difference between true love and superficial sex. The fact that I had no money and could stay at a *kibbutz* for free, exchanging labor for food and housing, definitely also helped.

I loved the trip. The whole experience was new for me. The airport (where I learned the hard way why it isn't smart to carry a connected camping gas stove in your luggage), the flight, my arrival and the smells and noises of the Middle East and the mix of Hebrew and Arabic. I tried my first hummus and falafel on Dizengoff, gazed at beautifully bronzed girls around Tel Aviv, and made the three-hour bus ride to Maoz Haim near Beit She'an in the Jordan

---

[55] https://johnwayne.com/quotes/

Valley—the *kibbutz* chosen for me by a volunteer organization. I immediately loved the atmosphere and thoroughly enjoyed myself.

A *kibbutz* is a communist-inspired alternative way for people to work and live together. Originally, the *kibbutzim* were very poor; all of the members would contribute in accordance with what they could produce and take from what was produced only as needed. All wore the same drab clothes, ate in communal facilities, sent their children to the same *kibbutz* school (where they would also sleep), and worked side by side, with basically everyone being equal. Shabbat was observed, but not nearly as strictly as it was by the orthodox Jewish communities around Jerusalem. In Maoz Haim, trouble and envy emerged when the *kibbutz* was becoming more prosperous and (for example) obtained one or two cars that people increasingly wanted to use for pleasure trips. As the kibbutz grew more successful, people began to want nicer clothes than the standard over-washed blue cotton uniform, or even extravagant luxuries like pets. The older *kibbutzniks* still had traumatic memories of the concentration camps they had survived in Eastern Europe. Perhaps suffering from survivors' guilt, some of the older members wanted all members to lead hard-working, sober, and frugal lives. However, younger members saw the rising standards of living in Israel and increasingly chose to leave the *kibbutz* to lead more frivolous lives under the bright city lights of Tel Aviv. All of this resulted in lots of heated debate and little structural reform.

I ended up sharing a room with a Japanese volunteer, Toshikuni Doi. As I had grown up on a farm, had some agricultural experience, and knew how to drive a tractor, I was assigned two important tasks. The first was to collect the community's garbage each morning and take it away to the garbage dump, conveniently located directly on the border with Jordan, so that the smell would drift eastward. Each morning, I would wave at the Jordanian soldiers across the border, who followed my every move with their binoculars. It took me at least a month to get them to start waving back. My second task was to join a team that was working to create an irrigation system that would automatically keep the lawns between the living quarters green as well as dripping water on plants in front of the, usually open, windows, to help cool down the rooms. In those days, air-conditioning was an unknown luxury in that part of Israel, although temperatures often reached 40 degrees centigrade. I was lucky to have two different tasks, and the tractor gave me some freedom and a chance to set my own timetable. Most of the volunteers were given monotonous tasks like clearing and harvesting the fields or working in the Poliraz plastic factory making bottle caps. There weren't many forms of entertainment on the kibbutz, and the nearest village and bus stop was a hot five kilometer walk away, so generally, life was quiet and unexciting.

When something did happen, the excitement was therefore greater. One day, just before the end of work and the beginning of lunch, I heard some brief machine gun salvos in the fields adjoining the *kibbutz*. A bit later, two bodies, their clothes drenched in blood, were dragged up in front of the infirmary. One person was clearly dead and the other was breathing heavily and looked very pale, the approach of death already visible in his eyes. He had been shot by a *kibbutznik* guard and was bleeding profusely from his belly. They were two smallish, very normal-looking Palestinian guys, no older than me (I was 20 at the time), who had illegally crossed the border from Jordan, armed with AK-47s, which they had not had time to use. Each had a small backpack with some bread and dates, T-shirts, underwear, a toothbrush, and a hand-grenade. The officer in charge of defence on the *kibbutz* tried to find out from the survivor whether they had been on their own or part of a bigger group. His Arabic was not that good and the guy passed out and died after disclosing only his name: Ishmael, which, ironically, was also the name of that Israeli officer. The *kibbutz* was declared secure again. Everyone was relieved that no one had got hurt (sic!), but that officer was unusually quiet for a good many days after that. And the Jordan border guards stopped waving at me.

We worked six days a week, from five in the morning until one in the afternoon, with Saturdays off. In the late afternoons, there were Hebrew classes; once in a while we had a day trip. Once a week, there was a movie night. I remember very well seeing the movie Entebbe, about a daring and successful raid the Israeli army had executed two years earlier. A plane had been hijacked by terrorists and flown to *Entebbe*, Uganda, where the hostages were later spectacularly freed by Israeli soldiers. One of the soldiers who participated in the raid was born on our *kibbutz* and, although he did not make it back, his parents were clearly very proud, the heroes of the day. During the movie, all of the typically stoical Ashkenazi *kibbutzniks* climbed on their chairs, cheering at each attack and booing at each counter-measure, in an atmosphere loaded with feverish nationalistic fervor. All agreed that it was a great movie and a great evening out. Catching their enthusiasm, I too was convinced that the Israelis were brave and fully within their rights to fight terrorism and discrimination.

One morning, a short time later, most of the young men and women of the *kibbutz* disappeared. They had been mobilized during the night. An anti-aircraft gun appeared out of nowhere in the middle of the *kibbutz*, people were nervous, and news became scarce. It turned out that there had been a raid or invasion, later named Operation Litani, into nearby Lebanon. That Saturday, all of us volunteers were invited to join an excursion in an open truck. We drove to the Lebanese border, which was not far away, passing the badly destroyed border post. We saw some smoldering vehicles and dead goats, and ended up in a nice meadow with a great view, where we had a simple picnic, practiced our hora dancing and chilled. On the way back, we passed more burnt-out vehicles, dead goats, some wearing boots, and damaged buildings and returned to the *kibbutz*. It was a bizarre and unsettling experience.

Once in a while, we had a long weekend off. We used those weekends to get to know the country. Israel is not very big and it has a great network of buses. The West Bank was considered safe at the time and we drove through it numerous times on our way to Jerusalem, the Sinai desert and Mount Sinai, and especially the snorkeling and scuba diving in Eilat, Nuweiba, Dahab, and Sharm Al Sheikh.

It is a beautiful country and every square meter is steeped in history. Masada, where some 960 Sicarii rebels fought to their death against the Romans or committed mass suicide during the first Jewish-Roman war, was perhaps the most impressive sight, together with the Wailing Wall and Yad Vashem, the memorial for the Shoah, the Second World War Holocaust.

I loved my experiences and adventures and I greatly admired the Israelis for being tough, resourceful, fair, and independent and for developing a backward, underdeveloped and scorched land into a blossoming country.

> *Sometimes when I was overcome by curiosity and desire for such exotic things, I envied the traveler who can see such wonders in their living, everyday context. But he becomes a different person. You cannot walk beneath the palm trees with impunity, and attitudes are sure to change in a country where elephants and tigers are at home.*[56]

> **—Johann Wolfgang von Goethe**

---

[56]   Johann Wolfgang von Goethe. *Die Wahlverwandschaftens* (Elective Affinities, 1809). North Charleston, USA: Createspace, 2015

One long weekend, I went with a friend from the kibbutz to look for the source of the Jordan River in the far north of the country, close to Banyas at the Golan Heights, which was military territory. We hiked all day and when night came, as we had done on previous occasions, we moved some distance away from the path, rolled out our sleeping bags under some trees, and fell asleep.

In the middle of the night, I was rudely awoken with the kick of a boot. As I opened my eyes, I was staring into an Uzi submachine gun. I was ordered out of my sleeping bag and onto my feet with my hands in the air. It was slightly embarrassing, as it was quite a balmy summer night and I wasn't wearing any clothes. We were surrounded by two armored vehicles, guns trained on us, and eight or ten soldiers, some of them female. Apparently, we had inadvertently penetrated into a military area and been spotted by an infra-red camera. We could consider ourselves lucky that the soldiers had not fired at us, or that we had not stepped into a nearby mine field. We could easily have ended up like poor Ishmael.

A couple of weeks, later my then close friend Toshikuni Doi was about to leave Israel and go back to his studies to become a reporter. As a last joint trip, I suggested visiting the Gaza strip to learn something about the many refugee camps there. Toshi found a UN contact and we were given a full-fledged VIP tour around one of the refugee camps. We got the opportunity to speak to some refugees, many of whom had been living in tents and shacks since 1949. We shared a meal with some of them and listened to stories about what had happened to them, their land, and their families.

On this trip, everything was very different. Most of the people in the camp watched us with deep mistrust. Suddenly almost all of the comments about the Israelis were negative; we heard many stories about abuse, violence, mistreatment, destroyed houses and livelihoods, and lost family members.

What had happened to my heroes?

We both felt deeply disappointed and perhaps even cheated. The experience made us somber. We had a night-long conversation, helped on by a bottle of whisky. In the end, we concluded that we had been blind-sided, or rather willfully blind, choosing to hear only one side of the story, weighing up only one set of facts. A story always has two, three, or even more sides—as many sides as participants. It was our own fault that we had listened selectively, sifting the news to suit our own one-sided ideas.

My friend Toshi ended up going back to Israel many times to make documentaries. He also filmed war atrocities in Israel (the Balata refugee camp) and Iraq (Fallujah). With each documentary, he focused more on the human side of the drama. It made him famous as well as a thought leader in Japan.

> *Then he made one last effort to search in his heart for the place where his affection had rotted away, and he could not find it.*[57]

—Gabriel García Márquez, *One Hundred Years of Solitude*

That same week, I also left the *kibbutz*. It hurt, as I had built some good friendships there. I was treated well and had lots of fun. But it did not feel the same anymore. I no longer wanted to be a part of the *kibbutz* system. I no longer wanted to help the Israelis in their heroic fight for their freedom and their God-given right to live in peace. There are many peaces in Israel and the other peoples involved have as much right to a peaceful and happy life as the Israelis do. My little self-proclaimed community service project in Israel turned out to not be that altruistic. I stuck with it as long as I could justify it within my own value system. It did not fit any more, so I could not stay.

I did not go back to Israel until 15 years later, when I was working on international tax planning for a new investment in Global Positioning Systems, research no doubt triggered by military needs. By then, the atmosphere in the country had changed completely and whatever relationship there had been between the Israelis and the Palestinians had completely broken down. I still have some Israeli friends. I still admire what has been achieved, but I cannot sympathize with people who become successful at the expense of others. There is a fundamental difference between standing on someone else's shoulders to reach higher, and trampling over someone to pursue your own success.

When should you admit to yourself that your ideas or convictions were wrong? And when do you change course or change sides?

---

[57]   Márques García, Gabriel. *One Hundred Years of Solitude*, New York: 1970. Originally published in Argentina, 1967 by Editorial Sudamericanos, SA, Buenos Aires, *Cien Años de Soleded*.

I find it difficult. However, as I get older, whenever I feel something nagging deep inside, warning me that something is not right, however irrational it may seem, I take it seriously and begin to analyze it. All of us are influenced by what happens outside us. I have a hard time admitting my mistakes and adjusting outdated ideas and allegiances.

Conversely, we are easily blinded by how great something looks from the outside. This unfortunately means that we spend little time looking at what is inside.

So, what did my experiences in Israel teach me?

The value(s) of charity and community service:

1) It is really easy to fall in love with a project, an idea, an ideology, or a set of values. To be sold on a story or an ideology that may objectively not be true. Every ideological leader, however extreme his (apparently never her) ideas has been able to gather a large following and get people to do whatever it takes to spread the cause.

2) Especially when an ideology comes close to your own values and belief system, it is easy to be blind-sided. Once you are on the wrong path, turning around is difficult. When a commitment no longer feels good, or when you aren't reaching your imagined destination, think about the premises you started out with and reach back to your earliest assumptions. They may have been wrong from the beginning, or at least one-sided.

3) Deep inside, sooner or later, you feel the eternal truths, the true values, the fact that we are all equally important and equally worthy. I subscribe to what Mohandas Gandhi said: "Many people, especially ignorant people, want to punish you for speaking the truth, for being correct, for being you. Never apologize for being correct, or for being years ahead of your time. If you're right and you know it, speak your mind. Speak your mind. Even if you are a minority of one, the truth is still the truth." Don't worry about what is en vogue or mainstream. Every change starts from a tiny minority, a few people who light the first small candle in a dark

room, eliminating darkness and ignorance. Do not be afraid to be part of the minority, even a minority of one. People who follow their hearts, their internal compass, will find ways to change and achieve satisfaction for themselves.

And once you do realize the truth, take action—move!

1) Life is short. A lot of people helped you to get where you are. Now this is your moment, your money, and your opportunity to realize your dreams and ideas. Whatever project or investment you choose, make sure that what you want and find important is reflected in your projects. Don't let other people's opinions limit what you can do with your life.

2) You always need to feel a sense of urgency. There is no better time than the present moment. Tomorrow, there will be other priorities, other things needing your attention. What you did yesterday doesn't matter; what you plan to do tomorrow—wait and see. It's all about what you actually get done today. It wouldn't be good to end your life in saudade, longingly remembering the past. The things you could have done—do them now. The present moment is the only moment that matters.

3) Many people will cross your path; there is no need to search for anything exotic. Be loyal to the people who are loyal to you, the ones who helped you get where you are. It does not matter whether they are family members, employees, neighbors, or members of the same religious sect. Nothing will be achieved in isolation; by starting with the people you love and trust, you will multiply your efforts. Anyone can help to make this world a better place. You can start with simple things: recycling old clothes or books, feeding someone, visiting elderly people, planting a tree, teaching someone a skill, treating people with respect, and even smiling. So many things in life don't require a big investment.

4) Develop a good plan, but don't hesitate or procrastinate. A good plan today is better than a perfect one tomorrow. Ask: what is good about this specific project? What are the assumptions and goals? If

we are not achieving the goals, were the assumptions correct? Was the effort adequate—were the goals realistic?

I would not have wanted to miss my experiences in Israel for anything. We can grow as human beings, develop new values and thoughts, and free ourselves from convention and the opinions of others in good and in bad times, through happy and unhappy experiences, and by meeting good and bad people—as long as we are prepared to step back, from time to time, to see our experiences for what they are. Each one enriches our lives.

Who was I now? I had the feeling that, after my farewell letter to Fidel, the comrades began to see me as a man from other climes rather distant from Cuba's specific problems, and I could not bring myself to demand the final sacrifice of remaining behind. I spent the final hours like this, alone and perplexed, until the boats eventually put in at two o'clock in the morning, with a Cuban crew who arrived and set off immediately that very night.[58]

A desolate, sobering and inglorious spectacle took place. I had to reject men who pleaded to be taken along. There was not a trace of grandeur in this retreat, nor a gesture of rebellion... just some sobbing as I, the leader of the escapees, told the man with the mooring rope to let go.[59]

—Ernesto "Che" Guevara, *on his escape over Lake Tanganyika, after his failed attempt to fuel change by starting a guerilla war in Congo.*

---

[58] https://www.theguardian.com/books/2000/aug/12/cuba.artsandhumanities Viewed September, 2016

[59] Hitchens, Christopher. *And Yet...: Essays.* Simon & Schuster: New York, 2015.

Chapter 11

A philanthropic project with long-term sustainability objectives.

When I give food to the poor, they call me a saint. When I ask why the poor have no food, they call me a communist.[60]

—Dom Hélder Câmara

Curaçao is a tiny island in the southern part of the Caribbean. For over fifteen years, it was our home. It was where our children were born, and where my first real business was launched.

As your plane descends towards the airport, your first impression, looking out of the window, is of drought, cactuses, and shrubs. It looks like the thirstlands in South Africa, Mexico, or Arizona.

Once you are on the soil of Curaçao, an autonomous country within the Kingdom of the Netherlands since October 10, 2010, you may feel that you have arrived in the only part of the Netherlands where the sun always shines. In many places, the red, white, and blue flag stands out against a stark, light blue sky, in the ever-blowing trade winds. Loud, sunburnt, Dutch people dominate the tourist trade as well as the financial sector. American influences are also obvious: ghetto music, big cars, shouting billboards, and American products in the supermarkets. Miami is never very far away. While the great majority of the population has darker shades of skin, the African influences take longer to notice: *tambu* music, the way society and politics work. Family life is matriarchal. Caribbean, Colombian, Venezuelan characteristics also emerge, in the magic realism of the region, the swinging rhythms, colorful foods and rich

---

[60] Hélder, Camâra. *The Gift: A Life that Marked the Course of the Church in Brazil,* Page 53, Editora Vozes, 2000.

pagan, Christian, and local traditions. Cuban Santeria and Haitian voodoo have local equivalents in Curaçao.

Of course, the island is a combination of all of these influences, even though many people live their whole lives in Curaçao in one particular culture, without ever being greatly influenced by the others. The island has four widely spoken languages, but many people manage happily without speaking much Spanish, Dutch, English or even Papiamento (the colloquial language spoken by 82 percent of the population). It is possible to stay in one segment of the melting pot, where most of the ingredients remain unstirred and unblended. Here you can you find Santa Claus, from a centuries-old Dutch tradition, as a black guy making himself white for the occasion, while his black helpers make themselves (more) black, to avoid being recognized by the local kids, or green and orange to adjust to more recent sensitivities on skin color. There are radio stations and newspapers in at least five languages, lots of political parties engaged in ever-changing coalitions, and more foundations, pressure groups, and special interest activities than anywhere else I can think of.

For many years, I lived in Curaçao, allowing the African and Latino influences to merely color my predominantly white world. Later, after living in South Africa, I realized that much of the island's background is actually African and I became more interested in those aspects. While spending time in Colombia, Venezuela, Santo Domingo, Haiti, and Cuba, I came to appreciate how the island fits into a unique regional culture, where each country or island is a separate expression of the mixture of cultures.

For such a small island, Curaçao has an unusual number of famous authors. A couple of times, at the Avila Beach Hotel, I was fortunate enough to meet Boeli van Leeuwen, one of Curaçao's leading writers and intellectuals. After the riots of May 30, 1969, which marked the transfer of power and authority from a small white elite to the black majority, he wrote,

Before everything, we must realize one thing: a nation that does not want to fight for her future, has no future. We should not let either the Netherlands or Venezuela put us in a dilemma. Self-respect and unanimity is our only weapon.

He was not particularly optimistic about Curaçao's geopolitical future: "The day will come that The Hague, Washington, and Caracas will decide about us, while we are fighting each other with village politics." This statement remains relevant today, although Beijing should probably be added to the list of places that decides what will happen in Curaçao.

The gossip circuit and newspapers are constantly full of grandiose plans to realize one great project or another, including scheduled flights from the airport to outer space. The island could easily be covered under a thick layer of reports, written about its future and prospective plans. As most of those plans never materialize, everything stays more or less as it has been forever. Curaçao attracts more than its fair share of romantic dreamers, naive investors attracted to the sun, and crooks and criminals of all kinds, exploiting other visitors and the rest of the population.

Almost all plans (perhaps providentially) suffocate from an absence of urgency or proactivity, stifling bureaucracy, corruption, nepotism, general inertia, or a wide-spread reluctance to put effort into anything that won't lead to instant gratification or end with a big party. There are more get rich quick schemes to be found in Curaçao than almost anywhere else in the world. Most would never work; fortunately, they rarely make it beyond the conceptual stage. The island has more lottery offices than proper investment institutions, more "lucky number advisors" than Hong Kong, more casinos than banks, more prostitutes than priests, and more *sneks* than restaurants. The two fixed events that appear on TV each night are wega di number (the lottery draw) and partisipashon di morto (death notices and funeral announcements). Funerals are major, time-consuming affairs and you need to participate in lots of them, including those of your neighbor's grandmother and grandmother's neighbor. At funerals of higher status people, business deals are sealed, gossip is exchanged, new networks are tapped, and participants end up at the nearest *snek* in a lively mood.

The "mentalidad di cangrew" is widespread. Just as one crab in a bucket can quite easily get out, two or more crabs in a bucket will prevent each other from getting out. By doing too well, you expose my lack of effort or success. For this reason, instead of celebrating your success, I will do what I can to belittle or hinder yours.

Somewhere, deep in the genes of the nation, there remains a feeling that we can't dominate or control what happens. The knife cut me—the bottle fell on the floor—the door hit me. Whatever happens is always outside our control. People in Curaçao rarely say to themselves: I cut myself with the knife—I dropped the bottle on the floor—I walked into the door and hurt myself. When a budget is made and the planned expenses exceed the projected income, the question is never how to cut costs or increase income, but whom we can find to pay for the deficit. This situation is not exactly improved by the unequal and mostly fictive partnership with the Kingdom, exhorting all parties to "rely on their own strength, but with the will to assist one another." On the Curaçao side, there is presently no solid or healthy self-reliance; on the Dutch side, there is no generous, selfless will to assist. As a result, the island residents' self-esteem remains very low and the country neither plans nor grows towards a sustainable economic model or proud independence. Had I been a *yu d'i Kòrsou* included in local society, this would have been a great and very useful development project to work on. It could begin by changing the focus from "respekt," a word used and misused in many contexts, to "pride and self-reliance." "Nos mes por" (the Curaçao version of "Yes, we can") must be transformed from a hollow phrase to a banner that unites the people. Respect, like progress, can only be created through hard labor. It becomes pathetic when begged for or received as a gift.

Of course, certain aspects of this mentality can be traced back to a long history of slavery. For a while, Curaçao played an important role in the transatlantic slave trade (in the typical Dutch spirit of self-flagellation, there is a slavery museum in Curaçao; Kura Holanda). Many dark skinned people on the island even today behave as if they had personally experienced slavery and thus deserve monetary compensation (or at least pity) from white people. Officially, the slave trade was abolished in 1803 and the ownership of slaves in 1863, with the government compensating all owners an average of 200 Guilders per slave. However, as former slaves owned no land and had no money, education, or choices, the de facto situation did not change much; former slaves continued to do the same jobs, albeit for a meager salary that they could spend in the plantation store. Real emancipation came only after a popular revolt in 1969. Since then, roles on the island have been reversed in many ways. It is often easier to get around speaking Papiamento and having a dark skin than speaking Dutch and having a white skin. Nevertheless, every time the (European part of the) Kingdom offers full independence, it is politely declined, as the Netherlands is where children go to study, most people go for medical attention, everyone has family, and all passport holders automatically qualify for social security.

There were two types of slaves in Curaçao, house slaves and plantation slaves. These roles created two very different types of mentality. House slaves were often docile and faithful to their masters—after all, they lived in or near the planter's or trader's house, wore decent clothes, and usually got proper food. When the Master was sick, a house slave would say, "we sick." Female house slaves were often unlawfully, and sometimes forcefully, impregnated by their masters, resulting in mixed race offspring whose adoptive names were often derived from those of the *shons* (the masters).

Plantation slaves typically lived outside and despised their masters, wishing death upon them and all they loved. Plantation slaves played inspirational music, and took part in uprisings and continuous acts of quiet sabotage. It was often said in Curaçao, for many years a thriving slave market, that those who could not be sold at the market became the forefathers of the local population. When the refinery construction started in 1914, the population grew exponentially, as people from all over the Caribbean, Latin America, and Europe felt attracted and moved to Curaçao. Nevertheless, many people like to trace back their roots as yu d'i Kòrsou to the days of slavery, and consider such families the true Curaçaolenos. However, on the day slavery was abolished, just 6,684 slaves were owned by individuals and 76 by the Government.

Looking back, I realize how many similarities there are between our aloe vera plantation in South Africa, and the lifestyle of the *shons* on Curaçao, two or three centuries ago. On payday evenings, we can hear from our plantation house the loud parties in the workers' compound, the music remarkably similar to *tambu*. There are knife fights and wounds that need to be stitched up; there are people unable to live in a normal family situation, as their homelands are far and our plantation, like all others, excludes children over the age of four and anyone who does not work there. When we arrived in South Africa in 2010, the plantation was still paying wages in cash, as none of the workers had a bank account. In any case, the nearest ATM and only shop, apart from the farm shop, was 20 kilometers away.) By law, part of a worker's compensation was in rations: staples like maize or sorghum meal (funchi in Curaçao, pap in South Africa) salt, cigarettes, some meat, offal, and vegetables. These would be distributed on Wednesdays, in Papiamento, Djarason, the day the ration was distributed. The notarial title deed to our farm, signed in 2009, fully fifteen years after the end of apartheid, refers to the belonger rights and obligations of employees born on and linked to the farm immediately after describing the plantation's land, house, farm equipment, goats and cattle, but before mentioning the antelopes, zebras, and wildebeest. Strangely enough, these belonger rights have never been abolished; instead, they are updated by law every single year. People who have them are envied for having some form of social safety net.

The author, Tip Marugg, in his novel, *The Roar of Morning*, incisively describes the mood of Curaçao and the world-weariness and occasional will-to-self-destruct of "Caribbean Man." In the story, a man sits on the doorstep of his home with a bottle of whisky, waiting for daybreak and contemplating suicide. He observes nature, thinks about philosophy, his childhood in Venezuela, his sexual dreams about women, and his life in Curaçao, where he feels out-of-place as a white Antillean. The novel contains an exceptional scene, in which the narrator watches scores of birds in flight crash into a steep rock face and die, a daily event.

In a subsequent meditation, Marugg says: *It is not the Jew but Caribbean Man who is the most tragic figure on earth, his destination is not Auschwitz but Disney World. He lives in hiding, even though the colonial occupation ended long ago. He suffers from night blindness and cures himself by spending the whole day in the sun. His life, a feast of laughing and dancing, is actually a lament, intoned to the sound of calypso, reggae or merengue: his mistrust is fed by skepticism about the likelihood of happy endings . . . The white man isn't white and the black man isn't black; both are aliens in this land where their umbilical cords are buried.*[61]

Gabriel García Márquez writes in a similar vein:

The Caribbean is a completely different country, another culture. And so, that brothel where I used to live was brimful of stuff from the Caribbean. And that port tavern where we'd go for breakfast when the paper came out, at four in the morning, where amazing fights and messes would break out. And the schooners that took off for Aruba, for Curaçao, loaded with whores ... I don't know, that left and came back with contraband... And Cartagena on Saturday afternoons, with the students, all that stuff. You see, I know the Caribbean, island by island, like that, island-by-island-by-island. And it can be synthesized in a single street, like the one that appears in The Autumn, which is the main street in Panama, in la Guaira. But above all, it's the business street in Panama City, filled with hawkers.

---

[61]   Marugg, Tip. Translated by Paul Vincent. *The Roar of Morning*, USA: Yale University Press.

The island of Curaçao, ever since being home to the Arawaks in the 12th or 13th century, has always been a center of commerce. The Spanish came in 1499 to capture a workforce and cut wood; the Dutch took over in 1634 to gather salt and trade slaves. Later, the island sold aloe vera, Panama hats, oil, and financial services (the upper slice of the famous Dutch sandwich). Lots of different nationalities can be found in Curaçao, mixing and mingling, usually for purposes of trade or conquest. And the mood of Gabriel García Márquez's *Macondo* is always discernable. Mother's Day is one of the biggest celebrations of the year, while Father's Day has been called "the day of great confusion." The most enjoyable annual event is the year-end celebration, when each business organizes a pagara, a Chinese style, very loud fireworks show to "burn money in order to make money" and chase away the *fuku* (bad luck). Hundreds of these parties being held on the same day, with people going back and forth between them, creates an Armageddon of noise and an inescapable smell of gunpowder.

The goal of year-end *tambú* parties is purification and cleansing. People play *tambú* to chase away *fuku* because bad things sometimes happen during the year. *Tambú* is widely considered the Curaçao equivalent of the blues. The way the locals dance *tambú* is more exciting than the way the Dutch have sex.

Where else in the world can you stay in a hospital where, in the midst of a treatment, a vendor selling *pastechis*, candy, and peanuts can walk into the treatment room to peddle his wares and chat up the nurses? Or where, if you ask the whereabouts of a nurse who has clearly forgotten about the thermometer she stuck into your arm-pit, the response is, "Don't worry about her. Her shift was almost over—she had to hurry off to some festivity, and she'll be back on Monday." Lots of heart-warming personal interactions.

My only family link to the island is this: in 1898, my great-great-uncle Friar Radulphus (my middle name refers to him), a very busy man who founded many schools and businesses, wrote the words to the national hymn.

Lanta nos bos ban kanta	*Let's raise our voice and sing*
grandesa di Kòrsou;	*the grandeur of Curaçao;*
Kòrsou, isla chikitu,	*Curaçao, small island,*
baranka den laman!	*a boulder in the sea!*
Kòrsou, nos ta stima bo	*Curaçao, we love you*
ariba tur nashon.	*above all nations.*
Nos bida lo ta poko	*Our lives would be little*
pa duna nos pais,	*to give for our country,*
luchando uní pa libertat,	*fighting united for liberty,*
amor i komprenshon.	*love and understanding.*
I ora nos ta leu fo'i kas	*And when we are far from home*
nos tur ta rekordá	*we all recall*
Kòrsou, su solo i playanan,	*Curaçao, its sun and beaches*
orguyo di nos tur.	*the pride of us all.*

My wife and I started our lives in Curaçao less than a week after we got married and emigrated to the West. It was a big adventure that we deliberately sought, wanting to get away from the over-regulated and over-protective Netherlands, where pressure from the government and your neighbors squeezed you from both sides, leaving only a small space to organize your life the way you wanted to. During my first day at work, Roosje Eleonora, the personal assistant assigned to me, uttered below her voice: "another *makamba* I need to teach the business to (makamba was the local equivalent of "gringo" in Curaçao). We ended up working together for 26 years until she retired. It took me a while to learn to ask the right questions. For example, when I asked whether a fax had been sent, the answer would be yes, even if the fax had failed to go through because of a wrong number. The correct question would have been: did the fax message reach the recipient?

My wife learned the hard way when she asked in a shop to see some dress fabric that was on the top shelf; the shop assistant said that she could not get that fabric as the guy in charge of the stepladder was out to lunch. We were taught that the right approach was to first describe the interesting occasion you needed a dress for: was it an upcoming wedding party with a great menu, or a famous musician in an original setting? Then, you should ask for suggestions in selecting the right color. Only then, as an afterthought, could you point at the fabric on the top shelf. If you followed this structure, the stepladder would be available immediately (or the shop attendant's lunch break would have ended). We were frustrated many times before we learned to navigate this way of life and ask the right questions. I got really good at formulating questions that could not be answered with "no." It was a skill that later served me well in India, where I had to learn to avoid questions that could be answered with "yes," as, in India, "yes" is a meaningless word; it indicates that your request has been heard but not whether it will be adequately dealt with. If you treat "no yes, no no" as a game, it works over time.

Four years later, Margaret Sankatsing and I, with Xander Arts, started our own trust business in Curaçao. For many years, it was at the heart of our financial services network. Our objective was to deliver the best possible personal service, providing state-of-the-art legal tax planning at reasonable fees. After five years, we took our still very small team of employees on a behind-the-scenes weekend trip to Disney World in Orlando. For our ten-year anniversary, we took a much larger group to Dallas to see the operations of Southwest Airlines. At 15 years, we realized that we could no longer cost-effectively gather all of our employees together for a weekend of celebration and learning. We polled our employees, who suggested replacing a fleeting festivity with something more tangible and sustainable; this made me very proud. Many of them had small children and wanted to create a childcare center. I wholeheartedly supported that initiative.

Brain-storming and implementation took the better part of a year, but we ended up with a wonderful daycare center, which had, at the time, no equal on the island. At its opening, many influential people showed up and spread the news. Afterwards, we freely shared our concepts, ideas, and experiences; now several really nice daycare centers have sprung up on the island, often sponsored or supported by corporations or government institutions. Many of our employees helped to renovate and decorate the building we purchased for the center (my wife painted a large mural with tropical flowers and birds), and to work on the curriculum and related tasks. The center's name, Tuma Mi Man (TMM), was selected through a contest. It means "Take My Hand" in Papiamento, which still seems very appropriate. In considering how our daycare project reflected our approach to philanthropy, I arrive at the following key points:

The value(s) and impact of a philanthropic project:

1) We wanted to carry out a project that would benefit our own employees, as well as other, less well-off, local families. We chose to create a daycare center because many of our employees in Curaçao at the time had pre-school age kids; they selected this option out of several. At the time, the island had no good quality daycare that covered our company's regular working hours.

2) We created the facility very close to the office, to be convenient for our employees, and we introduced extended opening hours to create maximum flexibility for parents.

3) We asked our employees to contribute toward their own children's care by paying an amount commensurate with their salaries.

4) We provided space for less-well-off children from often broken families living in the area where the facility was located. About one third of the children are those of our own employees, one third have parents who pay at least partial fees, and one third come from broken families without the financial means to contribute.

5) We hold regular fundraising activities, of which *Goals for Kids*, an inter-company weekend-long soccer tournament that has become an island classic. Over time, we hope that Tuma Mi Man can organize enough activities and generate enough income and funding to no longer depend on donations from our community foundation. A period of 10 years for becoming independent of donations is more or less an industry target.

6) As a company, we set aside 1 percent of our gross revenues for CSR, green initiatives, disaster relief, and philanthropic activities. Some of this money is used to make sure our daycare center meets the highest possible quality standards. However, the sooner our employees and the daycare staff succeed in generating more money, the sooner our community foundation can go back to funding new ideas and focusing on other initiatives. Our own contribution is earmarked mainly for management, administration, and organization. We do not want to give away fish forever; instead, we want to teach people to fish. Once a community can fish for itself, we move on to another location or another skill.

7) Each employee can earn 10 percent of his annual performance evaluation points by participating in corporate social responsibility or philanthropic activities. There are regular fundraising activities for Tuma Mi Man, as well as building maintenance, classes to teach, administrative work to be done, and subsidies to apply for. Those who participate receive points that go towards determining year-end evaluations, bonuses, career opportunities, and salary increases.

8) Employees can choose to participate in local activities (setting up a local project and running it), or in one of the larger projects organized and sponsored by the group. Many local projects help to raise money for group projects. We discourage projects that involve, for example, highly paid lawyers and accountants organizing a car-wash. However, fun that may sound, it creates unfair competition with those who rely on the car-washing business for a living. Lawyers can be more effective by doing legal work and then using the income from that work to support our community causes. As Don Corleone said, in *The Godfather*, "one lawyer with his briefcase can steal more than a hundred men with guns."

9) The performance of each of our offices (10 percent) is also judged on how active the office is in supporting CSR, green initiatives, and philanthropy. The overall coordinator for the group (the Director of Sustainable Development) is responsible for making sure that each office contributes. We believe that it is really important for everyone to have the opportunity to work on a CSR or philanthropic project, to enjoy the team building and spirit, and to encourage clients to get involved. Although some of the work takes place during office hours, most of it happens during our employees' spare time. As our work progresses, we are becoming more and more effective.

10) The Director of Sustainable Development is responsible for ensuring that each project becomes sustainable and independent, generating its own sustainable funding (income) and not relying on additional community foundation donations. Ten years is the target period within which each project should become sustainable and independent.

11) We do not force every employee to participate or be involved. Some employees have religious or cultural objections, and we do not force them to contribute. Once we organized a blood drive for a local hospital in Bangalore after a natural disaster, and some employees felt under pressure to give blood. That was obviously not the intention. In quite a few places, the initial enthusiasm for

CSR and philanthropy was limited (with many people already doing some form of charity work on their own time.) However, once people developed a taste for it, those who had initially been most skeptical often became our most committed participants.

12) Especially in local initiatives, we try to include vendors, clients, and suppliers. This helps to create a bond; informal contacts help us better understand the service levels required on both sides. We have launched various sponsor-a-child opportunities, and several of our vendors have sponsored kids. These initiatives also help projects to reach sustainability faster.

I think that education, any form of it, is easily one of the best ways to create a ripple effect and have substantial impact. Any educational success will multiply over time. If you train one professional, he or she may influence a whole business department. If you raise one kid properly, he or she may influence a whole family or sports club. If you want to change the world, then train and motivate as many people as you can.

There is much that does not work properly on Curaçao, where crime, nepotism, and corruption are rampant, while gossip, backstabbing, and other frustration-related behaviors are everywhere. You can easily spend a lot of time criticizing the system. Despite being part of the affluent Kingdom of the Netherlands and having a relatively high per capita GNP, in comparison with neighboring countries, Curaçao's social security system is close to non-existent. About half the population lives below the poverty line and good jobs are scarce. Lots of kids go to school each morning without breakfast, and some do not go to school at all. It is also a place of great wealth, full of grandiose houses, classy restaurants, beautiful yachts, wonderful parties, and warm and friendly people. There is always some social activity going on—always a reason for a drink, lots of dancing, and much pleasure. We have lifelong friends in Curaçao and often celebrate the holiday season there.

We started a business in Curaçao and later created Tuma Mi Man because people everywhere deserve decent childcare, proper education, and personal advancement. You might as well start by looking at the needs in your own environment. That is what we did, and we hope to inspire others to do something similar or better.

We achieved this with the support of many great people, despite the opposition of a few narrow-minded ones. It is important not to be disheartened by opposition, disapproval, sabotage, or negativity of any sort. Let me end this story with some words of encouragement from Mother Teresa, which gave me strength when I needed it most:

People are often unreasonable and self-centered. Forgive them anyway.
If you are kind, people may accuse you of ulterior motives. Be kind anyway.
If you are honest, people may cheat you. Be honest anyway.
If you find happiness, people may be jealous. Be happy anyway.
The good you do today may be forgotten tomorrow. Do good anyway.
Give the world the best you have and it may never be enough. Give your best anyway.
For you see, in the end, it was never between you and them anyway.[62]

---

[62] Kent M. Keith. *The Silent Revolution: Dynamic Leadership in the Student Council,* published in 1968 in a pamphlet.

Chapter 12

Outsourcing jobs to where they are needed and benefitting from the process to make a business more sustainable.

> *There is no reason to regret that I cannot finish the church. I will grow old but others will come after me. What must always be conserved is the spirit of the work, but its life has to depend on the generations it is handed down to and with whom it lives and is incarnated.*[63]

—Antoni Gaudí, the architect of La Sagrada Família Church in Barcelona, Spain

My first trip to India in 1979 was unforgettable. I arrived by intercity bus from Iran, via Pakistan after an epic journey, during which our bus was held up for ransom by Afghan Mujahedin in the Baluchistan desert. Our first stop was the Golden Temple in Amritsar, the scene of much bloodshed between the Indian army and Sikh worshippers and rebels. The world seemed to be in turmoil. Ayatollah Khomeini had just taken over Iran and the Russians had invaded Afghanistan. I bought my first Indian newspaper and read an article about the newly elected delegates to Congress. India had over 600 members of parliament, and many were elected from remote rural areas. At the time, many had no previous experience with flush toilets and some were photographed doing their business out of the windows of the Congress building. This upset the more civilized city people from higher castes, so special training was organized for members of parliament on how to use modern facilities, like flush toilets, electricity, and elevators. Even today, India is one of the few countries that has more cell phones than toilets.

---

[63] *Capacity Development in Practice.* Jan Ubels, Naa-Aku Acquaye-Baddoo and Alan Fowler, London: 2010.

Over time, I traveled the length and width of India, by bus, train, bicycle, and bullock cart, seeing many wondrous things. From a train in the early morning, you could see the backside of India, and the backsides of thousands of Indians doing their morning business along the tracks between piles of discarded clay cups and banana leaves. At the time, plastics were not ubiquitous. I loved Agra, Jaipur, and many of the old cities in the North, but I particularly remember Varanasi or Benares. Varanasi is a holy city on the banks of the Ganges River and one of the oldest in the world. In 1897, Mark Twain said, "Benares is older than history, older than tradition, older even than legend, and looks twice as old as all of them put together." It is without doubt the spiritual center of India. The city expresses life in its rawest and purest forms and it makes me realize how fragile and temporary, as well as how magically mysterious, interconnected, and complicated, our lives are.

All day long, but especially in the early mornings, the platforms descending to the river—the ghats—are filled to overflowing with an endless stream of bathing pilgrims, stoic beggars, wandering sadhus (holy men), busy hawkers, Brahmin priests, sacred bulls and holy cows, Hindu preachers, and busloads of tourists mostly too disgusted by the stench and filth to spend much time there, or to try to understand the sequence of events.

> *...crammed perspective of platforms, soaring stairways, sculptured temples, majestic palaces, softening away into the distances; and there is movement, motion, human life everywhere, and brilliantly costumed—streaming in rainbows up and down the lofty stairways...*[64]

—Mark Twain

Hindu legends suggest that taking a dip in the holy waters will offer salvation from sins and purification of the soul. In fact, one should attempt salvation and be freed from the cycle of rebirth by dying, or at least by bathing in the Ganges and being purified of all the sins and bad karma accumulated during current or previous births. I never could muster enough courage to actually dive into the Ganges River, so I guess I will have to continue to live with my sins.

---

[64] Mark Twain (1897: 496), who visited Banaras in 1895, Strathcarron, Ian. *The Indian Equator: Mark Twain's India Revisited.* Oxford: Andrews UK, 2013.

Especially interesting are the Manikarnika and Harishchandra *ghats*, where Hindus cremate their dead. At any hour of the day, one can see *rikshas* arriving with the bodies of the recently expired who are briefly immersed in the river before the cremation ceremony starts. They may be accompanied by one or many family members. They may be rich or very poor. You can tell who was rich and who was poor by the size of the funeral pyre. The *Doms* who guard the holy fires that bring muktha set a price for firewood and lighting the fire, based on the perceived wealth of the family of the deceased. They exert considerable power, as the fire cannot come from any other source. However, as they belong to the lowest sub-caste of Harijans, nobody will share a meal with them, let them into their homes, or even touch them. Sometimes the pyres are huge, built of massive tree trunks, with flames soaring into the sky. Sometimes, there are only a few sticks of wood and some coconut husks and the body shrouded in white cloth does not get hot enough for its fat to properly hiss and burn, assuming that the person managed to accumulate any fat during his or her life. All day long, one can hear chanting: *Ram naam satya hai. Ram naam satya hai* (truth in the name of God). The body after death no longer houses the soul and thus no longer has a name.

When the flames die down, the remains of the bodies are unceremoniously dumped into the Ganges River, where some extremely poor people eat the limbs that did not fully burn. Crocodiles always wait there, appearing most interested in the ceremonies of poorer people. Monkeys and dogs look for interesting scraps to eat. Untouchables carefully sift through the pyres for firewood that can be reused and the occasional valuable golden tooth or silver ornament. Just a few meters away, someone may devoutly be praying and bathing in the same river. Next to that person, someone could be defecating or brushing his teeth. As the water is considered holy, none of that matters. For germs, it must be Nirvana. I spent two full days on Shamshaan *ghat,* just watching the hustle and bustle and thinking about the value of life. This is India, no—it is the world, in its original, most naked essence of life and death, good and bad, pure and dirt, all right next to each other. I had lived most of my life in very clean and orderly places, and it took some time to adjust to the place. But this place was ideal for realizing that our lives are very short, and that, after death, we will again be just dust in the wind, while the universe moves on as if nothing had happened. It is quite obvious why people say that death and enlightenment are the primary business of Varanasi.

After the commotion of northern India, steeped in history and full of stories, snake charmers, great monuments, a hodge-podge of cultures, wonderful ceremonies and festivals, and endless traffic and noise, it was a nice change to travel to the fresh greenness of Goa and Kochin. There were endless palm-fringed beaches, quiet villages under the trees, lazy afternoons spent watching the waves crash on the coast, and the great Malabar kitchen serving a mix of Indian and Portuguese foods, one of my personal favorites.

This is where my guru, Sudhir Kakar, lives. As he is more than 72 years old, he is now in the *Sannyasa* phase of his life and is slowly detaching from obligations, possessions, and conventions. He has been named one of the greatest thinkers of our times and has authored many books. With his wife, Katha, he spends his days writing novels and sharing his wisdom from the porch of his Portuguese-era villa near the sea. From him, I learned that we all have an elephant inside us. It is the *dharma*, the way, and the purpose for which we have come. We must learn to understand that elephant, and to let it follow its path. We can nudge it a bit, but we can never force it to go where it does not want to. It is even worse to ignore it.

In the foothills of the Himalayas, Kashmir, Ladakh, Zanskar, Sikkim, Dharamsalah, Darjeeling, and Rishikesh have a totally different atmosphere. You may remember the Beatles song, On the *Road of Rishikesh*. It is one of the many songs they wrote there for the White Album or *Abbey Road* albums. In the summer of 1968, the Beatles were at the top of their fame. Encouraged by George Harrison, they decided to take a spiritual trip and attend an advanced Transcendental Meditation training session at the *ashram* of Maharishi Mahesh Yogi. They ended up in Rishikesh, now considered the yoga capital of India.

This trip changed music, European fashion, and ideas about Eastern philosophies. It introduced a whole generation to yoga, transcendental meditation, and Indian musical instruments like the sitar. It also forever changed the Beatles, as, whatever they found in Rishikesh, it was not love, health, or peace. This turned out to be their last international trip as a group. I never became much of a yogi, unfortunately, but I have been doing Transcendental Meditation on and off for most of my life.

Another widely known guru, Shree Rajneesh, (later known as Osho) had a popular but controversial *ashram* in Pune in the seventies, where his transformational tools, which included nude dancing, got many young foreigners interested in studying mysticism and his interpretation of the various religions and customs of India.

Mumbai is the commercial center of India. The first time I arrived at the Victoria Terminus (now the Chhatrapati Shivaji Maharaj Terminus) after a long overnight trip in Third Class on a steam train, I was completely overwhelmed by the enormous masses of people moving around there all day. On an average day, at least 3 million people pass through this station. The city is home to India's wealthiest business people, as well as some of its most miserable slums. If you read the book Shantaram by Gregory David Roberts, you may get a general idea of how challenging and desperate, and yet full of humanity and brotherhood, life in the slums can be. In November 2008, dozens of people were killed in a terrorist attack on the station, a hostage-taking at the nearby Taj Mahal Palace Hotel, and a shoot-out at our favorite Indian bar, Leopold's. For days, we could see from our office, courageously established by Niels van Linder, the smoke drifting from buildings. For years, Leopold's kept the bullet holes in its mirrors and walls to attract more tourists. The city houses temples of every faith, many of which I had never heard of. India has 3–5 million holy men, or sadhus, who give up everything in life, often going around naked or near-naked, and dedicating themselves to worship, while living solely on handouts. They never worry about where to go, what to do, or where their next meal will come from. Their philosophy instructs them to let things be, to live as animals live and let God and the universe provide. Some stand motionless for days, controlling their minds while defying gravity. There are libraries where each of our futures was inscribed on a banana leaf hundreds of years ago.

It is a country full of endless wonders and surprises. However, many Indians consider their age-old culture inferior to that of the West, as India has not produced as much scientific progress or material wealth. According to the Indian poet, writer, and Nobel Prize winner Rabindranath Tagore, the defining feature of Indian civilization, which Sudhir Kakar believes it is in the process of losing, is sympathy. Sympathy is a feeling of kinship that extends beyond our kin, a sense of "we" that extends beyond kinship. This feeling of kinship is not limited to human beings but extends to the natural world. The golden rule, that we should treat others as we would want others to treat us, is based on the presence of sympathy. Mohandas Gandhi agrees, writing that brotherhood is now just a distant aspiration: "To me it is a test of true spirituality. All our prayers, and observances are empty nothings so long as we do not feel a live kinship with all life." For Rabindranath Tagore, Indian civilization, unlike the West, is seeking to establish a relationship with nature and all living beings, not by cultivating power, but by fostering sympathy. I think he is absolutely right to say:

When we know this world as alien to us, then its mechanical aspect takes prominence in our mind; and then we set up our machines and our methods to deal with it and make as much profit as our knowledge of its mechanism allows us to do. For us, the highest purpose of this world is not merely living in it, knowing it and making use of it, but realizing our own selves in it through expansion of our sympathy; not alienating ourselves from it and dominating it, but comprehending and uniting it with ourselves in perfect union.[65]

In Chennai, there is an Urdu evening newspaper called *Mussalman*, which has been handwritten for 80 years or more without missing a single edition. The chief *katib* or copywriter, responsible for the front page, studied calligraphy and writes the news by hand. This daily newspaper contains just four pages, with a small section reserved for breaking news. The news has to come in by 3 PM for this section, so that it can be handwritten and printed in time. Although all of its competitors are digitalized and automated, this newspaper still holds on.

The Indian subcontinent gave birth to several of the world's major religions, including Hinduism, Buddhism, Jainism, and Sikhism. It has some of the most beautiful religious buildings in the world, including the Taj Mahal. Once every twelve years, most recently in 2013, Allahabad hosts the world's largest religious pilgrimage, Kumbha Mela; over a five-week period, some 20 million Hindus from across the world come together to bathe in the confluence of three sacred rivers: the Ganga, the Yamuna, and the Saraswati. Indians living abroad have popularized many aspects of Hindu philosophy, including meditation, yoga, *karma, dharma*, reincarnation, and Ayurvedic medicine. A plethora of Indian spiritual beliefs have spread around the world, more than from any other region.

The British era had a profound impact on India in practically every aspect of life. It also affected how people relate to their work. After more than 300 years of suppression, Indians became experts at peaceful resistance, often simply conserving energy while pretending to work hard. Over time, society became

---

[65]   Tagore, Rabindranath. *Creative Unity* (Macmillan, London, 1922), pp 48-9.

very hierarchical, layering the habits and rules of the British Army on top of religious rules and the caste system. Everything always needs to be stamped for approval by someone higher up the chain. Until recently, people in transit through an Indian airport would have their carry-on luggage tags inspected at least a dozen times, before boarding. Informal cooperation is frowned upon, as undermining authority. Creativity is not a highly prized character trait in the workplace. Lord Mountbatten left India through its Gateway more than 70 years ago, but the mentality he helped to promote unfortunately is still engrained. The British Raj lives on in the school system, management styles, and the way organizations are structured. When we launched our business in India, first in Bangalore and then in Mumbai and New Delhi, it took us a long time to realize that these habits weren't going to change anytime soon. I remember hundreds of meetings at our India office, in which we discussed the issues of the day. People would stare blankly at me; because I came from abroad, they expected me to have answers and solutions to just about everything, even though their colleagues who worked on these issues had had months to think about potential solutions.

Slavery is not always imposed, it can also be indulged in, as Mohandas Gandhi rightly remarked many times. The British Raj could not have used 40,000 civil servants and fewer than 100,000 British soldiers to suppress and reign over 100 million, and later, 200 or even 300 million Indians, had those Indians not let them have their way. It is high time for the British Raj to end, and the innate creativity and incredible entrepreneurship of Indians to merge with modern management techniques and better governance. By improving corporate governance, eradicating corruption, and ending stifling bureaucracy, India can and will become the next economic miracle of the world.

Although it struggles to provide its citizens with clean drinking water, electricity, sewage systems, public transportation, decent roads, a sense of hygiene, basic discipline, courtesy, and punctuality, India has a very entrepreneurial mentality. Many thousands of outsourced businesses (BPO) have been created everywhere, especially in the field of technology. Indian entrepreneurs now run huge parts of the West's back-office accounting, IT, and white-collar industries virtually; some see this as reverse colonialism, triggering pitiful tariffs and barriers.

In 2005, our accounting teams in Spain and Curaçao experienced a crisis; we thought we might miss the deadline for our annual audit. Once again, all forces united to make the obvious happen. We had two bright young accountants working with us: Kiran Kumar and Archana Pai. I also had friends from Bangalore and had always wanted to make a meaningful investment in India by creating jobs. So, more or less between one day and the next, we decided to establish an office in Bangalore, Karnataka, and to move our internal accounting department there. When I went there a few weeks later, Kiran Kumar and Archana Pai had already set up shop in the cellar of a hotel. A Ganesh statue was dangling from the ceiling to protect and promote their accounting activities. Ganesh is the Hindu God of Good Fortune, who brings prosperity, fortune, and success. He is also the God of beginnings and the remover of material and spiritual obstacles, which was exactly what we needed, as we had many. Initially, the whole office was the size of a meeting room, with eight people busily doing our internal accounting and trying to save the audit. During the next few years, we moved more and more back-office departments to Bangalore and the office grew to well over 300 people. Branch manager Manu Cheriyan brought in a British Raj-based, rigid management approach. Ganesh Babu Subramanian introduced the latest IT systems and homeopathic medicine; Binu Jose brought viewpoints and teaching methods from out of space. Our business was growing so fast that we had to move office at least every other year. We became very proficient at opening pujas and ceremonies.

I remember one particularly moving ceremony. Our offices had employees of many different faiths, and the lines between various religious attitudes were blurred. As the majority of employees were Hindus, all departments except IT tended to follow Hindu customs. At this event, we lighted an oil lamp, cut a ribbon, and sprinkled some flowers. Then a priest blessed the space, spoke his *mantras*, and started to sprinkle flower powder over all keyboards and ventilation panels on the desk tops to ensure their perfect functioning. Although the Hindus looked happy about this ceremony to enhance their computer equipment, in a corner, I could see the Muslim members of the IT Department wringing their hands at this abuse. Amazingly, the ritual did not permanently damage our equipment or cause a power outage.

The new office was much more spacious than the old one, with an enormous neon sign on the roof. Late in the evening after dinner, on the way back to our hotel, we used to ask the night manager to illuminate the sign for us as we drove by. We were so proud to see the name of our company on that huge neon sign, in the local Kanada script.

An office in India forces one to study and understand at least a little about Indian culture. One minor problem is that there is no single Indian culture. Instead, there are lots of religions: Hinduism, Islam, Christianity, Sikhism, Jainism and many animist sects as well as Buddhism, although I know that is not a religion. There are over 300 official languages in 29 states, each with very different cultural identities, food, holidays, and castes (although officially abolished, there are many glass ceilings in India). I remember a lunch in Kolkata with two Jain international tax advisors from "Big Four" firms. They entered the Jain restaurant (by definition, vegan) where we had our appointment, with little brooms, sweeping the floor in front of them to avoid accidentally stepping on an ant. In the Jain code of ethics and doctrine, ahimsa is a fundamental principle. The term means nonviolence, non-injury, and the refusal to harm any life form. Vegetarianism and other nonviolent Jain practices and rituals flow from this principle. Violence is usually associated with causing harm to others. According to the Jain philosophy, violence primarily involves injuring yourself—behavior that prevents the soul from attaining moksha (liberation from the cycle of birth and death). Violence against others ultimately harms your own soul. The Jains extend this concept of *ahimsa* not only to humans but to all animals, plants, micro-organisms, and beings with life or potential life; hence these incisive, cutting-edge tax advisors needed little brooms. All life is sacred and every creature has the right to live fearlessly to its maximum potential. Living beings have nothing to fear from people who have taken the vow of *ahimsa*. According to Jainism, protecting life, also known as *abhayadānam*, is the ultimate form of respect. *Ahimsa* was an important element of Gandhi's *Satyagraha*, which literally means "devotion to truth," remaining firm and actively but nonviolently resisting untruth, which he described as, "clinging to the truth that we are all one under the skin, that there is no such thing as a win/lose confrontation because all our important interests are really the same, that consciously or not every single person wants unity and peace with every other."

Ascetics observe the five vows below very strictly, embracing complete abstinence:

1) Satya   thinking, speaking, and living the truth

2) Ahiṃsā   not hurting or injuring any transient being

3) Honesty   not taking anything that does not belong to you

4) Celibacy   (for monks) and chastity (for householders)

5) Aparigraha   not getting attached to possessions

In Jainism, causing an injury, lying, stealing, lust, and attachment are *hiṃsā*, as indulging in these behaviors mars the pure nature of the soul. Strict Hindus (like Mohandas Gandhi) adhere to quite similar principles.

Coming from Europe, I found it difficult to understand how much more seriously people took their vows and religion in India. Setting up a dinner meeting was always a hassle. One person did not eat pork; the next one was a vegetarian or a vegan. The third could not eat on Mondays, or on the 11th day, or in the same restaurant with non-vegetarians. One person did not eat fruit and the next ate only fruit and raw vegetables. Fortunately, a big city like Bangalore could cater for all tastes.

One evening, I was invited to a traditional Muslim betrothal ceremony. A member of our IT department was celebrating his forthcoming marriage. We went to a party at the future bride's home. As we were foreigners, her family even provided one beer. Before we left, we were invited to meet the future bride, who was celebrating upstairs with the other women. We briefly shook hands, I looked her in the eyes and went back downstairs. "And?" the future groom asked. "And what?" I wondered. It turned out that our colleague had never actually met his bride. All of the arrangements were being made by the parents; the couple would meet for the first time at the wedding. The parents had more life experience and they knew best.

Another evening, I attended a house-warming party. My colleague's home was small, but cozy, freshly painted and spotlessly clean. I was more than a little surprised when, at the height of the ceremony, a cow entered and was persuaded to produce a cow pat: not a nice, neat pie, but one that splattered all over the clean floor. Millions of Hindus worship and revere cows. From the Mother to the Goddess, a cow is very auspicious and holds a special significance in Hinduism. It is the sacred animal, which provides life-sustaining milk. In many spiritual *yagnas*, there is a fire made from dried cow dung and ghee. For centuries, it has been assumed that burning cow dung with ghee is one of the best ways to purify and disinfect a home.

Well, scientific research has now confirmed that cow dung does indeed purify the air[66] and also has anti-pollutant and anti-radiation effects. In 2010, research carried out by independent groups in the University of Bristol and Sage College in Troy, NY found that cow dung also was an excellent mood-enhancing agent. Cow dung contains bacteria known as mycobacterium vaccae, which activate a group of neurons in the brain that produce serotonin—a neurotransmitter that contributes to feelings of wellbeing and happiness. It is also an excellent antidepressant. When I heard this, I remembered how as a kid, I always loved walking into our cow barn in winter and smelling the fragrant blend of hay, cow dung, and animal scents.

Gowri-Ganesha festivals are prominent in Southern India and celebrated with pomp and glory across Karnataka, where our main Indian offices are based. Over many years, families have competed with their neighbors by buying bigger and bigger Ganesha idols, which at the end of the festivities are ceremoniously thrown into the sea or a lake. Often these were made of plaster of Paris, which harms the environment, rather than the more traditional clay. A few years back, these environmentally dangerous idols were rightly banned from being thrown in lakes and waterways. Cow dung was a significant ingredient of Indian society once; families would dry it and spread it in front of their houses as well as using it to make their Ganesha statues. Nowadays, many people don't even want to touch cow dung. However, the old culture has come back and Ganesha idols made of cow dung are once more available.

Another growing trend is the use of cow dung to produce biogas, a cheap alternative source of energy that can be used as a fuel for cooking or even to produce electricity. Researchers at Hewlett Packard's Indian laboratories have found ways to power their data servers using cow manure. So it's not just milk, food, anti-pollutants, and anti-depressives, cows can even help us power our laptops and iPods!

Cultural habits, everywhere, slip into the work environment, and influence the way people think and work. Such habits aren't always easy for foreigners

---

[66]   D Girija, K Deepa, Francis Xavier, Irin Antony, and P R Shidhi. 5 January 2012; revised 21 May 2012. "Analysis of cow dung microbiota—A metagenomic approach." Department of Agricultural Microbiology and Distributed Information Centre College of Horticulture, Kerala Agricultural University, Kerala Veterinary and Animal Sciences University, Mannuthy, India. Indian Journal of Biotechnology, Vol 12, July 2013, pp 372-378.

to understand. The Indian unwillingness to say "no," for example, takes a good deal of time to get used to—especially since a wiggling of the head can mean "yes" as easily as "no." The answer to any question that can be answered with yes is always yes. The intonation may sometimes indicate a qualified or conditional yes, or a yes uttered just to please a listener or postpone a problem, even if only for five minutes.

For most of its history, India had one of the highest per capita GNPs in the world. However, when colonial powers conquered the country after 1750 CE, they stole India's wealth and deliberately destroyed its economic infrastructure, resulting in major famines in which millions of people died for no other reason than to assuage the greed of a happy few. Mohandas Gandhi had to fight grossly unjust laws that prevented Indians from making their own salt or producing their own cotton, just so that industries in the UK or operated in India by the British could make excessive profits. These policies led to mass unemployment and the displacement of people, encouraging racial and religious hate, destroying the social fabric, and causing mass starvation. On my first trip to Kolkata, I regularly saw garbage trucks in the morning picking up the bodies of people who had died of hunger or exposure on the streets during the night.

Creating meaningful jobs in India was, and is, a crucial way of helping people build a decent life. Although mass starvation seems a thing of the past, there is still dire poverty in India. Many villages have no electricity; whole regions have few if any proper schools, jobs, or opportunities. All of India's big cities have large slums where millions of people live in appalling conditions, surrounded by filth, stench, and disease. Walking through those slums reveals the extent of the problem: so many people lead desperate, empty lives because they lack schooling and opportunities. It would not be enough merely to replace the shacks with nicer homes. Slum living conditions will not fundamentally change unless education, jobs, and sources of income are also created. In many cases, caste restrictions must be lifted too.

To introduce the principles of corporate social responsibility to our Indian team, we decided to support the Parikrma Foundation, a first-class educational project for orphaned and semi-orphaned kids from the slums of Bangalore. Very professionally run by Shukla Bose, the foundation aims not only to take the child away from the slum, but also, and more importantly, to take the slum away from the child. For several years, we made donations, and many of our employees volunteered to do the accounts and to teach computer, art, and dance classes. My son spent some time there, working as a volunteer teacher. We conducted various drives to collect money and computer equipment. When, after a few years, some of our employees began to complain that the poor kids of Parikrma were a lot better off than their own children (a compliment rather than a criticism), the initiative slowly fell by the wayside.

We had numerous reasons for deciding to set up a Business Processing Operation (BPO) in the city of Bangalore. We chose India in part because I had trekked through the country more than 25 years earlier, getting a taste of Hindu and Buddhist culture. Having some familiarity with the country made it much easier to overcome the initial issues we encountered when setting up our business.

Why did we select the city of Bangalore?

1) Our first introductions were in Bangalore. When we compared Bangalore, Chennai, and Hyderabad, Bangalore was more diverse than IT-centered Hyderabad, and Chennai was really hot, so we picked Bangalore.

2) Having once been a British garrison (Winston Churchill was stationed in Bangalore before being sent as a war correspondent to the Boer War), Bangalore has good infrastructure and universities, dating from the time of the British Raj. It produces an abundance of university graduates, many of whom have more than one degree.

3) As the city is located on a mountain ridge in the middle of the country, its climate is moderate and pleasant.

4) A large international airport makes it relatively easy to connect from anywhere in the world.

5) Overall labor costs for accountants and lawyers (the people we needed most) were roughly 25 percent of their European equivalents, although double those in Davao in the Philippines. Even taking into account local inefficiencies and communication issues, the cost difference, especially initially, was very compelling.

Why did we choose Business Process Outsourcing (BPO)?

The fundamental idea behind BPO is to outsource large, repetitive, rule-based tasks to countries with cheaper labor costs. BPO enables companies to save money, without having to invest lots of communication time providing detailed instructions.

BPO works as long as there are clear delivery agreements and workflows in place and ways to measure tangible deliverables.

There is a huge number of service providers available, many competing mostly on price. Others specialize in specific niche markets.

BPO creates a level of flexibility. In India, it is relatively easy to hire large numbers of qualified people at short notice and to let them go again when a project is finished. The Indian attitude toward overtime work and pay, and long or uncomfortable hours, is much more pragmatic than in the West.

On the flip side, the outsourcing company runs a number of risks: data protection can be compromised; quality levels and delivery times must be clearly explained. In a country where many things, from the streets to political and business systems, are an absolute mess, demanding top quality requires constant attention. An understanding of what "top quality" means in practice may not come naturally.

The Values of Business Process Outsourcing (towards Worldwide Impact Sourcing):

1) We began working in Bangalore when our original teams in Barcelona and Curaçao failed utterly. We got off to a very good start. Our new Indian employees quickly picked up the key tasks and we met our audit requirements in good time. Having access to unlimited resources, after the limited resources of a small place, helped us tremendously.

2) As the cost of labor in India was 20–25 percent of what it was in the places our work came from, we could afford to hire additional people, ensuring that we had sufficient quality controls in place to do the work properly. Given these extra quality checks and the

additional communications required to work between two locations, it was necessary to roughly double the number of workers, making our initial savings close to 50 percent of labor costs; we also noticed improvements in consistency, completeness, and quality. Over time, the labor advantage eroded to a significant extent, as real wages, as well as taxes in India, went up considerably.

3) The flexibility of having access to a large labor pool and the improved efficiency and higher quality were important differentiators.

4) As we became more familiar with the Bangalore team, we experimented with moving more and more tasks there. When our tasks were standardized and rule-based, the cost differences were compelling. Outsourcing worked particularly well for straightforward tasks, and those that required grit and large amounts of time spent on repetitive activities (like Mutual Fund Administration, and producing financial statements and tax returns for HNWIs).

5) Tasks that required creativity, interpretation, or cultural and local knowledge, such as dealing with clients or bridging cultural differences, were much more complicated. Some of the more culturally sensitive work, as well as a lot of client-facing work, had to be moved back to where it came from. Using a call center to deal with your water bill or airplane ticket is one thing, but our business involves providing personalized services to millionaires. Many of our clients found it difficult to trust the credibility of anyone with a funny accent.

6) After overcoming some initial skepticism, everyone gained from being in contact with other cultures, norms, and values. Over time, in many of our offices outside India, little protective Ganesha statues began to appear; our colleagues started to appreciate Indian cuisine, and quite a few tried meditation and yoga. People started to travel back and forth to participate in their friends' wedding ceremonies and festivals.

I think, in the end, a better term than outsourcing would be "impact sourcing," leveraging our business in a conscious effort to reduce poverty by moving work and money into places that need the work and the money. The great thing about outsourcing, which (once you are used to it), really becomes "worldwide sourcing," is that you always have to ask what the best and most efficient place in the world would be to undertake a specific kind of work. As a result, our Bangalore 'outsourcing center' now outsources work to Davao in the Philippines . Worldwide impact sourcing is a very powerful tool for leveraging talent, improving productivity, and reducing work cycles across the globe. It lets each office do what it is best at, focuses creative people on creative tasks, gathers people who love to do repetitive tasks into one place, and frees up commercial people to serve clients with a personal approach, anywhere in the world.

Chapter 13

Stimulating impact investment in a country where it really matters.

I believe that there is no country in the world including any and all the countries under colonial domination, where economic colonization, humiliation and exploitation were worse than in Cuba, in part owing to my country's policies during the Batista regime. I approved the proclamation which Fidel Castro made in the Sierra Maestra, when he justifiably called for justice and especially yearned to rid Cuba of corruption. I will even go further: to some extent it is as though Batista was the incarnation of a number of sins on the part of the United States. Now we shall have to pay for those sins. In the matter of the Batista regime, I am in agreement with the first Cuban revolutionaries. That is perfectly clear.[67]

—U.S. President John F. Kennedy, interview with Jean Daniel,
October 24, 1963

As a teenager, I sometimes fantasized about whether, had it been possible, I would have had the personal courage to join Che Guevara and Fidel Castro on their dangerous but glorious adventures in the Sierra Maestra. I imagined the heat of the jungles of eastern Cuba, the hunger and fear, the random encounters with government fighters and death, the romanticism of living off the land and in the mountains, the beautiful girls in their tight fatigues, the encounters with illiterate and helpful or treacherous farmers. This adventure brought the *guerilleros* much danger and ultimately eternal fame. I still have a poster of Che Guevara hanging in my study, and I am still wondering what he and his mixed bag of ideas and deeds mean to me, and why I have always found him so intriguing. For many years, my personal motto has been the slogan he

---

[67]   **Senator John F. Kennedy** (1917-1963), (speech at a Democratic Dinner, Cincinnati, Ohio, October 6, 1960, during the 1960 Presidential campaign)

made famous: "Seamos realistas y hagamos lo imposible." (Let us be realistic, and do the impossible). Much later, I realized that Walt Disney had in mind something similar when he wrote, "It is kind of fun to do the impossible", as did the Queen in "Alice in Wonderland": "sometimes I believed as many as six impossible things before breakfast."

Time and again, life shows us that anything is only impossible until someone actually does it. Anything you can imagine can, and one day will, be done. The eternal challenge is to be the first person to do it. I am pretty sure that there are many more things not yet done than done, and many more things not yet known than known. For me, the key difference between humans and other transient beings is the fact that we have an imagination, and some of us actually use that great gift. Through imagination, we create things. "In the beginning was the Word, and the Word was with God, and the Word was God" (John 1:1). Our ancient forefathers set themselves apart from other mid-level or mid-sized predators when they discovered fire and invented weapons and the concept of hunting together in organized groups, freeing up more time for thinking and inventing new things. About 12,000 years ago, when the world reached its maximum carrying capacity for humans by supporting 6–8 million hunter gatherers, humans developed agriculture, which required scale and a social order, and therefore belief systems, religions, political systems, and means of exchange, like money. Developments went faster and faster and we quickly invented the methods and systems that now unite the world. Imagination made it possible for large numbers of people to work together on big developments and inventions, as well as in industries, political systems, and wars. Imagination allowed us to send people into space and bring them back safely.

We finally reached space in 1961. Yuri Gagarin was the first traveler to actually see the whole earth from beyond: "Looking at the earth from afar you realize it is too small for conflict and just big enough for co-operation."[68]

Ernesto Che Guevara wrote a series of diaries during his life. Two of them are famous and I have read them both. The first one, written in 1952, is called The Motorcycle Diaries. In it, he describes a trip he made on "La Poderosa II" when he was a 23-year-old medical student. He traveled with his friend, Alberto Granado, through much of Latin America. During that trip, Guevara, who came from a well-to-do background, slowly began to understand the plight

---

[68] Gagarin, Yuri. 1934-1968, Cosmonaut, first human being in space.

of the working classes, and the unfairness of the neo-colonial yoke that much of Latin America was suffering under. He began to dream about uniting all or much of Latin America into a single, strong country that could stand up to capitalism in general and the Norteamericanos in particular. Many diary entries focus on where to find transport (their motorcycle broke down after a few pages), food, and shelter, preferably for free. I leaf through the pages and take out my own (never named or published) diaries of the road trip through Latin America that I made with my girlfriend when I was 23—in 1983 and 1984—exactly 30 years after Che Guevara. When I compare notes, I must say that embarrassingly little had changed. We shared many experiences and most conclusions.

At the time, I felt a nagging awakening of my social and political conscience and a vague sense of guilt for just leading the "good life" without really doing anything to help the less well-off—very much what Che Guevara must have felt. My reverence for the might and brilliance of the great powers turned first into disbelief and then into lasting disgust. It is shameful and indefensible that all the major world powers, not just the U.S., misuse their technological advantage, unlimited resources, and influence to advance the pitiful material interests of a limited number of already rich people, instead of promoting a better life for all. However, I must admit, I never had the guts, grabbed the opportunity, or even felt a sufficient sense of urgency to pick up a machine gun and convert my deeper sympathies into action.

Does that put me into denial or make me a coward? A collaborator? A part of the misguided establishment? As Einstein said:

Those who have the privilege to know, have the duty to act. And even more dauntingly: The world is a dangerous place to live; not because of the people who are evil, but because of the people who don't do anything about it.[69]

In faraway South Africa, Nelson Mandela gave a brave three-hour speech during his Rivonia Trial in 1964:

During my lifetime I have dedicated myself to this struggle of the African people. I have fought against white domination, and I have fought against black domination. I have cherished the ideal of a democratic and free society in which all persons live

---

[69]   https://en.wikiquote.org/wiki/Talk:Albert_Einstein

together in harmony and with equal opportunities. It is an ideal which I hope to live for and to achieve. But if needs be, it is an ideal for which I am prepared to die.[70]

When the anti-Apartheid movement gained traction in the mid 1970s, my most heroic contribution was to participate in a protest march against the import of South African oranges from the Outspan company. My sign read: "Pers geen Zuid-Afrikaan uit" (Don't squeeze a South African dry). I also wrote letters for Amnesty International, asking politicians to campaign for the release of Nelson Mandela and other ANC Members. When I think back on it, my efforts look shamefully meager.

By 1966, Che Guevara, by then world famous as one of the key heroes of the Cuban revolution, had left his comfortable life, full of excitement and romance. In Havana, he wrote a moving farewell note that ended with the words: "Hasta la Victoria, Siempre," (ever onward, until victory), which were later immortalized in Fidel Castro's speech announcing his departure. After Che Guevara's death, "Hasta Siempre, comandante" became a world-famous song by Carlos Puebla. It still moves me, whenever I hear it. I especially love the Buena Vista Social Club's version of Compay Segundo. In Cuba, you hear it every day.

Aquí se queda la clara	*And what remains very clear*
la entrañable transparencia	*the charming openness*
de tu querida presencia,	*of your dear presence,*
Comandante Che Guevara.	*Commander Che Guevara.*
Seguiremos adelante	*We will go forward*
como junto a tí seguimos	*as we used to go with you*
y con Fidel te decimos:	*and with Fidel we say to you:*
Hasta siempre Comandante![71]	*Farewell Commander!*

The *Bolivia Diary* also focuses on how and where to obtain supplies, so that a small band of *guerilleros* fighting in a remote area in Bolivia can trigger a peasant revolt and convert the country into a more egalitarian and just

---

[70] From Protest to Challenge. A Documentary History of South African Politics in South Africa, 1882-1964. Volume 3, Challenge and Violence, 1953-1964, pp. 673-684, by Thomas Karis and Gail M. Gerhart, Hoover Institution Press, 1977.

[71] Song: Hasta Seimpre – Comandante by Cuban composer Carlos Puebla. https://en.wikipedia.org/wiki/Hasta_Siempre,_Comandante

society. This time, the peasants are not convinced. They don't bring supplies or take his side in droves; and as no grass-roots revolution can succeed unless it stirs the emotions of the population, El Che's efforts are doomed to fail. *The Bolivia Diary* ends abruptly when Che Guevara is caught in an ambush, slightly wounded, and executed the next day. One of his last entries, on the day of his 39th birthday reads:

I turned 39 today and I am inevitably approaching the age when I need to consider my future as a guerilla, but for now I am still in one piece.[72]

Getting killed in action, at the pinnacle of his fame, made Che Guevara immortal. He has become a symbol for generations of young people rebelling against the establishment, everywhere in the world. In the Bolivia Diary, one can sense a kind of yearning to die before the fame of having ignited the Cuban revolution wears off, in the face of governing, social, and economic realities.

In his last letter to his children, Che Guevara writes:

Above all, try always to be able to feel deeply any injustice committed against any person in any part of the world. It is the most beautiful quality of a revolutionary.[73]

The Cuban revolution was not a huge military conflict, when compared with similar events around the world. Cuba in the mid-1950s was an island with some six million inhabitants. During five years of guerilla and open warfare, some 20,000 people were killed. However, the symbolic impact of this particular revolution on the rest of the world went far beyond the borders of the country.

The history of the revolution reads like a classical tale. A small band of brothers fights against enormous odds, the future against the past. Initially, they are not very successful. The first military actions of Fidel Castro and his compañeros lead to disaster (the famous 1953 Moncada attack). Fidel is captured and jailed; he gives his famous "La historia me absolverá" (history will absolve me) speech. After leaving for Mexico, he returns clandestinely on the yacht *Granma*,

---

[72]   Che Guevara, Ernesto. *The Bolivian Diary: Authorized Edition (Che Guevara Publishing Project)*, Ocean Press, 2005

[73]   http://www.companeroche.com/index.php?id=33 – A letter Che sent to all of his children sometime in 1965. Viewed August 19, 2016.

with, among others, Camilo Cienfuegos, Che Guevara, and Raúl Castro, his brother. Although he has only 82 fighters, of whom all but 12 are killed or taken prisoner during the first few days of the invasion, he gradually wins the confidence and support of farmers in the remote Sierra Maestra region, by providing some literacy, medical aid, and socialist ideology. His band starts to win against ever larger military forces. The Batista regime completely alienates the population, becoming infamous for torturing and killing in cold blood anyone it suspects of being a revolutionary. The dead bodies of people believed to be revolutionaries are dumped at night in random parts of Havana and other cities, and found in the streets the following morning.

The Cuban government of Fulgencio Batista, heavily supported by the American government and clandestine FBI actions, was slowly pushed into a corner. Once the guerillas, under the command of Camilo Cienfuegos and Che Guevara, became strong enough to leave the mountains and conquer a swath of the center of the island, the Americans could see the writing on the wall. In December 1958, they withdrew their support. Batista was quickly and decisively defeated, and (after a famous New Year's Eve party) left the country with hundreds of millions of dollars in loot.

Expectations at all levels of the population, as well as in the international community, are high—initially, support from all parts of the establishment, as well as from the international community, creates high hopes and the impetus for major progress.

However, as so often happens, the skills needed to run a country are very different from the ones needed to run a relatively small band of *guerilleros*. Economic troubles soon reveal that a theoretically compelling egalitarian ideology may not work in reality to help regular people and their families lead normal lives.

Many of the cruel and murderous military and paramilitary men of the Batista regime were tried in military courts. Several of them were condemned to death in summary trials. These trials evoked powerful emotions, and the executions were widely publicized. Although the great majority of the people approved, these gruesome events quickly reversed the initially very positive international response to the revolution. As Che Guevara, himself actively involved in victor's justice, commented: "Cruel leaders are replaced only to have new leaders turn cruel."

In 1959, large areas of land were confiscated in an effort to achieve agrarian reform. Land reform was an essential element of the revolution. Society had demanded it ever since Cuba proclaimed its independence from Spain and occupation by the US in 1902. Only the big landlords (latifundistas) were affected by this nationalization, but the largest land owners were American companies, like the United Fruit Company, so this reform caused a strongly negative reaction from the United States government.

In June 1960, the United States cut off Cuba's supply of petroleum and the U.S. companies Texaco and Esso (which together with Shell controlled 100 percent of oil refining in Cuba) refused to process alternative crude coming from the Soviet Union. Subsequently, those refineries were nationalized by the Cuban government. There was a joke at the time among young revolutionaries about the refusal of these companies to refine Soviet oil and the resulting intervention: "Esso no pudo Shell y Texacamos de aquí." In Spanish, this sounds like "Eso no pudo ser y te sacamos de aquí," which means "This was not possible, and we expel you from here." I think this joke reflects the defiant mood among most Cubans and especially young people; it was applauded by many in Latin America.

Then President Eisenhower drastically reduced the sugar quota, which was vital for Cuba's foreign currency earnings (later, the quota was fully eliminated). In response, 26 American companies that operated in Cuba were nationalized, including a telephone company that controlled 100 percent of the Cuban telephone system, an electricity company that controlled 100 percent of the Cuban electrical grid, the three refineries, and the largest sugar mills belonging to American interests.

All of this happened before Cuba adopted a socialist system, which took place in April 1961, just hours before the Bay of Pigs invasion. Political isolation followed; a significant community of well-to-do Cubans left the country (initially temporarily) for Miami, while the youthful ideology drifted slowly but steadily towards a Marxist-socialist system.

After a badly planned and ill-fated attempt by some exiles, supported by the FBI, to overthrow the Castro government (the Bay of Pigs invasion), the American government enforced a range of boycotts and embargoes that slowly strangled progress in Cuba.

Six month later, there was another round of nationalizations of large- and medium-sized entities, including foreign and private Cuban banks.

It is interesting to note that investors' properties from countries like Switzerland, Spain, and Canada (including the Royal Bank of Canada and the Bank of Nova Scotia) were also nationalized. However, in those cases, an amicable settlement was reached and an acceptable compensation paid. With Cuba, the United States opted for a collision course, resulting in the longest lasting embargo in the world, as well as a shadow land register in Miami that has registered enough claims on Cuban land to make the country seem larger than Brazil.

For years, the country survived on preferential trade benefits provided by the Soviet Union. After the collapse of the Soviet Union, acute poverty set in. The situation became bleak and modernizations were needed to restart the economy and feed the population. In the five years after Soviet subsidies ended, the average Cuban lost 12 kilos in body weight, but gained 3–5 years in life expectancy, through a healthy combination of more exercise (due to a lack of public transport) and fewer calories (due to the food shortage). Many industries came to a standstill for lack of spare parts and money. The standard of living went down by at least 30 percent. At the same time, Cuba started to benefit from its excellent school system and exported the professional services of doctors, scientists, and teachers all over the world. Medicine and education, which initially were free of charge, are now Cuba's main source of foreign exchange income (more than tourism or exports of sugar and nickel).

My first visit to Cuba took place at the height of this Special Period in Times of Peace, in early 1992. I was working on a joint venture between the Havana dry-dock and the one in Curaçao. After that,, I briefly became involved in an attempt to establish a joint venture commercial bank. This joint venture, the Netherlands Caribbean Bank, negotiated between ING Bank of the Netherlands and Acemex, a financial and shipping group operating in Cuba, was established in Curaçao. As I had previously worked for Chase Manhattan Bank, I got involved on the planning and training side, teaching Cuban bankers about credit and risk, forecasting, and similar skills. Believe me, that was a difficult task. Some of the bankers had been appointed as they were successful tank commanders in the border wars against South Africa in Angola and Mozambique. None of them had really been exposed to international financial transactions for more than 30 years.

David Rockefeller, who worked in the Havana office of Chase Manhattan Bank before the revolution, would have been amused. He visited Cuba in 2001 and was really moved when my friend, Francisco Soberón, showed him his former office. He was surprised that, after so many years, it still looked more or less the same. Although critical of Cuba's lack of democracy and respect for human rights, he was impressed by the progress made in healthcare and education. Over the years, I have learned that every society I get the opportunity to visit has things to admire and things to improve—at least, I perceive that to be the case. You may admire or disapprove of completely different aspects. There isn't one clear path to a perfect society. Given this, a lack of perfection should never become an excuse for not becoming involved and working to improve conditions—quite the contrary.

I was enchanted with my experiences in Cuba. Living on the nearby island of Curaçao, I ended up going to Cuba quite often.

De Alto Cedro voy para Marcané　　　　*From Alto Cedro I go towards Marcané*
Llego a Cueto voy para Mayarí　　　　　*I get to Cueto, head for Mayarí*

This is the refrain of a great song by Compay Segundo (Buena Vista Social Club), who has been quoted as saying:

I didn't compose Chan Chan, I dreamed it. I dream the music. I sometimes wake up with a melody in my head, I hear the instruments, all very clear. I look over the balcony and I see nobody, but I hear it as if it was played on the street. I don't know what it was. One day I woke up listening to those four sensible notes, I put them a lyric inspired by a children's tale from my childhood, Juanica y Chan Chan, and you see, now it's sung everywhere.[74]

Cuba was and still is a magical place. As Pablo Neruda once said: "you can cut all the flowers, but you cannot keep the spring from coming.[75]" Whenever life in Havana became more difficult, the people fought back by becoming more sociable, more human, and deeper in their love and care for one another. There was music everywhere; in the evenings, in the street, from every bar and later paladar—even in hotels at breakfast time. Music seems to weave a *tantric* fabric

---

[74]　https://en.wikipedia.org/wiki/Chan_Chan_(song)
[75]　Nureda, Pablo. Twenty Love Poems and a Song of Despair. (Spanish and English Edition) Translated by W.S. Merwin. New York: Penguin Classics, 2006.

that keeps a country together and its people sane, in much the same way that science and literature keep Russia together. When the government and economy are far from perfect, music helps people stay proud of their country and culture. Cuba has the most romantic patriotic song of any country: *Guantanamera,* created by the Cuban composer and singer Joseíto Fernández, who brilliantly used the stanzas of a poem written in 1891 by national hero José Martí:

Yo soy un hombre sincero   *I am an honest man*
de donde crece la palma,   *from where palm trees grow,*
y antes de morirme quiero   *and before I die I want*
echar mis versos del alma.   *to pour out the versus from my soul.*

No me pongan en lo obscuro   *Do not put me in the dark*
a morir como un traidor;   *to die like a traitor;*
yo soy bueno y como bueno;   *I am a good person, and as a good person;*
moriré de cara al sol.   *I shall die facing the sun.*

The last few sentences proved to be prophetic; José Martí died with his face in the sun. In 1895, at the battle of Dos Ríos, he rode out towards the enemy on horseback, far ahead of the other troops. Fidel Castro decided to place his mausoleum right next to José Martí's, to save on the expense of a separate guard of honor.

I love the melancholic mood of La Tropicana, and the ambiance of La Bodeguita del Medio (birthplace of the Mojito), the walks in the old city and along the Malecón facing the Caribbean Sea—the breathing space of many habaneros living in cramped quarters without air-conditioning. Many Cubans are highly educated, well-read, and good debaters, as many chance meetings reveal.

My experiences in Cuba became dominated by two gentlemen, still two of my heroes.

The first is Frank Nathan Aldrich. Frank was an American bomber pilot in the Second World War. He was shot down twice, once over the North Sea and once in the Battle of the Bulge. He never expected to see his 23rd birthday, but he did. In 1948, he arrived in Havana, worked for the Bank of Boston, and married Dora, a Cuban girl. By the time the revolution began, he had risen to the position of branch manager and was Ernest Hemingway's private banker.

He used to hand-deliver bank statements to Hemingway in his favorite bar, El Floridita, thus getting to know the famous writer quite well. One day, he told me the story of how Hemingway was refused credit at El Floridita, where he used to go for his regular daiquiri shots. Infuriated and insulted, the author left the bar, only to come back a few weeks later having written and sold *The Old Man and the Sea*, to settle his bar bills and transform the evening into a big party. When we celebrated our company's 25th anniversary in Habana, coinciding with the 200th anniversary of El Floridita, we presented a plaque commemorating the event.

Frank was a staunch opponent of the Cuban revolution and the socialist regime it brought to power, as some of his friends and clients had ended up in jail after the revolution; others had lost most of their earthly possessions when leaving Cuba. Nevertheless, as branch manager of the Bank of Boston, he ended up in long meetings, listening to romantic socialist speeches on economic development delivered by the President of the Central Bank after the Revolution, Ernesto "Che" Guevara, who (to make matters worse), at the time, was dating a girl who lived upstairs in his apartment building. Meanwhile, the country slowly moved towards nationalizing the banks. When that ultimately happened in 1961, Frank left, vowing to never return while Fidel Castro was alive. In 1967, Castro himself, said: "I think that a man should not live beyond the age when he begins to deteriorate, when the flame that lighted the brightest moment of his life has weakened."

Frank Aldrich ended up in Rio de Janeiro and São Paulo, where, for many years, he headed the Bank of Boston, before acquiring his own small bank, the McLaughlin Bank, at an age at which many others would retire. He has been a wonderful, generous friend, tirelessly taking me around Latin America, and introducing me to friends, business relationships, and people of influence (or, as he put it, "the crooks and scoundrels I have known.") Our evenings invariably ended in some old neighborhood bar where stories and memories from the Cuban revolution, Paraguayan War, or Second World War would be retold over and over.

My second hero is Francisco Soberón. Francisco was for many years one of the highest-ranking non-military officials in the Cuban government. He managed the shipping industry with an iron fist during the difficult years of the Special Period in Times of Peace and was President of the Central Bank for

Toine with Francisco Soberón in Cuba

over 15 years. During that period, he was responsible for the monetary policy of the country, handling complicated issues, such as the decade-long circulation of dollars, and the replacement of the dollar with the peso convertible (the dollar-pegged Cuban currency) in 2004 side-by-side with the official Cuban Peso.

He has written several inspiring and profound books about finance. Whenever he visited Curaçao, he would come over for dinner; he introduced me to many business opportunities for foreign investors in Cuba. One of his better-known comments is: "To the extent that we do not achieve a steady improvement in people's standard of living and sustainable development, we risk that those formidable personalities (Fidel and Raúl Castro) become the only pillar on which our system rests."[76]

Both of these friends are gentlemen of the highest integrity and sincerity, despite being extreme polar opposites on the political and cultural spectrum. If they had met, they might not have become friends, but they would have respected each other. And Fidel might agree: "Men do not shape destiny. Destiny produces the men for the hour."

After helping to establish the first Cuban joint-venture bank, the next big project I became involved in was an international cement group's 50 percent investment in the largest Cuban cement production facility. This foreign investment was nearing its close just before Christmas, 1995. Two tankers with combustibles were cruising near Havana Harbor and would be entering the port once the joint venture agreement was signed. However, trust between the parties was low and the stakes were high, and so the cooperation agreements became very detailed; all of the points discussed had to be approved in Cuba at the level of El Comandante. Afterwards, all of those agreements had to be converted into articles within the joint venture company's deed of association.

---

[76]   Frank, Marc. *"Cuba begins to think about life after Castro."* Financial Times, January 3, 2006. Quote from Francisco Soberón Valdés.

As Christmas approached, no one wanted Havana to spend the holiday in darkness. Tensions built up, until at last, two days before Christmas, a full agreement was reached, with blessings from the top. I immediately herded all of the signatories into my car and we drove in great haste to the notary's office to sign the paperwork before anyone could change his mind. In our haste, we collided with a passing tree, seriously damaging my car. I hardly noticed: in my mind, I was watching the two tankers enter the harbor and dock, and the lights go on in many houses. I felt extremely proud of having contributed to a much more comfortable Christmas.

When I told this story to my dear friend, Frank Aldrich, he called me an apologist and a collaborator. Such words hurt, when spoken by a friend. I tried to explain why I felt it was right to have done what I did. He never agreed with me or condoned my clandestine activities, but continued to ask after the "progress of my collaboration." To me, his continued friendship and humor felt like absolution.

Much later, Francisco Soberón showed me a personal note, handwritten by Fidel Castro at that time, in which he was thanked for doing a great job, and presented with a cauliflower, grown in Fidel's own garden, accompanied by a long explanation of the many health benefits of that vegetable. Even many years after receiving this bonus present, Francisco was glowing with pride and gratitude. It made me think about reviewing our company's bonus system.

Poverty is not the fault of the poor, the ordinary compañeros in the street, who are victims of circumstance and cannot be held responsible for an idealistic, but hopelessly rigid and inefficient system—just as their parents and grandparents cannot be held responsible for the corrupt, cruel, and hopelessly unjust systems of Batista and the Spanish and American colonial days. In both cases, people have had very little food or electricity, and only one choice—to stick it out or leave everything behind and move to Florida. This was a difficult choice that no one should have to consider. The American embargo imposed cruel and indiscriminate hardship on Cuba and its population, without making the country any more just, fair, or democratic.

It was my personal choice to try to help where I could, and our team enthusiastically pitched in. I have never been a supporter of socialism as a political or economic system, but the ordinary people of Cuba deserved support in a world that has largely abandoned them for more than 50 years. I got to know so many of them: proud, austere, principled and loyal party members in the ministries, hard-working socialist field workers in the countryside, good-looking Caribbean girls in offices, people smiling, laughing, and joking in the bars and on the streets—and friends everywhere. There was nothing in their pockets, but their hearts overflowed with generosity. There are few places I feel so at home as in Cuba.

My weapon of choice has not been the indiscriminate machine gun. It became the pen and later the laptop.

I have been to Cuba many times since 1992. Unfortunately, on an economic level, not enough has changed since then. In 2010, even Castro admitted (to a startled U.S. journalist) that the Cuban model wasn't working anymore. Personal freedom remains restricted in many unnecessary and inexcusable ways, and yet the country is full of hope and progress.

Cuba has one of the highest rates of education in the world and has made, with very limited means, admirable progress in healthcare. However, food is still scarce. I recently visited with a foreign investor, who was interested in increasing the production of chickens on the island (an enterprise currently run by the military). By introducing modern techniques and better chicken feed, the goal was to double the monthly chicken ration each Cuban was entitled to, using a coupon book. Chicken is the main, and sometimes sole, source of protein for families in Cuba.

I continue to visit and to work to persuade other business people to invest in Cuba. I will do my part and my best to help defeat poverty and suppression, one investment at a time. After 25 years of engagement, we have persuaded more than 80 companies to invest; each one helps to build an economy that will one day benefit all Cubans. Our man in Havana, Eduardo Balmaseda, is kept very busy. Projects range from enlarging the Havana airport and cruise terminal, to building a citrus plantation, several new hotels, a construction company, a photovoltaic cell company, and increasing airline flights and funding for shipping.

We are thinking about launching an Alpasión Cuban rum to accompany a hand-made Vegas Robaina cigar. We have visited some rum manufacturers, very experienced and wise old gentlemen, looking stately in their *guayabera* shirts, and have developed ideas for some beautiful cigar and rum pairings. Sooner or later, our *Ron* Alpasión will hit the market.

On a recent road trip to inspect cigar facilities, we drove around in a brand-new, shiny Chinese Geely. Eduardo was behind the wheel, on a nearly deserted highway, racing past donkeys and bullock carts, while singing, drinking rum and smoking cigars. When we stopped for ice, and gas, a small *guajira* (rural music) band was playing *Hasta Siempre* very beautifully, while a group of scantily-clad ladies danced passionately in the background. What a life—to be an investor checking out opportunities! How beautiful this country will be when the old stately homes are converted into country hotels and one can look out over cane fields and enjoy the huge royal palm trees and birds. Cuba, having no money for pesticides, has an amazing bird life. Wherever one looks there are birds, ospreys, vultures, and hawks: the signs of a healthy eco-culture.

The world has quite a few places like Cuba. Howard Buffett's book, *40 Chances* talks about the meaningful agricultural projects he has kick-started all over the world, increasing productivity and the reliability of food supplies. His projects have helped to increase the life expectancy, wellbeing, happiness, and health of poor farming populations. Thoughtful investment in any underdeveloped nation or region through sustainable business activities can help to bring about real change and real progress. It just takes people like us, with the guts and grit to take on the challenge and get things in motion. To make the world a more integrated community, with opportunities and prospects for everyone, there must be open communication and fair engagement. In some cases, this can be initiated by organizing sports events or cultural exchanges. However, there is also great value in economic cooperation. When people work together, they learn to appreciate each other's cultures, qualities, and personalities. When inequality is reduced, even by a small margin, it reduces tensions and makes people's lives better. We, as people who are relatively well-to-do, have an obligation to help people in less favorable circumstances to have better lives. Business opportunities in Cuba, as in many other emerging markets, can be valuable and profitable in the long run. In the short run, it is just so much fun to be around Cubans, and to feel that you are adding meaningful value to their lives.

Investing to add value and impact:

1) Some people succeed against incredible odds; some impossible tasks are completed; with perseverance, some impossible dreams do come true. This can happen anywhere in the world.

2) It is important to choose locations that appeal to you, whether far or near. When you like a place and its people, it is easier to keep the interest and passion flowing and to stay the course.

3) Taking a lesson from Che Guevara's Bolivian adventure, you need to select places and people who will be receptive to your efforts. If there is no interest from the other side, your investment will fall on fallow land, and you better not waste any time on it.

4) There is value to be added anywhere in the world and at all times. The most important thing is to start today, wherever you feel you can add value. No place is perfect or undeserving of your investment.

U.S. President Barack Obama did the right thing by trying to end the stand-off with Cuba, starting to lift the U.S. embargo, and supporting initiatives to right past wrongs. The fastest way to bring about meaningful democratic reforms in Cuba is by going there, investing, paying salaries, demonstrating that economic progress works, and helping people earn money to pay for food. Fundamental change will follow from the inside out.

Without an outside enemy, it will be harder for the Cubans to hold on to archaic beliefs. In Che Guevara's own words: "It is a sad thing not to have friends, but it is even sadder not to have enemies." In discussing the meaning of these words with Francisco Soberón, we agreed that Che Guevara may not have meant that you need an enemy to justify your behavior, but that a person with values and principles who stands for what he or she sincerely believes in will always attract enemies. Not having enemies could be a sign that you are trying to please everyone and have no ideals or ethical principles that you are willing to commit to or defend. Although we may not all be capable or willing to fight or die for our values or ideas, at least we can be honest and defend them through argument!

The best people possess a feeling for beauty, the courage to take risks, the discipline to tell the truth, the capacity for sacrifice. Ironically, their virtues make them vulnerable; they are often wounded, sometimes destroyed.

—Ernest Hemingway

Chapter 14

A social enterprise that protects endangered species and restores nature.

> *Sometimes you look back at girls you spent money on rather than send it to your Mum and you realize, witchcraft is real.*

—Robert Mugabe

I was raised in a traditional Christian environment, but we nevertheless believed that we were all leaves on the same tree of life. We may feel closest to our family, but in the end, all humans are related and part of the same universe, in which hyenas and dung beetles also have a space and play an important part. It took me a while to overcome the assumption that humans are more important than other transient beings. We may be more self-aware and powerful than other animals or transient beings, in the same way that one race seems stronger than another, one caste more elevated, or one religion more forceful. Power, like beauty, only exists in the eye of the beholder. The people who belong to the dominant race, caste, or religion are not more important, just more powerful.

At this moment, humans are at the top of the food chain, the dominant species on planet Earth. We have become very self-important and see ourselves as masters of the universe. We consider the rest of the universe at our mercy. Even when we pretend to save something, we do so from the goodness of our hearts and the mistaken arrogance that it is ours to save (or not). We save the flowers and the bees, we save the rhinos and the elephants (from ourselves, I guess), and the greatest arrogance of all: we feel it within our power to save the planet. The planet fortunately is not ours to save, quite the opposite. The planet went through a lot worse than our presence over the billions of years of its existence and it will recover from our presence and continue to thrive long after we are gone and forgotten. It has survived considerable heating and cooling many times, been through massive earthquakes and huge volcanic eruptions that extinguished most life on its surface, while protecting organisms living up to 10 kilometers below, as well as plate tectonics, continental drift, magnetic storms, the magnetic reversal of the poles, collisions with comets and meteors, you name it, and it is still going strong.

What I am afraid of is that we may be changing the world so fast that we won't be able to adjust to those changes ourselves. We created pollution, climate change, and mass extinction, and we view these as the Darwinian right of a stronger species. However, we are now changing the world so fast that we may not be able to cope with the consequences of the changes we trigger, even causing our own (perhaps inevitable) extinction. We will ultimately create nuclear war, disease pandemics, overpopulation, and global warming, exhausting our natural resources. Any combination of these could put an end to human civilization and existence. This would not be a problem for Earth, which has lots of other species that could take over. And of course the planet can manage perfectly well without a dominant species—it is only a problem for us. We want to preserve our familiar, manageable lives and our own habitat. We want a clean and suitable place to live. It is pure and naked self-interest, although I do see some consolation in the observations of Werner von Braun:

Nature does not know extinction; all it knows is transformation… Everything science has taught me—and continues to teach me—strengthens my belief in the continuity of our spiritual existence after death. Nothing disappears without a trace.[77]

The planet will be here for a long time after we have become extinct through our own lack of self-restraint and will to self-destruct. The earth will continue to thrive and evolve, with new species of organisms dominating its surface. It will go on as if nothing had happened. Whatever its temperature or oxygen levels, however depleted of certain resources it becomes, some organisms will be perfectly suited for whatever habitat it provides. Our pollution and exploitation of the Earth's natural resources will automatically cease and be reversed, for the simple reason that we won't be here to cause problems. Given our recklessness, perhaps that will serve us right.

---

[77] This *Week Magazine*, January 24, 1960 (p.2)

So, on a larger scale, there is really nothing to worry about. The universe will take care of itself. It does not need you and me to save it.

On a smaller, more human, scale, however, the picture looks quite different. I refuse to give up on our planet or civilization—not on my watch. However, it is easy to assume that no individual can do anything to reverse climate change, mass pollution, the exhaustion of resources, or the extinction of species.

In the 1970s, the Club of Rome was predicting that the world would suffer mass starvation and would not be able to continue to feed itself. Genetically manipulated food sources, better grains, and much better irrigation, fertilizers, and farming techniques have partly solved that problem, as the immensely interesting book, Forty Chances by Howard G. Buffett describes.

In the 1980s, we feared that atomic and neutron bombs would destroy all life on earth. When the Berlin Wall came down and the Cold War ended, that fear diminished to manageable dimensions.

In the 1990s, acid rain was destroying our forests. We never hear about that now.

In 2000, the millennium bug (errors in software code) was supposed to bring the world to a halt. Of course, nothing actually happened; the issue turned out to be a hoax concocted by clever consultants who made a fortune, and strangely enough, got away with it unpunished.

Then we got global warming: an alarming increase in the temperature of the earth's atmosphere, leading to drastic climate change, a rise in sea levels, and many other dramatic effects. Now it seems that climate change is not affecting the whole world in the same way; the South Pole is not heating up, so sea water levels may not rise as fast as predicted. In addition, climate change has led to an increase in forestation, due to increased CO_2 levels. The only thing certain about the global warming caused by burning fossil fuels is that we do not yet fully understand the potential impact.

Every decade (or even every year), there is some major fear that the world will collapse because of one over-simplified major event. While I am writing this chapter, it is all about Brexit. I'm pretty sure that, by the time you start reading it, we will barely remember what that was.

It is a safe and comforting thought that we have the Kyoto Protocol to deal with global warming, the UN to avoid global war, the OECD to avoid financial collapse, and the Bill and Melinda Gates Foundation to eradicate polio. These are big organizations, the amounts of money involved are mind-boggling and thus all key problems are safely outside our sphere of influence.

For the ninety-nine percent of people who are not part of the small group that controls practically all of the world's wealth and resources—and even for the 1 percent (excluding the mere 1,250 billionaires who own eighty percent of the world's wealth), it is a comforting thought that others with more resources are solving the world's problems. But what if they are not committed enough or not interested or too busy? What if many of them are too greedy or self-absorbed to even care? What if there are lots of smaller problems that also need solving?

Here and now, I want to encourage people like you and me to realize that each of us, with whatever resources and influence we may have, can definitely make an impact and do something meaningful. Big changes happen because one person convinces a couple of others, and together, they slowly but surely create a tidal wave of change—sometimes for better, sometimes for worse. Every positive change or effort has an effect, and together, many small effects can become unstoppable. Mohandas Gandhi told his followers to "be the change you want to see in the world;" Mother Teresa said, "If you cannot feed a hundred people, start by feeding one." Small, even symbolic actions matter a lot, as they cascade down, triggering others to do their part.

Of course, we all can easily do the small stuff. We can refuse plastic bags at the supermarket, turn off lights, lower the air conditioning when we leave a room, stop overeating and over-spending, fly or drive less, and generally behave like good citizens. However, we all have the capability to do more and to take a more active part in creating change.

Good parents only exist as a side-effect of having great children. One night, over dinner at our farm in South Africa, we discussed as a family the rapid forced extinction of rhinos by poachers. We agreed that the problem was major and urgent; we couldn't do much, but needed to do something.

We decided to accommodate at least one breeding herd of rhinos (a crash) on our aloe vera farm. It had enough space (about 1,200 hectares), an excellent grass habitat, and plenty of different bushes and trees, which are part of the original habitat of both white and black rhinos. As a project, it would be both fun and meaningful to do.

We looked into the myriad of permits we would need to obtain, and the various conditions we would need to create, to safely host a rhino family. Electric fences, an anti-poaching unit, guns, two-way radios, drones with infra-red cameras, twenty-four-hour surveillance, veterinarians on stand-by, the lot.

In South Africa, as is right, people need many permits to transport, buy, sell, or own protected and endangered species—many more permits than are needed for hunting. Although many laws are broken in South Africa, the wildlife laws generally make sense and are enforced by dedicated people.

It seemed like a complicated but feasible idea until our neighbors came to complain. Bringing rhinos into the area would attract poachers and with them, trouble, danger, and risk.

I did not want to hear that, and the words of Bishop Desmond Tutu kept nagging me:

If you are neutral in situations of injustice, you have chosen the side of the oppressor. If an elephant has its foot on the tail of a mouse, and you say that you are neutral, the mouse will not appreciate your neutrality.[78]

On a separate occasion he also said:

If one day you stand before God and he asks you where are your wounds and you say I have no wounds he will comment was there nothing worth fighting for in your life?

I had a serious discussion with my son and we both realized that running a game reserve with valuable endangered species would incur serious risks, including the risk of getting killed by desperate people for protecting these animals. I applied the Che Guevara yardstick and accepted that living for certain ideas and dreams meant being willing to die for them. We agreed to accept the risks and to take things as they came.

---

[78]   As quoted in *Unexpected News : Reading the Bible with Third World Eyes (1984)* by Robert McAfee Brown, p. 19

So as not to create issues with our neighbors, and for a variety of other reasons, we ultimately decided to create a separate project, which many moons later became the Shared Universe Ventures Fund, Ltd.

The purpose of the fund is to attract people to invest in and jointly own a piece of African land as a nature reserve, restoring to the way it must have looked and felt before the big game hunters of the 19th century arrived to destroy larger game, like elephants and rhinos, eliminate predators, and make the area safe and cleared for cattle farming.

We were ready to launch by mid-2014. We established the legal structure of the fund, and raised enough money to buy two rundown farms with an old lodge on a property next to the Mapungubwe National Park in Northern Limpopo, close to where South Africa borders both Zimbabwe and Botswana.

The area was already named the Mapesu Private Game Reserve, after the Mapedu River that seasonally ran through the property; the lodge was called the Mopane Bush Lodge.

We opted for a strong focus on conserving rhinoceros, as this iconic species triggered our mission and adventure. However, we also wanted the reserve to have as many as possible of the original species that would have lived in the area, including elephants, various predators, and most of the common African wildlife.

Creating or, to use a better word, restoring a game reserve area is not as easy as I initially expected.

In nature, all animals have their proper space and purpose. There are animals like zebras that eat tall grasses and antelopes that eat shorter grasses. There are browsers, like kudu and nyala, which eat low bushes, and giraffes that go for the higher acacias. There are yellow-billed oxpeckers that eat the ticks off buffaloes, giraffes and kudus, and insects that live on only one specific type of plant or tree. It is a subtle balance that, once disturbed, takes time and effort to restore.

The balance is so subtle that, for example, the mopane tree (Colophospermum mopane,) not only emits an acid that will make a giraffe (or other browser) stop eating after a few mouthfuls, but also emits a pheromone (a chemical substance affecting the behavior or psychology of specimens of the same species), caused by emitted ethylene, that warns other branches and trees, forcing the giraffe to move to a completely different stand of trees to continue his meal. This keeps the mopanes healthy, thus preserving the giraffes' food supply in the long term. It also makes you admire the complexity and social altruism of the mopane tree, which can warn other trees in its immediate area. Understanding the situation, giraffes move upwind as they forage, outpacing the warning system of the mopanes. The mopane apparently understands that it will only survive if there are other healthy mopane trees in the neighborhood.

There is still much to learn about nature, and whenever we invent something new, sooner or later, we have to admit that a natural version already existed. Now that we have understood how to use the cloud to store information, it turns out that our bodies have stored memories and thoughts, in the form of energy fields, in the "cloud" all along. Someday, we will be able to access those energy fields electronically and create a whole new way of storing and sharing information between humans, and ultimately with animals and perhaps even trees.

Our game reserve currently encompasses a rather modest 7,221 hectares (we are hoping to continuously add more land). Although it is bigger than the largest nature reserves in the Netherlands (the Oostvaardersplassen is 5,600 hectares and the Hoge Veluwe is 5,500 hectares), as well as the Land van Maal in Curaçao (4,400 hectares), it is a fraction of the size of Kruger Park (2 million hectares) or the Serengeti Park/Masai Mara (jointly, some 3 million hectares). Even the largest parks are too small for nature to work as it should and has done for millions of years. Migration patterns have been disrupted by fences and habitat encroachment. In farms and towns, predator levels are often very low and animals who wander outside a protected area are likely to be shot by angry farmers or hunters. Some predators, like leopards, and elephants understand the situation. If hunting or poaching is up on the Zimbabwean side of our (Greater Mapungubwe Transfrontier Conservation) area, they move to Botswana and stay there until they think it is safe again, then they send out small groups to reconnoiter. The area is home to some 2,200 elephants, roughly double its carrying capacity (the natural maximum number of animals of a species a habitat can support with food and water). You can imagine what happens in times of drought, when the only green spaces in the whole area are the tomato, orange, and potato farms along the Limpopo River.

As wealth increases rapidly in Africa, people require more space for living, agriculture, and infrastructure; the habitat available to big game is disappearing at a much faster rate than the population is increasing. Many of the larger game species, such as elephants, hippos, and rhinos have seen over half of their habitat disappear in the past 30 years. As a result, their numbers are dwindling.

It has been calculated that, since the human cognitive revolution (which introduced learning, remembering, and communicating) began, some 70,000 years ago, humans have driven into extinction at least 100 of the roughly 200 genera of mammals weighing over 50 kilos, most of them disappearing even before the agricultural revolution of 10,000–12,000 years ago, in a time before sophisticated modern tools and weapons or large numbers of hunters. Of the surviving genera and species, all of the larger species have seen their numbers dwindle dramatically. Homo sapiens sapiens is now the most common mammal on Earth (over 7 billion individuals) followed by domesticated animals: over a billion cattle, a billion sheep, and almost a billion pigs. Genetically speaking the domesticated chicken has become the most successful species ever, with over 25 billion members. In nature, chickens live 7–12 years; nowadays however, most chickens lead terribly uncomfortable and uninteresting lives of quiet desperation in slavery. They barely live 35 to 40 days when bred for meat or a year when laying eggs, before being slaughtered. The number of horses on the face of the earth has dropped dramatically since their role in agriculture, transportation, and warfare was taken over by mechanized vehicles.

In addition to habitat loss, for game species, poaching takes a huge toll. The losses of plains animals, mostly antelopes that are taken for sustenance purposes by members of communities surrounding the nature reserves, can generally be replaced. Many species of animals up their birth rate when hunting or poaching reduces their numbers to below what the habitat can sustain. The more selective poaching of elephant tusk and rhino horn is, however, a totally different story.

> *There is that saying, we haven't inherited the planet from our parents, we borrowed it from our children. But borrow means you plan to pay back, and we've been stealing. And that is why I am working so hard with youth to create a critical mass of young people empowered to be guardians of our natural world. They are my hope for the future.*[79]

—Dr. Jane Goodall, Founder of the Jane Goodall Institute

Currently, there may be fewer than 400,000 African elephants left in the world. That is an over 60 percent decrease during the past decade. Per annum, some 12 percent of all elephants living in nature get poached for their tusks, and their carcasses are left to rot. Elephant tusks mainly go to China, Hong Kong, and Vietnam, where they are carved into ornaments and jewelry. In 2015, the Chinese government finally banned the ivory trade and began to eliminate all industries related to the carving and use of ivory. However, it will be a while before all legal stock is off the market and can no longer be replenished by smuggling in more elephant tusks. Nevertheless, I think it is a wonderful sign that the value of an elephant tusk (to those who are not elephants) has decreased since the Chinese ban was introduced 18 months ago, from US$2,100 to US$1,100 per kilo. If the Chinese government actually enforces its ban on

---

[79]   Bill Moyers the Journal, PBS interview of Jane Goodall, March 19, 2010

the whole ivory industry, which has existed in China for many hundreds of years, it will eliminate by far the largest market for ivory objects and the basis for much ivory poaching.

The situation concerning rhino horn is, if possible, even more alarming. There are probably only 25,000 rhinos left in Africa. Of these, there are some 5,000 black rhinos (Dicerus Bicornis), and the remainder are southern white rhinos (Ceratotherium Simum). The northern varietal of the white rhino went extinct just a few years ago. This population has fallen from 70,000 in 1970, although it has grown slightly since the 1990s. Black and white rhinos are actually the same color grey. The white ones have a wide beak, as they are grazers, and the black ones have a punt-lipped beak, as they are browsers. Black rhinos are more unpredictable and moody than white rhinos and can charge without notice. As they were once amongst the most difficult animals for big game hunters to hunt on foot, they made it into the all-important list of the big five. When I made my first trip to Africa, I thought that the big five referred to large audit firms, but they actually refer to the top animals in the safari business: elephant, rhino, lion, leopard, and Cape buffalo.

Rhinos are poached for their horns, predominantly in South Africa, where 80 percent of the world's remaining rhinos live. Between 2008-2016 over 6,000 rhinos have been poached in South Africa, half of them in the Kruger Park area. The horns are smuggled via Mozambique to Vietnam and sold as a detoxifying medicine, in accordance with the age-old principles of traditional Chinese medicine. Their popularity soared after a minister mentioned on TV in Vietnam that his rare cancer was cured by consuming rhino horn.

An additional problem is that members of Vietnam's wealthy elite see rhino horn as a status symbol, representing power and wealth, and also as a party drug and a cure for hangovers. It is now, in 2017, worth more than gold. A kilogram of rhino horn has a street value of about US$60,000 on the black market in Vietnam, whereas a kilogram of gold is currently worth a bit over US$40,000. Even if the Vietnamese government tries to stop the use of rhino horn, it will not have as much success as the Chinese government did in banning the use of elephant tusk for ornaments or shark fin as an ingredient in soup. An absolute ban on serving shark fin soup at government banquets (part of a larger awareness campaign) was promoted by famous actors like Jackie Chan, decreasing the demand for shark fin by 90 percent. In 2014, Vietnam signed the London Declaration to tackle wildlife crime. Trade in rhino horn became a criminal offense; Vietnam is now working with Mozambique and South Africa to chase and convict poachers and traffickers.

In South Africa, there is an ongoing debate about whether or not to legalize the trade in rhino horn. In 2016, a judged decided that, within South Africa, you would be free to buy and sell rhino horn that was legally harvested from rhinos or obtained from legally hunted rhinos, or those that had suffered a natural death. The hunting and farming community is divided, with many claiming that making the rhino horn trade legal creates a strong incentive for farmers to breed rhinos, which would quickly raise numbers. Rhinos can be bred as easily as cattle, although they have a long gestation period of 16 months. Their horns can be cut every few years, in much the same way that we cut fingernails, which then grow back.

The keratin in rhino horn is exactly the same as the keratin that makes up our fingernails and toenails. Even having the same slightly soothing "medicinal" effect as biting your fingernails, it would still be less effective than aspirin. One farmer in South Africa is breeding, herding, and protecting over 1,500 rhinos like cattle, in anticipation of a possible lifting of the rhino horn trading ban. At CITES meetings, the subject keeps coming up for a vote, with only the handful of countries that currently produce elephant tusk and rhino horn supporting free international trade. It is highly unlikely that the international trading ban will be lifted, as opponents of lifting the ban have a long list of objections. Some of the more convincing arguments include concerns that legal trade will be impossible to separate from illegal trade, and that potential consumers will continue to believe that rhino horn has medicinal value and that rhinos are not critically endangered, beliefs widely held in consuming countries, like Vietnam. I can see both sides. Ultimately, I think we should try to conserve these animals as they are and were intended to be. We should allow them to live with their horns intact, and not exploit them like pigs or chickens. I must admit that this argument is more emotional than rational or practical, especially given the relative success of domesticated species.

I have pursued criminals through the rhino killing fields of Kruger National Park, and across the South African border into Mozambique. I have observed shoeless, shabby poachers on their knees, heads hanging in shame while the elders from their local village berate them for dishonoring their families. I have held their weapons in my hands: axes and silenced .375 rifles, and I have felt the weight of poverty.[80]

—Jamie Joseph

We cannot blame Africans for aspiring a similar lifestyle to the one Europeans and Americans have enjoyed for a long time and Asians are now also enjoying (without much wildlife left). The African ecological footprint is still significantly smaller than that of the West, and we need to help protect what is left. Typically, in nature, if it pays, it stays. Wildlife unfortunately nowadays needs to be useful and add value to man to have a chance of survival.

If we don't do something now, soon we will only be able to see the big African animals in zoos, circuses, elephant safaris, and other forms of captivity and domestication. And what right do we have to lock up animals for life, just so that we can look at them?

We bought the farms and the lodge, immediately experiencing deep immersion into common African problems. The fencing around the property was in a terrible state; animals could easily get out and poachers in, resulting in a thoroughly depleted collection of only the most common plains animals.

There were some impalas, kudus, wildebeests, gemsboks, eland antelopes, a lone ostrich, warthogs, hyenas, and leopards.

My son Quinten, the general manager, set out to add new species and revive existing species that had not seen an influx of fresh genes for many years.

Over a period of two years, we replaced the simple cattle fence with a long and sturdy 34-kilometer, 21-strand, 2.40-meter fully electrified and electronically monitored fence. We built a smooth, fast road all along the fence, making sure there were no trees that an elephant could push down onto it to short circuit the electricity and let the animals escape. Elephants somehow know exactly how to do this. They have formidable memories, remembering water spots years after visiting them, and making annual visits of remembrance to places where their matriarchs have fallen, to perform family rituals. They can

---

[80]   Joseph, Jamie. "My war on poaching: reporting from Africa's trenches." *Element Magazine*, Monday, December 29, 2014, p 6-7.

typically recognize hundreds of other elephants from kilometers away, just by the rumbling sounds they make. They also remember kind human deeds for the rest of their lives. They sometimes retaliate for mistreatment in captivity with mahouts, even years after the fact, as we came to experience up-close.

When we were almost finished fencing the original area, the opportunity arose to add two more farms directly adjacent to our property, and so the project had to be extended. We were happy to stretch our resources.

There was no surface water in the reserve. Croetz, our farm manager, constructed a dam six hundred meters long, as a place for animals to drink and frolic in the water. Ultimately, it would be able to hold water all year round. The dam was constructed at the confluence of several seasonal streams and took several months to build. One shower of rain would fill it completely. Almost overnight, it made the land around it much greener. Water birds, including egrets and Nile geese, initially passed by but soon after, took up permanent residence. Zebras and wildebeest adjusted their habits to come and drink on a daily basis. Once the dam is fully stabilized, which will take at least two rainy seasons, the pressure of the water will reduce leakage by sealing the structure, and the dam will retain water permanently. It will then also become a home to the hippos and crocodiles that we plan to introduce at some stage.

All of the other water holes on the property lead to cattle cribs that will be replaced with elephant-tamper-proof and natural-looking water holes, powered by solar energy or wind energy.

In this part of the world, there is very little rain. What does fall comes down in a handful of torrential rainstorms once a year, creating huge temporary rivers, causing a lot of destruction and erosion, and turning the landscape into large empty pans with no topsoil or vegetation, and rugged, dry river beds. It is important to capture as much water as possible for the much longer dry periods. After each big rainfall, roads need repairing, fences cleaning, and passages through river beds rebuilding. A few years back, a big rainstorm flooded the rivers and washed away a nearby crocodile farm, which had fifteen thousand crocodiles of all sizes. They ended up all over the region, in rivers and water holes and people's swimming pools. One really big one was photographed in a supermarket 80 kilometers away in Musina, where he was making himself comfortable in the butchery section. It was a great subject for funny pictures.

The area has a stark beauty. It is very rugged, with big rock formations and lots of ancient baobab trees. Many trees have been felled by elephants; the area is now mostly overgrown with mopane trees. Whenever we visit the reserve, we try to combine our visit with a trip around the area. The Mapungubwe National Park is right across the road; it is the only wildlife park in South Africa that opens onto the frontier river and thus, effectively, onto the big open spaces of Botswana and Zimbabwe (across the river, the land is mostly communally owned and not fenced in). Some ten kilometers away is the Pitsani Farm and just beyond, the Tuli Block and Circle, with its abundance of wildlife. This is the area from which the December 1895 Jameson raid was staged, as well as early second Boer War skirmishes in 1899.

There is always lots to see in the thirstlands, with dramatic changes once the annual rains begin. Suddenly, yellow devil thorn flowers burst like a meadow and change the stark landscape, usually dominated by browns, ochers, and greys into a lovely view of bright greens and yellows. The mopane trees, for a brief period, are covered with shiny green leaves, and eight day grasses come up for brief periods. The impala lambing season kicks off, and given the Darling effect, all of this happens at the same time (with the moon dictating mating season). So, there's certainly a lot to see and get visitors excited about—in the bush, the most magical time is after a good rain.

One Saturday, we took a lazy late afternoon game drive in Tuli with the family and some friends. It was a very hot day and we saw nothing spectacular until we noticed a baby giraffe, its umbilical cord still hanging from its belly, with its mother and another female giraffe. We maneuvered our vehicle to get closer and observed the beautiful calf from nearby. It was, at most, a few days old; its walk was uncertain and it had huge eyelashes. Then we noticed two lionesses sneaking up on the giraffe calf. They had clearly decided to have the giraffe calf for dinner. The mother giraffe noticed the lionesses as well and immediately placed herself between her baby and the predators. The other giraffe ran off, quickly disappearing over the horizon. The lionesses split up, constantly outflanking the mother and trying to attack the calf. It was just a matter of time before they succeeded; indeed, it did not long take long before one managed to lure away the mother while the other jumped on the back of the calf and wounded it, before the mother realized her mistake and came running back to protect her baby. In the course of a number of similar attacks, the calf became seriously wounded and had trouble staying on its feet.

The mother valiantly attacked the lionesses and once or twice succeeded in kicking one of them with her heavy hooves, but she could not be everywhere at the same time. In between attacks, both the baby and the mother looked pleadingly in our direction. We were not supposed to interfere with nature, even if it had been possible. It felt terrible NOT to heed the words of Bishop Desmond Tutu, cited a few pages back. Nature needs to maintain all its species. Whoever cannot be fast ends up as food. It seemed cruel and I wondered what the difference was between the mouse and the baby giraffe. The best I could come up with was that the bishop's elephant has a choice and does not need to hurt the mouse, while the lioness needs to hunt to survive. It is her nature to hunt and kill for survival, while the elephant eats grass and has no business interfering with the mouse's life.

The sun slowly set. The calf was now so badly wounded, it could no longer stand up. The mother placed herself over its body and kicked in any direction where she thought there was a lion. It was a really sad sight. When it got completely dark, we went off to a tasteless dinner and a restless night. The future did not look good for that baby!

Before the sun rose the next morning, we were back in the game viewer and raced back to where we had left the mother and baby. From far away, we could see the mother standing in exactly the same position. The calf lay motionless between her legs and the lionesses were still circling. In the meantime, about 15 spotted hyenas and maybe seven or eight black-backed jackals had gathered around the scene. They were getting anxious and howling, adding urgency and sound to the so far mostly silent drama. It was as if they had been waiting for us to arrive. The hyenas made mock attacks on the lions, who stayed focused on their prize and chased off the hyenas.

Once the sun was fully up and the mother giraffe saw that she could not expect any help from us, she looked at us again with her big brown eyes with their long eyelashes, and a sense of despair made my heart sink and my stomach turn into a huge knot. Then she stepped away from the baby's body and slowly walked off. After about 15 or 20 steps, she turned around once more to give us that look and then slowly, with dignity and her head held high, walked away. I felt terribly powerless. The lionesses had waited for this moment and immediately fell on the calf's carcass. We assumed it was already dead, as it no longer moved. In seconds, the calf's entrails were hanging out and in less than half an hour, the lionesses had taken their fill. In the meantime, the hyenas were getting ever more nervous that there wouldn't be enough food for them. They started to nag the lionesses, who eventually got fed up and moved off to rest and digest in the morning sun some ten meters away. The hyenas started to rip the carcass apart and were soon joined by jackals stealing bits and scraps. Less than half an hour later, the whole carcass had disappeared. Not even a piece of skin or bone was left, and the two lonely African white-backed vultures who were waiting in nearby trees looked on without taking any action. There was nothing left for them!

Over the years, I have witnessed many predator kills. It always amazes me that, once the predator wins the chase or the fight, the victim resigns itself to fate and prepares to die without further struggle. Leopards catch impalas so that their cubs can play cat and mouse for prolonged periods, until eventually they kill their prey. The herd may initially be disturbed that one member has been chased and caught, but the moment the battle is lost, the herd settles down; minutes later, all are back to grazing as if nothing had happened, while the predators are quietly having their meal amongst them.

Every day, there is a new adventure. At night, we hear hyenas, as we are sitting around the fire in the *boma*. Locally known as "Kalahari TV," staring into a fire makes people tell stories, just as our homo sapiens forefathers transmitted information, culture, and skills for 150,000 years—and other hominoids for some one million years before them. We invented writing and reading 5,000 years ago; but only in the last 150 years have a large number of people actually been able to read and write. Stories were our ancestors' primary way of transmitting knowledge and values. Our brains have evolved to expect stories with a particular structure, with heroes and villains, a hill to be climbed or a damsel to be rescued.

Nowhere else on earth are we so close to nature and our origins as in Africa. The first humanoids originated from present-day Ethiopia. One day, in Addis Adeba, I visited Lucy, also known as AL 288-1 or *Dinkinesh*, meaning "you are marvelous" in Amharic. Lucy was a female australopithecus afarensis; she acquired her name from the song "*Lucy in the Sky with Diamonds*," by the Beatles, which was played loudly and repeatedly all evening after the excavation team's first day of work on the recovery site. A petite lady, 1.1 meters tall, and weighing only 29 kilos, she once lived for not much more than 20 years on the

Ethiopian savannah. She has now been dead for over 3.2 million years. She is world-famous for being the oldest upright-walking hominid ever found, but her remains are unceremoniously kept in a glass case in a dusty museum, where she is surrounded by kids on school trips for most of her days.

A similarly sorry fate is shared by *Mrs. Ples,* the first truly upright human, a lady from Sterkfontein in South Africa. She is about 2.15 million years old. Her skull was blown to pieces when she was excavated, and she now lies lifeless under a glass ceiling. Her claim to fame is that, in spite of the excavation mishap, she has the most complete skull of any australopithecus africanus ever found. Some of her descendants, homo sapiens, spread all over the world, although most stayed closer to home. The KhoiSan are the oldest identifiable inhabitants of the area and also the oldest human group on the face of the earth. They are, genetically speaking, the most diverse people in existence. All the peoples of the world outside Africa descended from a tiny group of emigrants who crossed the Red Sea into the Middle East and from there, colonized the four corners of the earth, long after the original KhoiSan were already in place.

African skies are very clear; at night you can see thousands of stars. For the KhoiSan, these represent totally different images and stories than they do for us.

In certain KhoiSan stories, the Moon represents a man who one day made the Sun angry. The Sun's sharp light retaliates by cutting off pieces of the Moon until almost the whole of the Moon is gone, leaving only one small piece. Ultimately the Moon pleads for mercy and the Sun lets him go. From the small remaining piece, the Moon gradually grows again until he becomes a Full Moon. Some KhoKhoi spoke of the Pleiades as the Stars of Spring and called them the *Khunuseti.* They were the daughters of the important Dawn, or Sky God. One day, the story goes, the *Khunuseti* told their husband (represented by the star Aldebaran) to go out and hunt the three zebras (Orion's Belt). As requested, the husband went out, but took only one arrow with him. He aimed and shot at the zebras, but missed. His arrow (Orion's Sword) fell beyond them, and still lies there today. Although he wanted to retrieve the arrow, he couldn't: there was a fierce lion (Betelgeuse) nearby, who was also watching the zebras. So the poor man sat there, shivering from the cold and suffering from thirst and hunger, unable to return to his wives, who would be angry that he hadn't completed his mission and couldn't collect his arrow.

The KhoiSan are extremely good at tracking animals. It is something they learn from a very young age. The famous big game hunter Frederick Selous, who lived with them for years, found out how their bushcraft became so superior: the answer began in infancy. Given small tortoises to play with, two-year old children learned, as a game, the art of tracking animals across traceless stone. As they released a tortoise, it crept off across the rock and the children crawled after it, learning to follow the little reptile by using the imperceptible marks of its claws crossing the stone.

There are many Bushman sites in the area of our reserve, including rock art of amazing creativity. The Kaoxa site, some 15 kilometers from our gate, has over 200 pictures and is one of the most well-known sites in all of South Africa. We were very excited when we recently also discovered on our property, under an overhanging cliff, previously undocumented paintings of elephants, rhinos, wild dogs, and hyenas that have been carbon-dated back 3,000–4,000 years. Of course, these pictures were known to the local Northern Sotho inhabitants, but they never were of much artistic interest to white researchers, especially during Apartheid. It was a huge boost for me to learn that our property was part of an ongoing interaction between man, spirit and nature.

Every picture has its meaning. Originally incorrectly interpreted as attempts to exert power over animals to be hunted, interviews with bushmen in remote areas have unveiled a rich spiritual world in which each animal has its meaning and each ceremony links humans, animals, and the phenomena of a larger world at a spiritual level. The KhoiSan frequently dance until they reach exhaustion and dehydration, and then enter into a trance to convert into an animal of spiritual potency and achieve a state of *Num*. By doing so, they temporarily take on all the spiritual properties of the animal. In some of the pictures on our reserve, you can still see how the Khoisan expressed that *Num* by depicting the animal itself in black pigments and then adding in the *Num* as a red line over the back of the animal. The concept is remarkably similar to the *kundalini* concept in Hindu culture, where *kundalini* is a primal energy (or Shakti) lying in wait as a coiled snake at the base of the spine for the purpose of reaching spiritual awakening through meditation, yoga, or *pranayana*. The rock art drawing of the elephant in our reserve clearly shows the same red *Num* line over its back. Sitting at that rocky overhang, one can hear the activity at a nearby hyena den, and can easily picture where and how the KhoiSan must have done their singing, dancing, and rituals, all those thousands of years ago.

The KhoiSan originally occupied the whole country; as they were unfamiliar with the concepts of ownership and leadership, they were perceived as a threat to farmers (excellent trackers and hunters, the KhoiSan saw domesticated cows and sheep as particularly stupid antelopes.) They themselves were hunted almost to extinction in the Cape Area around 1870 and marginalized to remote areas in the Kalahari, where the Government sold and issued permits to hunt KhoiSan until the 1930s. Nowadays, there are fewer than 100,000 KhoiSan left, mostly living in extremely poor conditions in Namibia and Botswana. As Nelson Mandela pointed out, "of all of the civilizations in Africa, the KhoiSan have been wronged the longest and the most by others." And the great tragedy of the KhoiSan is still hidden and rarely spoken of in South Africa. After all, had they been treated fairly, they would have had the most legitimate claim to ownership of the land.

In our area, the KhoiSan were succeeded mainly by Bantu people of the Mapungubwe Kingdom; between 1075 and 1220, the first real city on South African soil was created not 10 kilometers from our reserve. In Mapungubwe, one can see the first traces of a society with different status levels, signs of centralized leadership, an extensive organized spiritual life, and lively trade and handicrafts. When the area became over-populated and over-exploited, the population moved on to found the nearby Great Zimbabwe Kingdom in present-day Zimbabwe, leaving behind many artifacts, including glass beads and gold objects, which proved that they were trading via the port of Kilwa in Tanzania with people as far afield as the Arab peninsula, India, and even China.

After the Mapungubwe people left, the area was largely deserted until the time of the great hunters in the 19th century, after which the land was parceled out into marginal cattle farms that provided a meager existence, constantly threatened by droughts and floods. By the year 2000, the last commercial cattle farmers had more or less given up.

Jan Smuts, several times Prime Minister of South Africa and well known to the area, owned a house on a neighboring farm and proposed the first trans-frontier park there in 1922. An official start was made, with the creation of the Dongola Wildlife Sanctuary in 1947. Jan Smuts lost the 1948 election to the Reunited National Party of Daniel Malan, the government that institutionalized Apartheid. Decisions regarding the park were reversed and the area was once again used for cattle farming until the next power change. In 2007, the Mapungubwe National Park was opened.

The northern Limpopo area, combined with the adjacent areas of the Tuli Block in Zimbabwe and some very large Zimbabwean farms, forms the Greater Mapungubwe Transfrontier Conservation Area. An area roughly half the size of the Kruger area, but with fewer than twenty good lodges, as compared with many hundreds in the Kruger Transfrontier area. In the Mapungubwe area, you will never find 20 game viewing vehicles around a lion kill, called together by apps and radio contact, or even many asphalt roads or game viewers.

When we bought our lodge, it was very run-down. We renovated and extended it from eight to twelve *rondavels* (cottages), accommodating up to thirty guests at any one time. We added some art, and tried to make it more comfortable. We also involved local people, hiring them as employees or buying their art to sell in our little shop.

As a company we adhere to the ten principles of The World Fair Trade Organization (WFTO), as updated most recently in 2013:

Principle One: Creating Opportunities for Economically Disadvantaged Producers. We help with poverty reduction through trade and by supporting marginalized small producers, whether these are independent family businesses, or grouped in associations or cooperatives. We seek to enable these suppliers to move from income insecurity and poverty to economic self-sufficiency and ownership.

Principle Two: Transparency and Accountability. We are transparent in our management and commercial relations. We are accountable to all of our stakeholders and respect the sensitivity and confidentiality of commercial information supplied. We involve employees, members, and producers in our decision-making processes.

Principle Three: Fair Trading Practices. We trade with concern for the social, economic and environmental well-being of marginalized small producers and do not maximize our own profit at their expense. We are responsible and professional in meeting our commitments in a timely manner. We recognize the financial disadvantages producers and suppliers face. We recognize, promote, and protect the cultural identity and traditional skills of small producers, as reflected in their craft designs, food products and other related services.

Principle Four: Payment of a Fair Price. A fair price is one that has been mutually agreed by all through dialogue and participation, which provides fair pay to the producers, and which can also be sustained by the market.

Principle Five: Ensuring no Child Labor and Forced Labor. We adhere to the UN Convention on the Rights of the Child, and national/local law on the employment of children. We ensure that there is no forced labor in our workforce and/or at the workplaces of suppliers and home workers.

Principle Six: Commitment to Non-discrimination, Gender Equity and Women's Economic Empowerment, and Freedom of Association. We do not discriminate in hiring, remuneration, access to training, promotion, termination or retirement based on race, caste, national origin, religion, disability, gender, sexual orientation, union membership, political affiliation, HIV/Aids status or age.

Principle Seven: Ensuring Good Working Conditions. We provide a safe and healthy working environment for employees and / or members. We comply, at a minimum, with national and local laws and ILO conventions on health and safety.

Principle Eight: Providing Capacity Building. We seek to increase positive developmental impacts for small, marginalized producers through Fair Trade. We develop the skills and capabilities of our own employees or members.

Principle Nine: Promoting Fair Trade. We raise awareness of the aim of Fair Trade and of the need for greater justice in world trade through Fair Trade. Honest advertising and marketing techniques are always used.

Principle Ten: Respect for the Environment. We maximize the use of raw materials from sustainably managed sources in our range, buying locally when possible. We use production technologies that seek to reduce energy consumption and where possible use renewable energy technologies that minimize greenhouse gas emissions. These seek to minimize the impact of the waste stream on the environment. Fair Trade agricultural commodity producers minimize their environmental impacts, by using organic or low-pesticide production methods wherever possible.

The lodge and reserve employ approximately fifty people. That is a lot of salaries to pay each month, and so much of the initial focus has been on making the commercial side of the project work. One of the ways we do that is by using the reserve to breed Cape buffaloes. These massive and unpredictable animals (Syncerus caffer) easily multiply; as their aggressive nature protects them from predators, they increase rapidly; surplus animals can be sold at auction. In South Africa, the original population of Cape buffaloes carried all of the common bovine diseases, such as foot-and mouth disease. As a result, cattle farmers killed Cape buffaloes; at one time their numbers were very low. The South African government has established strict rules limiting the areas in which diseased buffaloes can roam and separating them from areas where cattle are being raised. Currently, they are restricted to roughly the greater Kruger area; in the rest of South Africa, and increasingly also in neighboring counties, buffaloes must be disease-free. If animals are transported, they are tested at least three times and, where needed, kept in quarantine. If diseased animals are found within the cattle zone, they are destroyed and the area is quarantined for several years. Those measures have created a large, stable demand for disease-free buffaloes. Letting them freely multiply on the reserve and then selling the surplus can help to cover some of the costs of the nature reserve.

Every year, a game count is carried out by helicopter, and the game plan for the reserve is adjusted. For each species, there is an optimal number of individuals related to the carrying capacity of the grass or foliage. There must also be a careful balance between prey-animals and predators. The predators help to cull the wounded, sick, and old. Too many, and they will deplete whole populations and then starve. For many species, fresh blood must be introduced from time to time to maintain genetic diversity in fenced or isolated populations. As a result, there is an active animal trade between conservancies and auctions, keeping animal populations as genetically diversified as possible and avoiding inbreeding and degeneration. You will find apps in South Africa with the latest market values of wild animals.

Initially, we wasted a lot of time and money on an attempt to re-wild elephants from distressed situations such as zoos, circuses, and misguided elephant safaris. The latter are fortunately now getting closed down in South Africa. We got stuck in a swamp of paperwork. Some people still believe that highly intelligent elephants actually enjoy being locked up, chained, and used for forced walks with tourists, because they get sugar lumps in return. Such beliefs fall into same category as using a picture of a smiling Nelson Mandela on Robben Island, and saying he actually enjoyed his 27 years in captivity.

In September 2016, we achieved an important milestone and received our first wild elephants, translocated from an over-populated reserve close to the Kruger Park. Trans-locating elephants is a complicated and hazardous adventure. A family herd of seven was carefully selected. The amount of paperwork involved was easily as voluminous as the elephants themselves. A conservation plan was needed, as well as lots of permits for catching, moving, and releasing elephants. The translocation was supervised by someone from Nature Conservation and a veterinarian. Elephants are very dependent on their family support systems. If moved, it is important to move a complete family. Our herd is headed by a beautiful 25-year-old matriarch. It has a bull of a similar age, set to grow out to become a majestic tusker, a few youngsters, and a baby or two.

Capturing elephants is not as easy as one would think. This small herd was tracked for several days, to determine for sure which members belonged to the family group. On the actual day of the translocation, it still took several hours to relocate the herd in the morning, as it had moved a lot during the night. Then a helicopter herded the elephants to an open spot not far from a road, a stressful and potentially dangerous process, as elephants are not used to running longer distances. They were then shot with darts from the sky. The first was the matriarch. When she collapsed, first on her knees and then on her side, the rest of the herd, apart from one young bull, rallied around, as if to protect her from the helicopter dart guns, making themselves easy targets. The young bull dashed off and fell a few hundred meters away.

Up close, one can see how majestic and big these animals are. Once they are asleep, you have to make sure the trunks are not in any way obstructed, as this is the only way they can breathe. In normal circumstances, they sleep no more than two hours a day, and can easily go for two to three days without any sleep. We still do not understand how or why. When they lie down for longer periods, their eyes must be covered against the sun, and their blood pressure must be monitored. A trunk is kept open by inserting a twig. With the animals demobilized, you can feel their powerful hearts beating through the pulsing of veins in their ears, and feel how soft their feet are, even though they walk on thorny bushes and rough stones all the time. You can also see how vulnerable these animals are. They are easy to track, used to human presence, and make large, easy targets for any hunter with a steady hand. We do not often think about how close they are to us; they have the same range of emotions we have: they joke, play, fight, flirt, mourn, and are jealous, obnoxious, unreasonable, and naughty. They do not like bees or pepper plants (both create invisible barriers against them). They save the weak and young of their own kind and occasionally save or protect animals of other species, and they also make tools. They use twigs to scratch themselves, sticks to dig for water or tear down branches of trees; they even find ways to get through electric fences.

The professional crew worked quickly and efficiently (unfortunately, translocation is a growing business in Africa, so the team was experienced) and it took less than two hours to stabilize all the animals, collar the matriarch, lift them all onto flat trucks, and cage them in. Once on the truck, the animals were given an antidote to wake them up. One by one, they woke up, puzzled and struggling to get back on their feet. That struggle caused lots of noise, as the drowsiness wore off gradually. We made an impressive 3D movie inside the truck, between the confused awakening giants. But the most important thing was that they all got up, ensuring their new lease on life! Not too long ago, large animals in overpopulated reserves faced culling as the only alternative to starvation.

When all were well again, the three-hour drive to the Mapesu Private Game Reserve began. There, all was prepared for their reception. We had built an electrified enclosure within a second enclosure within the actual reserve, effectively creating three barriers between the elephants and freedom. Some of the staff were really nervous and afraid that the elephants might run amok and cause a problem. Others drank gin and tonics and watched the preparations for offloading as if it were a routine event. I climbed to the top of the truck and felt the powerful elephants pounding against the full metal walls, as they tried to orient themselves and prepare for whatever might come. One elephant trunk came through the skylight and touched my leg—was it a greeting or a warning? Finally, the first, small elephant was pushed out with a prodding rod to take her first step in the Reserve. She was the first elephant on Mapesu for at least 100 years. The matriarch followed slowly; once she was out, the others all walked out of the truck, just as if they were getting off a bus after a routine commute. They walked in single file towards the nearby fence, apparently to check whether the electricity was properly on (it was). This action made the alarm go off on at least six phones containing the monitoring app, and it was funny to see six people simultaneously reaching for their phones. It was good to confirm that the app really worked, as it turned out it was the last time they ever touched the fence. The elephants followed the fence until they reached a water hole. The next day, we found them still in the same place. According to the experts, they were showing displacement behavior, pretending to eat, while privately trying to figure out what the hell had happened, a bit like the way we grab our cell phones and start pushing buttons if we find ourselves in an awkward situation.

Soon, the matriarch started sending out low rumbling sounds or vibrations to connect with all other elephants in reach and as far as 40 kilometers away. Once they understood where they were and that they were safe, they calmed down and seemed to settle in. I, sitting on the porch of my *rondavel* at the lodge, could hear them breaking tree branches and pushing over the mopanes, just the way they should. I felt an overflowing of pride—I was so privileged to have had the opportunity to witness this extraordinary home-coming. The nature reserve immediately felt more complete. Yes, the elephants raised the risk of breakouts and poachers, but we were willing to pay that price to restore nature and wildlife.

> *Something is different now in the Mapesu Nature Reserve. There are large circular tracks in the dust, each of them etched with a labyrinth of delicate wrinkles. Mopane trees are scattered and splintered in certain places, and reddish brown balls of dung lie scattered on lonely game paths everywhere. There are elephants here, once again.*[81]

—Andrew Rae

The damage that elephants do to trees and the grass helps to diversify the biosphere and maintain open grasslands. The number of mopane trees goes down and the number of antelopes goes up. More antelopes feed more predators and the whole circle of life becomes more complete than before. In a healthy, natural environment, one sees only perfect animals; the weak ones are taken out quickly. The abundance of bird, animal, insect, and plant species adds value to each—not in a planned way, but for the benefit of the bigger picture. It is easy to imagine a genetic master plan present in the animals' genes. Why otherwise would one painted dog or buffalo risk its life protecting another from a lion, or one acacia tree warn the next that a giraffe was coming, or a zebra warn vervet monkeys about a leopard, or an elephant protect one animal from a predator but not another? Why would baboons catch dog puppies and feed them for months until they are old enough to act as guard dogs under the trees they sleep in overnight?

I have not found a definite answer yet, and perhaps I never will. But I hope to maintain the right environment for asking questions, by maintaining the habitat of these animals the way it is supposed to be. We hope to reintroduce rhinos to our reserve soon, and hippos after that. We are also working on a program to grow our herd of Cape buffaloes. When that is all in place, the larger predators are the last on the list. Hyenas have been there forever; there are at least three hyena dens on the property. Leopards are doing well and we regularly see leopard cubs trailing their mothers. Lions or cheetahs (I prefer the latter) can and will be added when, in line with our game management plan, the populations of prey animals, especially impala and wildebeest, have

---

[81] Andrew Rae, owner and operator of Rae Safaris

had time to recover in sufficient numbers and there is enough prey to support a stable pride of larger predators. If an adult lion eats the equivalent of two impalas a week, then that is 100 a year and 1,500 over a lion's fifteen-year life-span. A healthy pride easily comprises six to ten adult lions, and quickly produces lots of cubs. Birth control nowadays is very important for these animals, as overpopulation will quickly lure animals off the reserves and onto farms where reputational damage for the reserve as well as existential hazards and certain death await the predators. The conservancy is not large enough for wild dogs, which live in big packs and need territories of many hundreds or even thousands of square kilometers.

Is all this worth all the effort? Bishop Desmond Tutu was a road warrior until old age prevented him from preaching. He said, "Instead of growing old gracefully, at home with my family—reading and writing and praying and thinking—too much of my time has been spent at airports and in hotels."

Of course, it's worth it! It is work that must be done—if not now, when? And if not by us, by whom? There are lots of obstacles. We encounter corruption; people try to take advantage of us and our relative wealth, through theft, embezzlement and fraud—you name it. However, we also enjoy people's reactions to their first safari, employees happy with stable jobs, the nature we see slowly recovering, the area we see gaining in economic strength. We are also protecting this natural heritage for our grandchildren, so that they can see the majestic animals of Africa in their natural habitat and not behind bars. Many of our investors and donors have visited the project. They all leave very happy and satisfied to be helping restore the great African wildlife and scenery, while building memories that can last a lifetime.

Over the first two years of the project, we collected an amazing set of characters and created the Shared Universe Foundation, a charitable foundation with tax-effective feeder foundations in the Netherlands and the UK, to help Shared Universe Ventures with its wildlife research, volunteer program, and tracking and collaring of animals. One of our investors, James Hill, was interested in creating a veterinary training program on the property. Of course, wild animals do not need much veterinary care, but things do happen, requiring lots of birth control and inoculations. Rudi Viljoen, a motivational speaker and trainer, activated a local Rotary Club and is spearheading a project to have our own rhino ambulance that can pick up baby calves from a wide area if their mothers get poached. Charles Perry is working to persuade non-governmental institutes to make significant donations. Tara Lal, another investor, is particularly interested in wild dogs and cheetahs and is working to introduce them to the project in due time, along with researchers interested in studying their habits. Many of our staff members put in extra hours to get marketing materials ready in time, as well as impressing our guests, telling stories around the camp fire in the *boma*, and making the conservancy a little bit better and more beautiful every day.

Axel Primmer is organizing a volunteer project to give young people from all over the world a chance to help the conservancy track the many hundreds of species of birds who are native to this area or pass through on their annual migration. Being at an overlap of two major climate zones, there is an amazing variety and mix of bird life.

I recommend becoming involved with this type of impact investment project. Some of the key returns on investment are listed below; they cover financial, strategic, social, emotional, and legacy motives.

The value of impact investments:

1) Financially speaking, there is the expectation of a long-term capital gain. No more land is being made; the land around the Kruger Park is worth at least 20 to 40 times more per hectare, only 3–4 hours away. Over time, land dedicated to proper conservation is bound to increase

in value, as the surrounding land, once abundant, is used much more intensively for infrastructure, agriculture, and other human use.

2) The lodge, as a tourism project, is profitable; it already covers many of the running costs of the project. Increased tourism, related activities, and a volunteer program should generate enough cash to expand the impact of the project.

3) The planned veterinary training program, as well as the sale of surplus animals (especially Cape buffaloes), if properly handled, can add extra income.

4) Huge cash dividends are not to be expected, but after an initial investment period when the lodge is refurbished and occupied, and the reserve is well stocked with a balanced variety of species, it should not be too hard to beat the return on T–bills.

5) There are some clear corporate social benefits. We contribute to the training and development of lodge and reserve employees, hardworking guys doing bush clearing and making charcoal, local artisans and trackers, and communities that benefit from the presence of the reserve. Not to mention the pride and commitment of all who learn that conservancy is valuable and pays off.

6) By setting an example and promoting the reserve widely within our sphere of influence, we will encourage others to do similar things. Our aim is not to have as many people as possible participating in our project, but to have as many people as possible doing something, whenever, wherever.

7) There are some clear benefits for the soul. There is no way to measure the inner pride and calm it brings to see your own nature reserve grow and flourish and the animals and birds return to leading the lives they were meant to live in freedom and in their natural habitat. At the same time, it is a playground and laboratory for shared adventures with friends and family.

8) There are benefits to our ecosystem. Helping to save endangered animals protects biodiversity and maintains unique animals, birds, and plants for the benefit and enjoyment of future generations.

9) There are also more personal emotional benefits. Being able to brag to your friends that you co-own and protect elephants and other endangered species, will impress them more than showing off the latest luxury handbag or watch.

10) Happiness and satisfaction, and a true tangible heritage to leave to your children. To own a farm in Africa is a long-term investment that can help you bond with your children, siblings, and friends. It is a perfect way to foster respect for nature, build on family values, have enjoyable family vacations, and work together on something meaningful that has more appeal and many more different layers of return on investment than a passive investment portfolio.

Now is the time to act; Africans are becoming more prosperous and more and more land is being developed, restricting nonproductive animals to ever smaller pieces of habitat. It is quite likely that, over time, the value of the land in the Mapungubwe area will rival the value of land in the Kruger area. In theory, one can make serious money there, but I am convinced that intangible returns on investment are worth much more.

Doing good by doing well means that you can invest in a conservation project, have lots of fun developing it, and know that your grandchildren will ultimately reap the fruits in two ways. They will have the chance to see for themselves many majestic animals and birds in their natural habitat, as well as learning about them and having the chance to own and protect a piece of nature that will become sustainable and more valuable. Game reserves in Africa will attract visitors from further away than South Africa or Europe. Asians are starting to flow in, never before having had the opportunity to travel to places as far afield as Africa. Tourism will be concentrated in fewer and smaller areas, meaning that lodges in places like Mapungubwe will attract more and more tourists. Creating jobs and income for local people both protects the project from potential threats of nationalization and creates interest in and respect for communities that prosper as a result of a successful project.

For me, my wife Paula, and our two children, Quinten and Florence, this has been a very rewarding adventure so far. We each get different things out of it and we each enjoy it in our own individual way. It bonds our family and helps us meet interesting people, learn about nature, and experience unique adventures that are less likely to happen in the middle of Singapore or Amsterdam.

I feel enormous pride that I am in the position to do something tangible—and that what I do really makes a difference to a community and some endangered species of animals. I learn more every time I go out with the game rangers, animal conservation team, or anti-poaching crew (each more fun than private bankers). I really enjoy the time I get to spend with my son on something he loves and considers worthwhile. How often does one have such feelings? How do they stack up as return on investment?

We gather for sundowners on a *koppie*, or for dinner around a fire in the *boma*, or just somewhere in the wild under the starry sky, and we talk as a family or with any investors or visitors who are present, about what we can do to make the nature reserve grow. Putting money into a new dam to attract more wildlife and birds, investing in animals, and improving infrastructure feel very different from spending money on lavish consumption. Even from that point of view: an elephant is much more exclusive, gives more status, and will look more beautiful than a new car. If well cared for, it will last a lot longer and have offspring.

Consumption is a drug. It will give you a brief high that quickly wears of and leaves a hangover, caused by the money spent. Making a durable investment, on the other hand, is a one-time potentially stressful moment of heightened awareness when you take the plunge, followed by positive emotional returns every time you see it grow and flourish or realize how much you contribute to the conservation of animal species.

Chapter 15

Nepal – Bhutan: sustainable development

Nature is our home; we need to take good care of it to have a safe living environment.

Climate change is destroying our path to sustainability. Ours is a world of looming challenges and increasingly limited resources. Sustainable development offers the best chance to adjust our course.[82]

—Ban Ki-moon

When I was about ten years old, one November night there was a particularly heavy winter storm. The family was huddling together in our farm kitchen, and my mother fired up the wood-burning stove and made hot chocolate. The big old farmhouse was creaking, puffing, moaning, and groaning under gusts of the wind, as it had for many generations enduring winter storms. From time to time, we heard some of the tiles on the roof slide and then fall off. As the storm grew in strength, my father began to worry about the big wooden gate into the farmyard, which was in poor condition and creaking and bending in the wind. If the gate collapsed, the storm would crash into the heart of the farm and the roof would blow off. At one stage, he ordered the whole family—my mother, sister, younger brother, and me—to stand with him and push against the wooden gate with all the power in our bodies. We stood out there in the cold rain and onslaught of wind and pushed with our backs against the gate, as hard as we could, for at least two hours. Finally, the sun came out between the storm clouds and we felt the wind subside. It was a very cold, wet, and scary experience, but also a very powerful one. As a family, we had been able to beat the storm and save the farm (or at least most of it). I was convinced that our will power and mental energy as a family, rather than our bodily strength,

---

[82] UN Secretary-General Ban Ki-Moon. Remarks to the General Assembly on his Five-Year Action Agenda: "The Future We Want", January 25, 2012.

held the gate that night. That night, I acquired a healthy respect for the forces of nature and for the wisdom of my father. Neither has ever left me.

There are few places in the world where I feel as connected to nature as in the Himalayas. The whole area of Ladakh, Zanskar, Nepal, Sikkim and Bhutan has a magical appeal for me. Once, in Thailand, I did a regression, learning that I had, in a previous life, been a porter in Nepal, living in a small house on a mountain slope with a wife and about ten children, each of whom had a vague but undeniable resemblance to someone in my present life, which gave me a very comforting feeling; seemingly, we had all met before and would meet again. I was a porter on the centuries-old trading routes that connect Tibet and India, carrying salt and herbs down and textiles and utensils up. One day, I slid off the path and drowned in a fast flowing, ice cold mountain river at an age when my older children could easily take my place. It had been a simple, good life and a peaceful death. I learned that day that the only people who should fear death are the ones who have regrets, who have not lived their lives to the fullest. I believe that, if you live fully and do what you are capable of, you are always ready for the next experience, including death and whatever follows. Now, whenever I meet someone from my Nepali family, I experience warm feelings about the past, and remember being with them in Nepal.

I am a rational person and it took me a while to accept this regression experience for what it was. It felt much more real and powerful than any dream I had ever had and it stayed with me vividly afterwards. If I walk the streets of Patan or Kathmandu in Nepal, I seem to know what is around the next corner. I intuitively know the meaning of many of the temple carvings and the designs, colors, and smells are all very familiar. Even its language, although I never got much beyond "Namaste," has a familiar ring to it.

On my first trip to Nepal, I walked the famous Jomsom Trail. It was 1979 and tourists were few and far apart. It was a magical coming-of-age experience. In the course of several weeks, we walked from the road head in Pokhara over a range of mountain passes, staying in small country inns until we reached the Tibetan plateau at Muktinath, and then on to the Thorung-La Pass. In the mornings, we started out early, in the cold before sunrise, in order to get a big head start on the Sherpa porters who used the same routes, walking slowly with their heavy loads. As the day progressed and we had to stop more and more frequently, they invariably overtook us. By the end of the day, they had always covered a much greater distance than we had. The snow-capped mountains, including some of the highest peaks in the world, are truly impressive, especially if you are at the bottom of a rift, looking up at the path disappearing around a mountain. Our need to find out what was behind that corner was always stronger than gravity or the desire to just have a cold beer and relax. After the trail, it was great to indulge for a few days in hot showers, the famous space cake of Chai and Pie, and the many smoky places on Freak Street in Kathmandu, which, after trekking in the great outdoors, seemed places of great luxury.

The founder of the U.S. National Parks system, John Muir, said over a hundred years ago: "Thousands of tired, nerve-shaken, over-civilized people are beginning to find out that going to the mountains is going home; that wildness is a necessity."

He was right. People have always stood in awe of mountains. The strength and sturdiness of the rocky crags and smooth slopes of peaks around the globe have inspired creativity and kindled courage. Mountains have been venerated by many cultures, which worshipped great summits as gods and sacred beings. In their looming presence, humanity has seen power, steadfastness, and resolve. Whenever you visit or approach a mountain, you tap into this vast energy of commanding grandeur.

Apart from this hike on the Anapurna circuit up to 5,416 meters, I recall with great pleasure, now that my tired legs are forgotten, hikes to the Mount Everest base camp, also in Nepal, at 5,364 meters, Sikkim in India at 4,450 meters, Mount Kenya at 5,199 meters, Mount Bromo in Indonesia at 2,329 meters, Mount Sinai in Egypt at 2,610 meters, the Inca trail in Peru at 4,200 meters, Cordillera Blanca, Huarez at 4,250 meters, Torres del Paine, Chile at 2,000 meters, El Avion de los Uruguayos, Argentina at 4,200 meters, Kilimanjaro, Tanzania at 5,895 meters, and quite a few others. Hiking is obviously one of my favorite pastimes. It is a great way to get to know people, including yourself, really well. As they say: "it's not the altitude, it's the attitude!"

Some of my friends are collecting the seven summits (climbing the highest peaks on each continent). They have invited me to come along. Enticing as that sounds, unfortunately some peaks are just too high for me. While hiking Kilimanjaro, some of the porters (we had 35 for our group of 10 climbers) were already making fun of me, as I was a lot more weighty than any of them.

Jambo! Jambo bwana!	Hello! Hello sir!
Habari gani? Mzuri sana!	How are you? Very well!
Wageni, mwakaribishwa!	Guests, you are welcome!
Kilimanjaro? Hakuna matata!	Kilimanjaro? No worries!
Tembea pole pole. Hakuna matata!	Walk slowly, slowly. No worries!
Utafika salama. Hakuna matata!	You'll get there safe. No worries!
Kunywa maji mengi. Hakuna matata!	Drink plenty of water. No worries!

All hikes are memorable and, for one reason or another, end up being unique and usually spiritual experiences. To measure yourself against the forces of nature makes you feel how small and insignificant you are in the larger scheme of things, and how easily nature could wipe you out. I increasingly believe that the universe protects us, as it protects every other transient being, preventing us from slipping and allowing us to be what we are supposed to be. I wish we could do the same for nature and the animals around us. Hiking makes you realize that, with guts, grit, and time, you can conquer any mountain, any obstacle, and any setback. In nature, everything is perfect. There are no ugly vistas or landscapes; all trees are beautiful, even when wind-swept and crooked. All animals are perfectly adapted to their environment. What is not perfect, healthy, and fully adapted will be gone in a heartbeat and replaced by something that is.

On my second trip to Nepal, in 1993, I came as a young businessman hired by USAID, the U.S. Ministry for Development Aid. In the true spirit of aid for underdeveloped countries, I flew business class and stayed at the posh Yak and Yeti Hotel. It was a very different experience. When I transited with my briefcase in a *riksha* from a business meeting to the hotel, I kept looking around and hoping that nobody I met 14 years earlier would recognize me. I felt like a traitor to my group of poor backpackers, frequenting Freak Street and the Chai and Pie shop and opposing bourgeois society. I thought about "*The Godfather*," which I had watched on the plane, and how Don Corleone had said, "one lawyer with a briefcase can steal more than a hundred men with guns."

I was being paid by USAID to research whether or not Nepal should become an offshore financial center. I felt a little apprehensive about that, given my earlier trekking experiences. Shouldn't this country stay as it was, rather than being modernized and destroyed by wealth and progress? I knew this was a selfish response, but I couldn't stop thinking about it. I conducted interviews with almost everyone in the financial services sector, including the Minister of Finance. While we were speaking in his office, we were interrupted every few minutes by someone coming to use the phone. When I looked annoyed at the umpteenth interruption, someone explained to me that the Ministry had only one phone. All official Ministry business, as well as the Ministry of Finance's international contacts, had to be conducted from that one phone.

I visited all the banks and every financial advisor. Then I went to see the Stock Exchange. This was a really fun visit. The Exchange was not much more than a shack with a tin roof. It employed some 20 people, most of them equipped with sturdy bicycles. When an order came in to purchase shares (i.e., a buyer walked into the premises), the hand-written stock register of the relevant company was checked, and the broker-dealers went out on bicycles to find a willing seller. If one of them found a willing seller, they brought that person on the back of a bike to the Exchange. Negotiations took place and the deal was sealed with a handshake. The shares were purchased and sold on the spot, cash changed hands, the register was adjusted with pen and ink, the stock exchange retained its margin in cash, and the old school blackboard in the corner with all the listed shares was updated with chalk. "You see", said the CEO of the Kathmandu Stock Exchange, "same-day settlement and delivery, just as at the London Stock Exchange". I could only marvel at the simplicity and efficiency of that low-impact system.

I asked why the names of certain companies on the blackboard were crossed out. Apparently, those companies didn't make it. The Nepalese textile business at that time was suffering heavy competition from its neighbor and main trading partners in India. During the few weeks I spent in Nepal, there was political unrest created by anti-monarchist Marxist groups; people were killed on the streets while protesting, the border with India was closed to prevent smuggling, and the newspapers were full of stories about Indian politicians hiding money in Nepal.

I therefore had no choice but to report that Nepal did not meet the minimum requirements to become an offshore financial center. When I was back (in Curaçao), I finished my report and sent it off to the USAID in Washington and to various financial contacts in Nepal. I did not hear anything back from the Nepalese Ministry of Finance; when I enquired, a few weeks later, it turned out that the DHL donkey had got caught in a mudslide and I needed to resend my report. In the end, the Nepal Government decided against developing a financial center and selected more nature-oriented development aid projects. I felt very relieved. I love the country, and prefer to see it as a spiritual center and base for hiking and exploring the mountains and Buddhism, rather than as a center for devising new financial strategies.

It took me another 20 years to make it back to Nepal. The city had grown beyond recognition. There was incomparably more wealth; people and cars were everywhere. I looked for Chai and Pie but couldn't find it. Freak Street had disappeared from all the maps after a government clean-up. It was full of Indian-owned clothing shops and massage parlors; progress had reached Nepal. But the pace of life, and the many temples around the Durbar squares in Kathmandu and Patan were still the same, although the cities had grown together into one. This time, the nature of the project I was visiting Kathmandu for seemed even more ambitious: financially structuring a subway system for Kathmandu, to alleviate killing traffic in a city that, by then, had grown to more than a million inhabitants. The project moved slowly. Shortly after I left, a big earthquake destroyed many of the age-old buildings I had learned to recognize and enjoy.

The reason the Earth is shaking and trembling is because she just cannot bear the weight of people's greed, suffering and misbehavior any longer, a priest writes in a matter-of-fact manner. People have become selfish and forget about their communities. They forget to worship and be thankful for their existence.[83]

Needless to say, that explanation put the subway project off the cards for years to come. The spirituality of the land forced me into soul-searching and reaching out toward what was beyond my comprehension. I thought about the enormous task of resurrecting the mighty tantric structures in Kathmandu's Durbar Square, a job I feared was not progressing quickly. Nepal needs much better planning before it is too late for sustainable development, a process that would meet human development goals for its rapidly growing population, while sustaining the ability of natural systems to continue to provide the resources and ecosystem services on which the economy and society depend.

---

[83] Tree, Isabella. "No Nepalis, Earthquakes Send Humans Warning From the Gods", National Geographic, May 14, 2015.

Neighboring Bhutan is ahead in many ways. Any flight into Bhutan's Paro airport is spectacular. The Druk (Dragon) Airplane, coming in from Calcutta, swirls between the mountains like a true dragon and must lean on one wingtip and then on the other to reach the tarmac between the mountain tops.

Bhutan is a very traditional and interesting country. It deliberately (by law) holds onto many of its old traditions, clothing, and housing styles, while at the same time being thoroughly modern in some of its policies.

In 1916 (a full 100 years ago), the first King of Bhutan, Ugyen Wangchuck, promulgated a ban on the filthy and noxious herb known as tobacco. Individuals were allowed to import tobacco and tobacco products only for personal consumption, according to limits set by the Tobacco Control Board, subject to duties and taxes. Those who brought their own tobacco or tobacco products into Bhutan had to show proof of taxation. They could only bring in goods that displayed the required health warnings, and could not bring in goods that promoted tobacco using false or misleading information, or anything likely to create an erroneous impression of its characteristics, health effects, or hazards (for example, by describing it as "light or mild"). Foreign visitors were allowed to smoke what they brought in, provided they carried with them at all times the original receipt from a foreign provider. Marijuana, which grows as a shrub in Bhutan, was only used to feed pigs before the introduction of television. When I looked around the country, I saw cannabis (marijuana) plants growing everywhere. Several times, when I entered a temple, I saw those plants being used as sturdy brooms. I found it an interesting thought that in a country of plenty, the economic value of marijuana was reduced to zero. Unfortunately, in recent years, the number of people arrested for trading and smoking marijuana has gone up.

The number one contribution to Bhutan's Gross Domestic Product (GDP) comes from selling clean energy (hydro-electric power) to India. The number two contribution is tourism. Remarkably, however, Bhutan is less interested in counting its GDP than its GNH or Gross National Happiness, a measure of the collective happiness of the nation.

The term was coined in 1972 by Bhutan's fourth Dragon King, Jigme Singye Wangchuck. Originally, the phrase represented a commitment to building an economy that would serve Bhutan's culture, based on Buddhist spiritual values, instead of Western material development.

> *Today, GNH has come to mean so many things to so many people. To me, it signifies simply—Development with Values. Thus for my nation today GNH is the bridge between the fundamental values of kindness, equality, and humanity and the necessary pursuit of economic growth.*[84]

—Jigme Dorji Wangchuk

GNH measures the progress of Bhutan as a nation on the basis of parameters such as:

1) Sustainable development

2) Preservation and promotion of cultural values

3) Conservation of the natural environment

4) Establishment of good governance.

The GNH concept has evolved, through the work of international scholars and researchers, into a socioeconomic development framework. The GNH policy now serves as a unifying vision for Bhutan's five-year planning process and all the derived planning documents that guide the country's economic and social development plans. Proposed policies in Bhutan must pass a GNH review based on an impact statement (by coincidence, very similar to the impact study needed when creating a nature reserve in South Africa, calculating the carrying capacity and ecological footprint of each and every species introduced.)

In July 2011, the United Nations passed a resolution (number 65/309) that was adopted unanimously by the General Assembly, placing happiness on the global development agenda and defining the four pillars in relation to eight contributing factors: happiness; physical, mental, and spiritual health; time

---

[84] His Majesty Jigme Singye Wangchuck, the Fourth Druk Gyalpo, King of Bhutan. His Majesty the King, on his first State Visit to India, delivered a talk titled "Changing World and Timeless Value" in Madhavrao Scindia Memorial Lecture hall in New Delhi about Gross National Happiness (GNH).

balance; social and community vitality; cultural vitality; good education; decent and fairly equal living standards; and a sound environment.

Hiking is a serious affair in Bhutan. The country contains the highest unclimbed mountain in the world in terms of elevation: Gangkhar Puensum, at 7,570 meters. It is on or near the border with China. In Bhutan, climbing mountains higher than 6,000 meters has been prohibited since 1994. The rationale is based on a combination of respect for the Bhutanese people's traditional belief that mountain peaks are the sacred homes of protective deities and spirits, and, of course, the lack of high-altitude rescue resources.

We settle on a very modest but steep climb to Taktsang, a monastery glued against the side of a rocky cliff above the Paro valley in Bhutan. The going is fairly easy if taken slowly, as the path is well-constructed and maintained and the mountain air is fresh and cool. The pilgrimage to Taktsang, also known as Tiger's Nest, is the highpoint of most travelers' visits to Bhutan. For us, it was the final stop on a trip that had taken us around the western part of the kingdom, visiting *dzongs* (monastery fortresses), temples, and the wintering grounds of white-bellied herons and black-necked cranes. We had had plenty of time to acclimatize to the altitude and there had been at least two long walks through farms and villages to prepare us for the climb to the Tiger's Nest. We knew that, at the end of a day of climbing, there would be a traditional Bhutanese wooden bathtub containing water heated by large mineral stones that had been kept in open fires for hours and placed in the tub as required for the amount of heat needed.

Taktsang is the holiest site in Bhutan. It's where Guru Rinpoche, also known as Padmasambhava, materialized some 1,300 years ago on the back of a flying tigress. Finding shelter in a series of caves, he meditated for some three years and then set about converting the Bhutanese to Buddhism, still the state religion. The monastery that commemorates this auspicious beginning was built nine centuries later, in the 1600s, although the buildings have had to be replaced several times. But, as the Bhutanese point out, buildings are temporal and meant to be renewed; the ideas and philosophies they represent cannot be destroyed.

The final approach to the monastery, after a two-hour climb to some 3,000 meters, is over a bridge across a waterfall. The entire area is wrapped in prayer flags in five colors, arranged from left to right in a specific order: blue, white, red, green, and yellow. The five colors represent the five elements and the five pure lights or wisdoms. Different elements are associated with different colors for specific traditions, purposes, and *sadhana* (mind and soul in practice towards a spiritual goal), and are used to promote peace, compassion, strength, and wisdom for all directions and all beings. As they disintegrate over time, their essence gets absorbed by the environment. Old prayer flags may not be discarded when finally removed, only burnt.

Meanwhile, crevices in the rocks are crammed with cute *tsa-tsas*, small reliquaries containing ashes of the dead. I could not resist the temptation to take one back with me. My wife later, back home, was upset when she found the *tsa-tsa* in my toilet bag, and forced me to take it back on my very next trip. Unfortunately for this Bhutanese spirit, my next trip happened to be to Abu Dhabi, and there is now one lonely *tsa-tsa* dwelling in Qasr al Sarab, facing the desert. I hope he likes the scorching heat and unobstructed view of the desert.

Entry to the sanctuary was granted, if shoes, cameras, cell phones, and other electronic equipment were left at the gates. A security guard patted us down and instructed us to dust and straighten our clothes out of respect. Inside, I visited the various temples and chambers crammed with Buddhist icons and heaped offerings of food and money. Flickering traditional butter lamps cast a warm, ethereal light. In one temple, we encountered a monk watching over the door that sealed the cave used by Padmasambhava all those centuries ago. It is opened only once a year in a special ceremony. The monk blessed us and poured saffron-laced water into our hands; we had to bring it to our lips and splash it onto our heads. In the next sanctuary, we found a monk chanting from sacred texts who invited us to come and meditate.

Meditating in a temple in the clouds, three-thousand meters up on the side of a mountain deep in the Himalayas, is not difficult, even though I am getting too old and fat to enjoy sitting cross-legged. I do not even attempt the lotus posture. It is a matter of letting go of all thoughts, memories, worries, wishes, and dreams.

Wherever you are, be there totally.[85]

—**Eckhart Tolle**

---

[85]   Tolle, Eckhart. *The Power of Now: A Guide to Spiritual Enlightenment,* Canada: Namaste Publishing, 1997.

As I was engulfed in silence, staring into the fierce eyes of one of the statues, I let my mind wander to the need for sustainable development everywhere, so that these magical places, and everything they stand for, do not disappear.

Having spent much time in nature, I often encountered man-made degradation and destruction. Over time, I composed the following list of relatively easy-to-achieve sustainable improvements for some of the places I have been involved in, including the Mapesu Private Game Reserve, the Aloe Farms, Alpasión, the Chile Forestadora Project, and the Bali Community Center project.

Sustainable Development, organic farming, and conserving our natural environment:

1) We aim to depend as much as possible only on sustainable energy, like solar power, and to go completely off the grid, if possible. In Curaçao, we built parking lots at our new office that were covered by solar panels to create both shade and electricity; we did something comparable at the aloe factory, covering over 95 percent of our electricity needs with clean solar power. When too many others on the island followed our example, the government reacted by imposing a solar tax, taking away most of the financial advantage. The sun now no longer comes up for free in Curaçao.

2) At the Mapesu Private Game Reserve, we strive to reach, within a reasonable timeframe (we are clearly not there yet), the stage of zero fossil fuels, other than for vehicles, achieving this by a combination of solar power and wind mills for pumping water, replacing diesel pumps that need to be checked and refilled regularly, creating energy efficiency, for example by heat exchange and durable light bulbs, and minimizing the use of energy-inefficient equipment, such as air conditioners by using time- or movement-related switches.

3) We want all of our farming to be organic, relying on fertilizers of organic origin such as compost, manure, green manure, and bone meal. We want to emphasize techniques such as crop rotation and companion planting. Biological pest control, mixed cropping, and the fostering of insect predators are encouraged. In general, organic standards are designed to allow the use of naturally occurring substances

while prohibiting or strictly limiting synthetic substances. Naturally occurring pesticides are permitted, while synthetic fertilizers and chemical pesticides are avoided. Genetically modified organisms, nanomaterials, human sewage sludge, plant growth regulators, hormones, and antibiotic use in animal husbandry are prohibited. The advantages of organic farming include sustainability, openness, self-sufficiency, autonomy, health, food security, and food safety. We apply as many organic principles as possible in both our aloe vera and grape production. The ultimate result of natural farming is not just the cultivation of crops, but the perfection of human minds. In addition, if you eat healthy ingredients and organic foods, after death, your body will decompose properly and contribute to the quality of the topsoil.

4) In the dry areas where we operate, we drip-feed plants, separate water circuits for clean, grey, and black water, apply water recycling and reuse grey water. The Desa Les Community Center will eventually use the rain and waste water of the community center to feed and grow fish, which in turn will reappear as Ikan Bumbu Bali on the menu of the center.

5) We apply waste management (re-use, recycle, reduce), by being very serious about recycling, using absolutely no plastics in construction (other than for piping), in packaging, or in day-to-day consumption, and creating as little landfill material as possible. We push the use of reusable bottles, bags, and other packaging. You would be surprised how much you think about waste management, once you live 50 kilometers from the nearest garbage dump. We also recycle food and butchering waste (some people keep pigs for that; we raise crocodiles in Africa), compost and use worms, collect manure, and make biochar to fertilize the aloe vera and lucerne lands.

6) We produce significant quantities of biochar, charcoal used as a soil enhancer. Like most charcoal, biochar is made from biomass (in our case surplus mopane wood) via pyrolysis. Biochar produces negative carbon dioxide emissions and thus has the potential to help mitigate climate change via carbon extraction. Independently, biochar can increase the fertility of acidic (low pH) soils, increase agricultural

productivity, and provide protection against some foliar and soil-borne diseases. It also reduces pressure on forests. Biochar is a stable solid, rich in carbon, which can endure in soil for thousands of years.

7) We try to eat and serve in our lodge and restaurants food grown in our immediate environment. The sustainable permaculture garden in Bali grows crops and herbs on-site in their natural environment, provides healthy, good-margin, fresh vegetables and fruits year-round, supports local farmers, and helps to avoid wasting fossil energy transporting food. We adhere to the Balinese spiritual calendar and follow the auspicious days for cleaning the land, seeding, pruning, and harvesting.

8) We support farmers near the Desa Les Community Center and will teach them the principles of permaculture. Permaculture has been defined as a philosophy of working with, rather than against, nature; of protracted and thoughtful observation, rather than protracted and thoughtless labor. It involves looking at all of the roles played by plants and animals, rather than treating any area as a single product system. In permaculture, we avoid using non-renewable resources or synthetic fertilizers and pesticides; we do not remove topsoil or reduce biodiversity. There is no ploughing in permaculture; we strive for a tantric balance between needs and production, making sure that we return to the earth everything it needs to sustain itself and us; as a matter of principle, we don't take more than we need.

9) We continuously work on soil restoration. At the Mapesu Private Game Reserve, we restore nature by replacing the shrub cover (mostly mopane and sickle bush) caused by overgrazing with new grassland, using harvested trees for bush-packing (fighting soil erosion), fencing, and making charcoal and biochar. We plant trees to restore biodiversity, build gabions to prevent topsoil erosion, and create water catchment areas to collect scarce rain water.

10) We offset the CO_2 used in driving and flying; where possible, we use electric rather than fossil fuel-driven equipment.

11) We conserve office materials, always printing on both sides of acid-free paper. The office is as green and as sustainable as possible. It is

better to save a tree than to cut it down to make paper and print a story about the tree.

12) We are always looking for sustainable funding or income. At some point, every development project must become self-sustainable. The Mapesu Private Game Reserve must attract tourists; the Desa Les Community Center needs help from restaurants and hotels that it also adds value to; the vineyard must sell enough wine to be profitable; the aloe project must sell enough cosmetics to pay for health drinks. Each year, the economic merit of each project must be evaluated; if it cannot be made self-sustainable, it must be terminated.

Sustainable activities may at first seem a bit futile, given how much waste is produced and how minimal one person's efforts may seem. However, after a while it becomes a challenge to create the smallest ecological impact possible. Recurring choices (such as eating vegetables or meat) are easier to make once we understand the impact of those choices (a meat-based meal has 3–5 times the ecological impact of a vegetarian one).

Think about your ecological footprint, and do something about it. Your ecological footprint is a measure of your impact on the earth's ecosystems. It's typically measured by assessing the amount of wilderness space or natural capital consumed each year to maintain a human population, including the area needed to assimilate human waste. The average world citizen has an ecological footprint of about 2.7 global average hectares (9 hectares in the US and 1.8 hectares in China) while there are only 2.1 global hectares of bio-productive land and water per capita on earth. This means that humanity has already overshot the global bio-capacity by 30 percent and now lives unsustainably, depleting stocks of natural capital. As Mohandas Gandhi said many years ago: "our earth produces enough for everyone's need, but not enough for everyone's greed."

I would urge each company, family, and individual to adopt a sustainability strategy! There are so many of us, and together we have only one Earth. Any adjustment towards a more sustainable approach makes a difference. Mohandas Gandhi said that:

There are but two roads that lead to an important goal and to the doing of great things: strength and perseverance. Strength is the lot of but a few privileged men; but austere perseverance, harsh and continuous, may be employed by the smallest of us and rarely fails of its purpose, for its silent power grows irresistibly greater with time.

Apart from what we all can do for ourselves, we can also enhance and multiply our efforts by investing in projects that reduce our ecological footprint. There are many such projects, in almost every vulnerable part of the world.

Chapter 16

Investing in green consciousness—the consequences of humans' impact on the environment.

If I knew that today would be the last time I'd see you, I would hug you tight and pray the Lord be the keeper of your soul. If I knew that this would be the last time you pass through this door, I'd embrace you, kiss you, and call you back for one more. If I knew that this would be the last time I would hear your voice, I'd take hold of each word to be able to hear it over and over again. If I knew this is the last time I see you, I'd tell you I love you, and would not just assume foolishly you know it already.[86]

—Gabriel García Márquez

Forests, for me, have a certain magic. From afar, they seem dignified and cool (often up to ten degrees cooler than the surrounding land); when they engulf you, they seem to breathe, listen, and watch as a collective, rather than as a collection of individual trees. In a big forest, I always lower my voice and feel watched. Most stories set in forests have some mystery. The truth is, we don't know nearly enough about what goes on in old-growth forests. If we spent more time understanding the complex interactions in forests, we would have more productive forests and more space to properly enjoy old-growth forests. Henry David Thoreau, a hundred years ago, sadly captured our one-sided view of forests when he wrote:

If a man walks in the woods for love of them half of each day, he is in danger of being regarded as a loafer. But if he spends his days as a speculator, shearing off

---

[86] Márquez, Gabriel García. *Love in the Time of Cholera*, translated by Edith Grossman, London: Penguin Books, 2007.

those woods and making the earth bald before her time, he is deemed an industrious and enterprising citizen.[87]

Recent scientific research has finally proven what people who live in nature have known all along—that forest trees communicate with each other through smells (various gases emitted to meet different needs), sounds (mostly underground), and by exchanging chemicals through interconnected root systems. The underground root-like filament systems (rhizomorphs) of fungi are used as a forest-wide Internet to spread information faster and further than the one-centimeter-per-hour speed of chemical information exchange. To maintain a healthy ecosystem, trees of the same species support each other (as African acacias do); sometimes deciduous and coniferous trees cooperate. This is not pure philanthropy. As Adam Smith wrote in 1776: "It is not from the benevolence of the butcher, the brewer, or the baker that we expect our dinner, but from their regard to their own interest."[88] The same applies to animals and trees. In beech forests in Europe and North America, stronger trees connect via their root systems with weaker trees and support them for tens of years with nutrients and sugars, in order to maintain a closed and even canopy and prevent other species from invading their space.

Fungi can grow quite big; the largest one known, an Oregon honey mushroom (Armillaria ostoyae), spreads across 10 square kilometers of ground; it is at least 2,400 years old and weighs at least 1,600 tons. It feeds on and lives in harmony with an entire forest.

Humans favor their own children. An experiment was conducted to determine whether trees do the same: whether Douglas firs recognize their own kin, as bears recognize their cubs. Mother trees grown near their own and unrelated seedlings did recognize their kids. The mother trees colonized their kin using larger mycorrhizal networks (fungal links for exchanging water, minerals, and carbohydrates). They even reduced their own root competition to make room for their kids. When mother trees were injured or dying, they sent messages of wisdom to their seedlings. Isotope tracing has been used to trace carbon and defense signals moving from an injured mother tree down her trunk into the

---

[87]   Thoreau, Henry David, Foreword by Richard Francis Fleck. Citizen Thoreau, Portland, Oregon: Graphic Arts Books, 2014.

[88]   Smith, Adam. The Wealth of Nations, Simon & Brown: 2012. Originally published March 9, 1776.

mycorrhizal network toward her neighboring seedlings. These two compounds increased the resistance of those seedlings to future stresses. So, trees actually do communicate and do what they can to strengthen and protect their offspring. They also store minerals like nitrogen and phosphate when they anticipate future shortages due to climatic variations. On Mapesu, our private game reserve in South Africa, fever trees (Vachellia xanthophloea) store salts and toxins in sacrificial limbs, branches that concentrate unwanted minerals and then die and break off. In Argentina at the Alpasión vineyard, open spots in the vineyard are filled by leading branches of neighboring vines into the soil to take root and form a new plant. After a while the connection between the two plants need to be severed as ALWAYS the mother plant keeps feeding its kid long after needed and to its own detriment.

Every tree stores millions of calories in the form of sugar, cellulose, lignin, and other carbohydrates. In addition, trees hold water and CO_2, provide shelter to animals and birds, and feed lots of insects, mushrooms, and fungi.

To ensure they can procreate effectively, beeches produce flowers and beechnuts only once every 3–5 years. When they do produce nuts, they are so abundant that wild boars, deer, and other seed-eaters can't possibly eat them all. Lots of seeds germinate or are squirreled away for future germination. The abundance of beechnuts in one year will lead to a birth wave of wild boars or deer the following year. When the beeches don't produce seeds, the boars go hungry and don't multiply as rapidly. In this way, nature keeps a balance that benefits both the trees and the wild boars. Similarly, the wildebeest on the Serengeti plains all calve at the same time of year; because they overfeed the lions, most calves survive to embark on their annual great migration, where they repeat the same trick when crossing the crocodile-infested Grumeti and Mara rivers. By presenting the crocodiles with too many food choices at the same time, most wildebeest make it across.

Large forests are the lungs of the world, but there are only a few really big ones left: the Amazon Basin and the birch tree forests of Siberia are two of the most important. The wooded areas of North America, the Congo, and Indonesia are rapidly disappearing. Those that remain are often in marginal areas for food production; they must be maintained and expanded, so that they can generate enough oxygen for all of us to breathe.

Trees that are planted (on plantations and in production forests), instead of growing naturally from seeds, develop very differently. Not only do they grow more slowly (and benefit less from the experience of older trees in managing resources), they also seem to work less well together, becoming more susceptible to diseases and insect damage. When there is more in-depth research on the ways trees function and whole forests co-operate, we may be able to produce more wood per hectare of forest. However, this could negatively impact the trees' quality of life, just like our treatment of animals raised for food. At the very least, we can treat them with respect and harvest them under humane (sic!) circumstances.

Major sources of greenhouse gas emissions include the burning of fossil fuels (for example, by flying or travelling by car) and the outputs created by industries that rely on fossil fuels (coal, electricity derived from coal, natural gas, and oil). The major greenhouse gases are carbon dioxide, methane, nitrous oxide, and hydrofluorocarbons (HFCs), all of which increase the atmosphere's ability to trap infrared energy, thus affecting the climate and heating the atmosphere.

To offset the negative impact of these greenhouse gasses, the concept of carbon credits was introduced, reflecting our increasing awareness of the need to control emissions. The IPCC (Intergovernmental Panel on Climate Change) determined, after lengthy discussions and even lengthier position papers, that polluters would have to pay; those who come up with the solutions can benefit. A new market mechanism could therefore arise whereby simple greed is harnessed to protect our climate.

The mechanism was formalized in the Kyoto Protocol, an international agreement between more than 170 countries, succeeded by the Marrakesh Accords and the Paris Agreement, within the United Nations Framework Convention on Climate Change (UNFCCC). The agreements address greenhouse gas emissions, mitigation, adaptation, and finance, starting in 2020. The Paris Pledge for Action of November 2016 was the world's first comprehensive agreement between all civilized countries to keep the increase in the earth's temperature below two degrees (counting from pre-industrial levels).

At some stage, before all this humbug, we decided that our small company should become a green company, having no negative impact on the local or global environment, the community, or the economy. A green business also engages in forward-thinking policies about environmental concerns and policies that affect human rights.

We quickly found out that we were too small to buy or produce carbon credits for the official international markets (a pretty cumbersome and expensive process for smaller organizations), and so we decided on a simple in-house solution. In 2013, we agreed to track, report, and offset the production of our group's CO_2 from air travel. The Ami-Carbon CO_2 Offset Project became an initiative in our Green Consciousness Program.

Green Consciousness Initiatives:

1) We started by buying video-conferencing equipment for each of our offices, to reduce the need for flying, especially for internal training and meetings. Separately, we ran an internal awareness campaign to inform all employees about the why, where, what, when, and how of reducing their carbon footprints; we also showed them how to book carbon neutral flights through our Travel Desk.

2) We made sure that we had green processes in every office. We printed paper on both sides, avoided acidic paper, recycled printer ink cartridges, use re-usable cutlery, and kept plants for oxygen.

3) We did the math on oxygen consumed in air travel, based on the production of CO_2 per flight (long flights and bigger planes are per person per kilometer more economical than short flights and small planes). Based on the speed at which trees grow in Chile, the type of trees chosen, and the amount of oxygen they can be expected to produce over their lifecycle, we committed to planting 1 tree for every 1,000 kilometers flown by any of our employees, and began making financial provisions with each and every flight we booked.

4) We chose Chile as a place for planting, as we had an office nearby to keep an eye on the project. Chile was the best place to carry out this long-term project safely, securely (no risk of nationalization), and at relatively low cost compared to other countries (such

as Brazil, Ecuador, Thailand, and Indonesia). There were costs associated with the land (in Chile, we could own it outright), labor, and bureaucracy.

5) With each flight reservation, our travel desk notifies each employee how many kilometers his or her flight is and how the flight will be offset. The numbers are quite simple: for each unit of 1,000 kilometers, we set aside U.S. $5 to allocate land and plant and nurture one tree. The trip discussed below would require the planting of 10 trees and set aside U.S. $50 for that purpose.

The text reads:

Soaring High, Living Green

This 9,789-kilometer trip produces 989.60 KGs of carbon from jet fuel emissions that harm the environment, per traveler. It takes the oxygen produced by 10 trees during a year to minimize this impact. The company commits on your behalf to plant a tree for every 1,000 kilometers of all your air travel. We will do this for you and with you in a joint effort to stand out for a greener tomorrow. Fill these miles with smiles.

Wishing you a safe trip—Fly, Plant, and Rebalance

6) By December 2013, we had traveled 6,353,993 flight kilometers, producing about 657 tons of CO2 that required 6,354 trees to offset. From January to December 2014, our air travel increased to 10,109,451 air kilometers, almost 40 percent above the previous year (by that time, nobody could fly outside the system anymore). That produced 808 tons of CO2, which in turn required 10,110 trees to offset. 2015 and 2016 showed similar patterns of air travel. We can therefore assume that our company needs least 10,000 trees to neutralize our CO2 impact each year.

7) In 2015, we acquired about 50 hectares of land on the Pacific coast of Chile, some 5 hours south of Santiago. As the area is blessed

with very favorable conditions to plant trees, we will use it to offset our CO2 emissions from now on.

8) About 35,000 trees (mostly Radiata pine and eucalyptus) already planted on the land will immediately offset some of the emissions we have incurred since starting to track our air miles.

9) Next spring, we will plant an additional 70,000 Radiata pine trees. Employees and interested parties are encouraged to participate in the actual planting. The attributes of Radiata pine include fast growth, and an ability to sequester lots of CO2 and release oxygen. Once the trees have reached an optimum size, they can be harvested and used in the construction and paper industry; the land will then be replanted.

10) The idea is to regularly plant and add more land over time. In this way, we support our own lungs by consistently neutralizing our carbon fuel footprint.

11) We are offering clients and serious third parties an opportunity to participate in and strengthen the project. If we can add only 50 hectares a year, this will become a sizeable forest over time.

12) There already is a small block hut on the land; we are planning to improve it and add another one, both off the electric grid, powered by solar energy, so that visitors (two families at a time) can stay there, fish in the river, go horseback riding, and enjoy the fresh forest air, just ten kilometers from the Pacific Ocean.

It will take some time for the trees to be fully grown and able to fully offset our annual CO2 usage. In time, we be able to offset not only our own impact, but also that of any clients who would like us to plant and maintain trees on their behalf.

Although we will ultimately harvest and replace the trees, when they have reached maturity and their growth rate is reduced, this will happen gradually. At the same time, we will continue to increase our forest area.

The most difficult thing is the decision to act, the rest is merely tenacity. The fears are paper tigers. You can do anything you decide to do. You can act to change and control your life; and the procedure, the process is its own reward.[89]

—Amelia Earhart

---

[89]   http://www.ameliaearhart.com/quotes/

Chapter 17

Suppression and Exploitation
- freedom is not free

Standing up for our values will help to strengthen them.

Once more the passer-by will stop in front of a house and ask: What is this, why is the gamelan silent, why are no girls singing? And once more the reply will be that a man has died.

And he who travels through the villages, will at dusk sit with his landlord, and around him the sons and daughters of the house, and the children from the village, and he shall say:

A man died who promised to be righteous, and he sold righteousness to anyone who gave him money. He fertilized his fields with the sweat of the laborer whom he had called from his own fields. He denied the laborer his wages and ate the poor man's food. He became rich from the poverty of others. He had plenty of gold and silver and precious stones, but the neighboring farmer could not satisfy his child's hunger. He smiled like a happy man, and there was gnashing of teeth for the man who complained and wanted his right. There was satisfaction in his face, but no milk in the breasts of the mothers.

And the inhabitants of the villages will say: Allah is good... we curse nobody!

Chiefs of Lebak, one day we will all die!

What shall be said in the villages where we had authority? What will be said by the passers-by who behold the funeral?

And what shall we answer, when we have died and a voice speaks to our souls, asking: Why is there weeping in the fields, and why are the young men hiding? Who took the harvest from the sheds, and from the stables the water buffalo which was supposed to plough the fields? What have you done with the brother whom I expected you to guard? Why is the poor man sad and why does he curse his wife's fertility? [90]

—Max Havelaar, speech to the Heads of Lebak

Suppression exists in many forms. The above quote, written in 1860, is probably the most famous and influential example in Dutch literature, exposing the excesses of colonialism. It galvanized public opinion in the Netherlands and set the stage for a more humane and (arguably) less exploitative phase of Dutch supremacy in the Dutch East Indies (now Indonesia), by creating the foundation for a New Ethical Policy, which used some of the profits made in Indonesia to improve schooling, healthcare, road and railway systems, and scientific research—mainly as a way to justify continued suppression.

Colonialism is defined as the establishment, either through military or financial force, and the exploitation and maintenance of *de-facto* control in one territory by a political power from another territory. It contains a set of unequal relationships between the colonial power and the colony and often also between the colonists and the indigenous population, usually maintained by brute military force. Investments that develop people and create infrastructure to exploit the wealth of the colony are often used to justify exploitation. Such justifications fall into the same category as trying to defend the gas chambers by pointing out the beautiful Autobahns created under Nazi rule.

By definition, colonial powers always extracted much more from their colonies than they invested in them (in the Dutch East Indies, through the *Batig Saldo* or Net Return on Investment Policy). Generations of wealth accumulated in the Netherlands, and much of its 19th and 20th century infrastructure, were financed by exploiting the people of the East Indies. Colonialism gave birth to the world's first multinational company divided into shares (the Dutch East Indies Company or VOC, which was active between 1602 and 1800), and the world's first stock exchange (founded in Amsterdam, also in 1602).

---

[90] Dekker, Eduard Douwes. *Max Havelaar, Or the Coffee Auctions of the Dutch Trade Company*, USA: ReadHowYouWant, 2008.

There have been and still are many instances of colonialism in the world. We are all familiar with the hundreds of years of Dutch exploitation of Java and the Spice Islands of Indonesia, the British Raj and its precursors in India, and the Spanish and later American exploitation of Cuba and much of Central America. But the near complete eradication of Native Americans in the US and the First Nations in Canada, the marginalization of aborigines in Australia, the long-lasting suppression of the Khoi San and Bantus in South Africa, 20th-century Japanese efforts to create a greater East Asian "Co-prosperity Sphere," the Russian conquest of Siberia and the traditionally Muslim territories of Southern Russia, and the German attempt to create Lebensraum in Eastern Europe, all fall into this category as well. In all cases, the colonized countries have suffered as a result.

Jawaharlal Nehru, the first Prime Minister of India, commented as follows on the economic effects of British rule, in his book, *The Discovery of India:*

A significant fact which stands out is that those parts of India which have been longest under British rule are the poorest today. Indeed, some kind of chart might be drawn up to indicate the close connection between length of British rule and progressive growth of poverty.[91]

Around the year 1500, India commanded about 33 percent of the world's GNP; by 1947, this had collapsed to 4.3 percent. It will take a long time for India to recover its global average (at least 15 percent of the world's GNP). Foreign interference in China had a similarly devastating effect. From 35 percent of GNP in the 1820s, it dived to less than 5 percent in the 1940s and 1950s; however, China has shown a strong recovery since Deng Xiaoping declared that "to be rich is glorious."

I was lucky to grow up after colonialism's more blatant excesses had been eradicated. Many African and Asian countries had obtained sovereignty (although, in practice, many of those newly independent countries remained for years economically subservient to European or American powers.) A vague sense of collective guilt continues to haunt the Netherlands. Even seventy years after a popular revolt in Indonesia brought Dutch domination to an end, this revolution, which took the lives of hundreds of thousands of Indonesians

---

[91] Nehru, *Discovery*, 296-9, 284. See Clairmonte, *Economic Liberalism*, ch. 2, for much confirming evidence.

(known as "ploppers") and 6,000 Dutch, as well as many British and Japanese people, is still defended as a police action.

When I first visited Indonesia in 1980, I saw the country very differently from others. I somehow felt that part of it was mine; although I never traced any family member back to Indonesia, I felt some misplaced sense of entitlement. After all, it was still referred to as "our" Indies. It is easy to forget how slowly civilization progresses, or how we judge the past with the benefit of hindsight.

Until 1865, one could legally buy and sell people in large parts of the U.S. (black people only, of course; white ones were never for sale). Until 1964, there was segregation; a black man could not sit next to a white man in a bus. In South Africa, some aspects of segregation lasted until the country's first free elections in 1994. Although South Africa did not promote or condone slavery to the same extent as the U.S., until 1935, the government issued official permits and paid bounties to shoot Bushmen (now known as the KhoiSan) as "vermin." Their bodies could also be stuffed and displayed in trophy collections (embarrassing for the heirs to such collections nowadays). Indian scalp hunting in the U.S. ended in 1885; the State of Massachusetts having paid the highest bounties.

Some countries, such as India, abolished slavery over 2,000 years ago (yet India is widely accused of having forms of slave labor even today). Many did so in the 18th or 19th century. The last countries to allow slavery (most of them in Africa) abolished it during the past few decades; some twenty to thirty million people in the world still suffer some form of slavery or bonded labor. The Australian government stole Aboriginal children until 1985; as many as one-third of the total number of Aboriginal children in the 1950s and 1960s were taken away from their parents by force.

I have great sympathy and admiration for people who suffered these kinds of abuse and still found the strength to forgive (but not forget). People like Nelson Mandela, who after spending 27 years in jail, found a way to work with the government of President de Klerk and negotiate a way out of Apartheid; if achieved through armed struggle, this could have taken years, cost many lives, and destroyed the country. The challenge is described very clearly in these words of Bishop Desmond Tutu:

Forgiving and being reconciled to our enemies or our loved ones are not about pretending that things are other than they are. It is not about patting one another on the back and turning a blind eye to the wrong. True reconciliation exposes the awfulness, the abuse, the hurt, the truth. It could even sometimes make things worse. It is a risky undertaking but in the end, it is worthwhile, because in the end only an honest confrontation with reality can bring real healing. Superficial reconciliation can bring only superficial healing.[92]

Of course, it also took admirable courage for existing leaders to give up power and put their trust in the transition they had helped to set in motion.

Modern-day forms of slavery include the sweatshops (from Morocco to Bangladesh) where most of our clothes come from, the plantations where bananas, coffee, and palm oil are grown, and the factories in China and elsewhere that make labor-intensive products. On the beaches of India and Bangladesh, many price-competitive ship-breaking businesses lack even the most basic safety measures; they cause heavy pollution and daily accidents. As Muhammed Shahin of Young Power in Social Action in Chittagong has explained:

Explosions of leftover gas and fumes in the tanks are the prime cause of accidents in the yards, other accidents are caused by falls—because the men are not given safety harnesses—or workers being crushed by falling beams or plates, or electrocuted. Most workers wear no protective gear and many work barefoot. There is hardly any testing system for the use of cranes, lifting machinery or a motorized pulley. The yards reuse ropes and chains recovered from the broken ships without testing their strength. Fires, gas explosions, falling steel plates, exposure to poisons from bunker oil, lubricants, paints and cargo slop have left thousands with respiratory diseases.[93]

The disabled and dead are easily replaced: for each open position there are at least ten job seekers.

We, as consumers, must demand to see the fair trade credentials of every product. The measures in place in the fair trade coffee market should become

---

[92]   Tutu, Desmond. "Truth and Reconciliation." *The Greater Good Science Center at the University of California, Berkeley* September 1, 2004. Online. https://greatergood.berkeley.edu/article/item/truth_and_reconciliation

[93]   John Vidal, "Bangladeshi workers risk lives in shipbreaking yards", Bangladesh, *The Observer*, May Saturday 5, 2012.

commonplace. Asian and European egg cartons tell shoppers how well the chickens that produced the eggs were treated—why not do the same for human beings? I want to see labels certifying that clothes were not made with child labor, certificates on buildings guaranteeing that safety measures were implemented during construction. We should demand best practice for all aspects of the economy.

We all now know that colonialism, child labor, abusive labor conditions, and the exploitation of employees are absolutely unacceptable; just a few generations ago, these were considered smart business practices. However, discrimination on the basis of gender, religion, cultural or ethnic background, sexual preferences, and clothing remain rampant today and have not markedly decreased. Some countries prohibit gay marriage, allow unequal pay between the sexes, and discriminate against religious groups, excluding them from sectors of the economy, or even the country as a whole. We talk a lot about fairness and equality; the reality is that when our personal (financial or other) interests come into play, we can rationalize lots of forms of abuse. I have heard people say that refusing to buy products made by child labor or people working for unfair wages in terrible conditions would put those people out of a job. Others say such conditions are inevitable—"if I don't do this, someone else will." Such excuses are commonly used by people selling drugs, and engaged in the trafficking of human beings and protected animal parts. We must protest against this way of thinking, and initiate concrete action to change the prevailing mentality.

Future generations may criticize us for poisoning our kids with unhealthy sodas and processed and fast foods, and for being hopelessly unfair in our treatment of domesticated animals for human consumption. We are naturally carnivores/omnivores, despite the understandable preferences of vegetarians and vegans. However, there is no reason, apart from pure stinginess, why calves, pigs, and chickens should spend their already artificially short lives in cramped, dark spaces, with no semblance of a normal social life.

As we start to learn more about how trees and plants behave and act, we may want to treat nature more considerately. If we destroy our own ecosystems, we will ultimately trigger our own extinction. By looking after nature, we will ultimately enhance the quality of our own lives.

In the end, our own mindset and carefully selected thoughts will determine the norms we want to live by, as a society, as a culture, as a generation and as individuals. It is easy to judge previous generations by the norms we apply today; someday, future generations will judge us by future norms. We should anticipate that, for our own sakes.

> *Carefully watch your thoughts, for they become your words. Manage and watch your words, for they will become your actions. Consider and judge your actions, for they have become your habits. Acknowledge and watch your habits, for they shall become your values. Understand and embrace your values, for they become your destiny.*

> **—Mohandas Gandhi**

None of us can correct all the wrongs in the world alone, but each of us can do something. It does not require a huge force to create a sea-change; it can be done by promoting and implementing an idea whose time has come, a truth that cannot be denied. As Mohandas Gandhi said:

We are our own slaves, not of the British. This should be engraved on our minds. The whites cannot remain if we do not want them. If the idea is to drive them out with firearms, let every Indian consider what precious little profit Europe has found in these.[94]

When Fidel Castro and his *guerilleros* landed with the Granma for the invasion of Cuba, they fell into an army ambush, in which 70 of the 82 invaders were either killed or taken prisoner. It took several days for Fidel Castro to meet up again with his brother Raúl and the few other survivors. When they finally met, Fidel asked Raúl how many rifles he had brought. "Five," Raúl answered. "That is great," said Fidel, "We have two, so together we have seven; now we will certainly win the war!"[95] Even his own brother considered this level of optimism a bit over the top. But less than 26 months later, Fidel had won the

---

[94] Gandhi, Mahatma. *The Essential Writings*. Edited with an Introduction and Notes by Judith M. Brown. Oxford World's Classics: New York 2008.

[95] Army General Raúl Castro Ruz, President of the Councils of Sate and of Ministers, during the closing ceremony of the Sixth Session of the Seventh Legislature of the National People's Power Assembly at Havana's Conference Center. December 18th, 2010, "Year 52 of the Revolution. http://www.radiorebelde.cu/english/news/full-text-of-speech-delivered-by-cuban-president-raul-castro-20101222/

fight and was in full control of all of Cuba. Perhaps this was partly the result of a string of lucky events, but it was mostly down to guts and grit and being totally committed to a just cause.

The important thing is to always be aware of what is happening around us; we must take pride in taking a stand on things that contradict our values. The worst thing we can do is imagine that we have no influence and cannot change the world. We all have it within our power to change the world; our inactivity is what keeps social and economic injustices in place.

> *Nothing better protects a human being against the stupidity of prejudice, racism, religious or political sectarianism, and exclusivist nationalism than this truth that invariably appears in great literature: that men and women of all nations and places are essentially equal, and only injustice sows among them discrimination, fear, and exploitation.*[96]

—Mario Vargas Llosa

It remains amazing how we, as human beings, seem to relish reducing our own personal freedom with limiting thoughts—even though, at the same time, we claim to crave freedom of movement, of thought, and from conventions.

We reduce the potential of our societies and companies by restricting access to the tribe or in-crowd through random segregations involving race, color, educational level, religion, caste, sexual preference, and gender, despite knowing full well that, by doing so, we are limiting the potential of the group. Hierarchy and continuous suppression feed our egos and promote feelings of superiority and security.

We create artificial limitations within society that initially seem to create order and organization, but soon get out of hand and limit most people's opportunities to benefit a small elite. Laws, rules, regulations, mores, workflows, and habits control just about everything. Such self-inflicted rules make life complicated and restrict our personal freedom. Many of our rules are not needed and only limit our potential.

---

[96]   Llosa, Mario Vargas, "Why Literature: The premature obituary of the book." *New Republic.* May 14, 2001. Online https://newrepublic.com/article/78238/mario-vargas-llosa-literature

However, they do provide security. We humans appear to enjoy self-imposed limitations to our freedom. We love to create our own prisons by hiding behind approvals, workflows, and regulations to avoid making decisions. We love restrictions on our authority that protect us from accountability and responsibility. We give up on success because "he who is born for a dime can never be a quarter." Only lucky or dishonest people willing to break the rules can be successful.

Schools help to rank people: a few good or outstanding individuals and lots of average and failing ones. Once a person has been labeled a failure, it is difficult for him or her to escape the stigma, except by rebelling or single-handedly building a multinational organization in a garage.

We buy the same sorts of cars as other people in our social environment, join the same golf clubs, and aspire to similar houses, lifestyles, clothes, and sex lives. Year after year, we take the same routes every day to work, vacation in the same places, sit in traffic-jams to get to work at the same time, eat the same food, have very similar opinions, join similar religions, choose to believe in the same Gods and priorities, and move through life in a largely pre-programmed way. Similarly, we aim to build a fortune for an old age that is already well-taken care of, and to feather the nests of our kids. The point is not that we don't have choices. The point is that we don't want choices.

Einstein said, "Common sense is nothing more than a deposit of prejudices laid down in the mind before you reach eighteen."[97] We love to follow the herd, be conventional, blend in, do what everyone else does, and think what everyone else thinks. We create our own prisons in our own minds, put the keys in our own pockets, and forget about them. We decide or accept early on what our professional and personal lives should look like, what to believe spiritually, politically, and economically, and what we want to look like. Once we have locked ourselves in, we may be bored to death, lose all passion for our work or partners, and still find it extremely difficult to take the prison keys from our pockets, unlock our cells, and exploit other thoughts, dreams, and limitless opportunities!

---

[97]   Quoted in Eric T. Bell, *Mathematics: Queen and Servant of Science*, Mathematical Truth (p. 42) McGraw-Hill book Company, Inc. New York, USA. 1951

Our limiting beliefs have created wars between all the major "one true" religions. They have led to the colonization of 80 percent of the world at one time or another, the murder of whole races and populations, the destruction of nature, animal species and whole ecosystems, and the prosecution of gays, Freemasons, and anyone thinking outside the box.

At some stage, we will have to learn that restrictions exist only in our own minds. All species of transient beings are in the same boat; insecurity and impermanence are part of our reality. We share a common fate and are essential components of a common universe. Without you, me, or any of us, the universe would not be the same. Our lives would be richer if all other elements of this universal ecosystem were valued and supported. Yes, nature will ensure that all individuals die and that their genes are shared and recycled. Some species disappear to make space for more evolved inventions of evolution; sooner or later, this may happen to us. In the meantime, we all depend on each other. We need and can add value to each other.

Enormous personal satisfaction can be derived from making sure that the people we interact with get a fair chance and can be their authentic, true selves, without facing restrictive discrimination, regulations, or conventions.

The universe has enough resources for all our needs, if not all our greed. We must break away from conventions and limiting beliefs. We must not accept crap from anyone. We must not buy crap for any reason. As mentioned before, we can always choose our own attitude in any given set of circumstances.

When our children finally find out that Santa Claus, the Easter bunny, the tooth fairy, Satan, the big bad wolf, God, and all of our other imaginary friends and foes do not exist, they rarely get angry. They are glad to know something that smaller children don't know. The same is true for all forms of limiting belief.

> *There is a way to be sane, just by being a simple witness of your thought processes. It is simply sitting silently, witnessing the thoughts passing before you. Just witnessing, not interfering not even judging, because the moment you judge you have lost the pure witness. The moment you say this is good, this is bad, you have already jumped onto the thought process.*

It takes a little time to create a gap between the witness and the mind. Once the gap is there, you are in for a great surprise, that you are not the mind, that you are the witness, a watcher.

And as you become more and more deeply rooted in witnessing, thoughts start disappearing. You are, but the mind is utterly empty.

That's the moment of enlightenment. That is the moment that you become for the first time an unconditioned, sane, really free human being.

—Osho

When we begin to truly understand that the world outside us is just a reflection of the world inside, we may wonder whom to blame for the problems in our lives. If one's childhood was difficult, how should one take responsibility for that? The same question arises in work and current relationships. We all know that blaming others is the exact opposite of taking responsibility, but we don't always understand how to take responsibility for things we don't truly feel responsible for. We may blame our parents for our low self-esteem, or our current partners for exacerbating it. We may blame our colleagues for things going wrong on the work floor. Objectively, this seems to make sense. After all, it is not our fault if our parents were irresponsible or unkind, or our partner badly-behaved. Anything that fails at work can be pushed onto a colleague's plate by hiding behind titles, responsibilities, rules, workflows, or job descriptions. Some people even think it makes them look good, if they can point out someone else's mistake.

You can get discouraged many times, but you are not a failure until you begin to blame somebody else and stop trying.

—John Burroughs

The problem lies with the act of blaming. Whether we blame others or ourselves, there is something aggressive and unkind about it. It sets up a situation in which it becomes difficult to move forward under the burdensome feelings of shame and guilt that arise. It also puts the resolution of our suffering into the hands of someone else. Ultimately, we cannot force others to take responsibility for their actions; they must make that choice when they are ready. In the meantime, if we want to move forward with our lives instead of waiting around for something that may or may not happen, it is wise to take the situation into our own hands. Our lives become instantly easier and healthier if we see everything as our own responsibility (to explore this idea further, read Joe Vitale's book on the Hawaiian healing process of Ho'oponopono). Influencing others is really difficult, but adjusting our attitude to practically anything is quite easy. It is like deliberately flipping a switch in our mind. The moment we decide to take responsibility for something, the issue is already half solved, as we start listening to various sides of an argument, look into root causes and consequences, and begin to see how to change the situation. The positive energies we create in this process generate solutions and make them happen. Being reactive, by assigning responsibility outside ourselves, wastes time on negative behavior. By contrast, being responsive, by actively looking for solutions, improves the atmosphere and makes it straightforward to resolve the issue at hand.

> *When you plant lettuce, if it does not grow well, you don't blame the lettuce. You look for reasons it is not doing well. It may need fertilizer, or more water, or less sun. You never blame the lettuce. Yet if we have problems with our friends or family, we blame the other person. But if we know how to take care of them, they will grow well, like the lettuce. Blaming has no positive effect at all, nor does trying to persuade using reason and arguments. That is my experience. No blame, no reasoning, no argument, just understanding.*[98]

—Thích Nhất Hạnh

The best thing we can do to improve the world is to stand up for our values, be missionaries of truth, help explain values, fight ignorance and limiting beliefs, and spread tolerance. The worst thing we can do is to do nothing. Theodore Roosevelt once said:

To sit home, read your favorite paper, and scoff at the misdeeds of the men who do things is easy, but it is markedly ineffective. It is what evil men count upon the good men's doing.[99]

---

[98]   Nhat, Hanh Thich. *At Home in the World: Stories and Essential Teachings from a Monk's Life,* Berkeley; California: Parallax Press, 2016.

[99]   Roosevelt, Theodore. "The Higher Life of American Cities," *Outlook,* December, 21, 1895

As masters of our souls, in full control of the universe, we can and must stand up for everything we feel strongly about. There are lots of actions we can undertake to spread our values, repay others, and fearlessly expose popular defects, at any time and wherever we are, with whatever we have!

Civil action, community service:

1) Join or start a pressure group or special causes group; become a member of a (political, religious, social) party in your local community and work on improving your community.

2) Join networks of people who spread the right ideas. The thought impact of organizations like the World Wildlife Fund, Peace Parks Foundation, and Médecins Sans Frontières has been enormous, far outpacing the impact of their actual activities.

3) Write books, articles and commentaries on the issues that motivate and stimulate you, and engage the people around you in discussions. You will be amazed at how good ideas resonate. And you will be even more amazed how little people seem to think about issues that matter to all of us. Or if they think about those issues, how little they convert their thoughts into action. Over the centuries, the impact of writers has far exceeded the impact of military commanders. Think of Karl Marx writing *Das Kapital* or Jean-Jacques Rousseau, whose *Contrat Social* introduced the principles of *liberté égalité fraternité* that underpinned the French and American revolutions.

4) Strongly oppose bureaucracy, anywhere, and everywhere you go. Bureaucracy robs life of its fun and kills initiative. It is also terribly expensive; both in a corporate and government environment, it steals resources from all stakeholders, clients, shareholders, and citizens. There is no excuse for even a limited amount of bureaucracy; it blunts intellect, kills initiative, adds costs, wastes time and resources, and makes our world a lot less pleasant.

5) A special form of bureaucracy is corruption and nepotism. It is illegal in most places and immoral everywhere. To pay people extra

for inappropriate reasons is plainly wrong and must be avoided at all times and at all costs. Even low levels of bureaucracy and corruption must be fought, as people get used to them and begin to tolerate more and more abuse. Expose corrupt people whenever and wherever you can.

6) Convert your ideas into practical examples. Convince supermarkets to eliminate plastic bags, municipalities to limit harmful activities, businesses to restrict pollution and engage in corporate social responsibility, and governments to produce the right type of legislation. Small ideas can have a large ripple effect.

7) Do not covet or display ostentatious wealth. Beyond a certain level of comfort, additional wealth will not make you happier or more satisfied—quite the contrary. Use your well-earned wealth to care for those who came before and after you, as well as society and spiritual needs. You will be appreciated more for driving a modest car and truly caring about others, than for driving a Rolls Royce, but adding little value to society.

8) Serve the community. Volunteer work is one of the best ways to expose yourself to a new medium of helping other people. There are tons of volunteer opportunities out there, from assisting elderly people at care homes, to working with delinquent kids, mentoring kids at orphanages, helping out at animal shelters, cleaning up the beach, shopping, gardening, and doing laundry for elderly or infirm people, and keeping the dying company. Volunteer work doesn't have to involve grandiose acts. As long as you offer a part of yourself pro bono to the world (skills, knowledge, time, effort, or money), you are volunteering. The return is that you will live a longer and happier life.

9) Protest loudly against what is wrong. The anti-Vietnam demonstrations in the 1960s ultimately had an effect, as did the anti-Apartheid demonstrations of the 1980s, and the anti-nuclear missile demonstrations of the 1990s. There are always things worth protesting against and rallying for.

10) Rage against lack of quality and inefficiency. Poor quality products waste precious natural resources, as well as time and money. Our life on earth is too short to accept half measures, potholed streets, poor electrical connections, cold coffee, bad wine, boring meetings (or worse, people rudely reading iPhones during dinner conversations), unprepared colleagues, half-done assignments, compromises, and lack of care or passion more generally. The lack of time or money is NEVER an acceptable excuse for a lack of quality.

11) Refuse military service; fight for world peace in non-lethal ways. Refuse to be part of any government or corporate activity that threatens the rights or lives of other people. Use your inner moral compass to stand up for the truth and what is ethical and just. Never close your eyes to injustice, abuse, or the misuse of power and authority.

A human being is a part of the whole universe, a part limited in time and space. He experiences himself, his thoughts and feeling as something separated from the rest, a kind of optical delusion of his consciousness. This delusion is a kind of prison for us, restricting us to our personal desires and to affection for a few persons nearest to us. Our task must be to free ourselves from this prison by widening our circle of compassion to embrace all living creatures and the whole of nature in its beauty.[100]

— **Albert Einstein**

The point here is that civil action, standing up for your beliefs, does not require capital to the extent that meaningful charity, philanthropy, corporate social responsibility, and social businesses do. Civil action and community service are accessible to all of us. They just require some of your time and some personal courage, depending on what needs to be achieved. If more people had had personal courage in Europe in the 1930s, they could have countered the rise of fascism. If more people had had personal courage in the 1950s and 1960s, segregation in the U.S. and Apartheid in South Africa would have ended much sooner. The ills of our times may not look as repugnant as those of earlier times, but the same thing was true then. Look around you; there is a lot of social

---

[100] Einstein, Albert. *The World as I See It.* Philosphical Library: New York, 1949.

injustice and inequality. Many people never get the chances they deserve. Every day, people die of easily prevented diseases and disasters, or the lack of proper drinking water and simple forms of care and help. There is plenty of nature to protect, and many habits to be changed. If you cannot find anything to improve around you, question your own personal courage and moral values! Later in life, you may regret the chances you ignored today.

> *It is not the critic who counts; not the man who points out how the strong man stumbles, or where the doer of deeds could have done them better. The credit belongs to the man who is actually in the arena, whose face is marred by dust and sweat and blood; who strives valiantly; who errs, who comes short again and again, because there is no effort without error and shortcoming; but who does actually strive to do the deeds; who knows great enthusiasms, the great devotions; who spends himself in a worthy cause; who at the best knows in the end the triumph of high achievement, and who at the worst, if he fails, at least fails while daring greatly, so that his place shall never be with those cold and timid souls who neither know victory nor defeat.*[101]

— Theodore Roosevelt

---

[101] Roosevelt, Theodore, in his speech, "The Man in the Arena", Sorbonne, Paris France, April 23, 1910.

Chapter 18

Invest in friendship as the cornerstone for achieving something together.

My love, suddenly your hip is the curve of the wineglass filled to the brim, your breast is the cluster, your hair the light of alcohol, your nipples the grapes, your navel pure seal stamped on your barrel of a belly, and your love the cascade of unquenchable wine, the brightness that falls on my senses, the earthen splendor of life.[102]

—Pablo Neruda, *The Essential Neruda*

One fateful morning I woke up knowing that I had to do something about my intellectual development. I'd been dreaming again about imposter syndrome (where you wake up bathed in sweat, believing that you never completed your formal education) and I felt I was getting stuck with routine solutions to the challenges I faced at the time. Reminded of Einstein's warning that "we cannot solve our problems with the same thinking we used when we created them," I decided to enroll for an Executive MBA at INSEAD in Fontainebleau. For me, this course confirmed that Einstein had a point when he said: "an education is what remains after you have forgotten everything you learned in school."

The Executive MBA was totally different from what I had expected. I ended up taking no class notes, but gathering lots of new-found wisdom and insights, as well as a wonderful group of new friends, including two of my professors, Manfred Kets de Vries and Sudhir Kakar, both great thinkers. The Challenge of Leadership (COL) course, as it was called, basically used us as business cases, and charged us for that. Each of us shared the remarkable episodes and struggles of our lives, while the others, after a few clarifying questions, commented on

---

[102] Neruda, Pablo. *The Essential Neruda: Selected Poems,* edited by Mark Esiner, City Lights Books, 2004

236

how the story made them feel, what associations it triggered, and how they would advise the narrator to change his or her life. The recommendations were the most interesting part, holding the answers to the questions bothering the person acting as advisor rather than the person advised. I finished the course with the clear and comforting conviction that, whatever lives we lead, we share the same key challenges, which we struggle with in very similar ways.

By the end of those weeks spent in Fontainebleau, Singapore, and Mulu, Borneo, we had become very close, having learned everything important about each other: every fear, dream, desire, love, and hate. During the day, we spoke about business and career-related challenges, our "inner theatres," in the evening, our discussions at the IBIS bar explored the personal, hidden, and darker sides of our lives. We wanted to make sure that we stayed in close contact—and so we did. For the past seven years, we have had memorable annual reunions at places around Europe. We enjoyed a beautiful closing dinner in a French country-style restaurant called Bas Breau in Barbizon, near Fontainebleau. Over the course of that evening, we agreed to develop a joint investment project. And as none of us knew anything about wine, beyond being expert or amateur drinkers, we agreed on Bill Fisher's idea (and my secret dream), to invest into a vineyard and develop our own brand of wine. The hidden or forgotten dreams of many of us came together in the courage of a fleeting spiritual moment. To use the words of Walt Disney, "all our dreams can come true if we have the courage to pursue them."

> *People who dream when they sleep at night know of a special kind of happiness which the world of the day holds not, a placid ecstasy, and ease of heart that are like honey on the tongue. They also know that the real glory of dreams lies in their atmosphere of unlimited freedom.*[103]

—Karen Blixen, *Out of Africa*

Eight members of our group were interested in pursuing the concept. Defining the scope of the project turned out to be more complicated than we had originally thought, not least because piloting a non-existent ship with eight captains was uncharted territory for most of us. We organized a couple of fact-finding trips and looked at small, existing wineries in France, but quickly realized that we could not afford the nicer ones. At the time, Chinese investors

---

[103]   Blixen, Karen. *Modern Classic Out of Africa*, Penguin Classic; New Ed Edition, 2001.

were buying up all the wineries they could lay their hands on. The situation in Italy was not much better.

We then made a very interesting trip from Porto to Beja in the Alentejo area, east of Lisbon to look at a beautiful place called Herdade do Vau. We flew out there in a tiny plane with one door missing (it was a plane used mainly for cartography), when the morning mists still lingered in the Douro Valley. The pilot was new to the plane, and possibly also to his role as a pilot; every step of the way, he had to consult his flight manual. This seemed odd to me and alarming to my son, who dislikes small planes anyway. We kept asking the pilot questions to make sure he knew what he was doing. However, we landed perfectly and had a great three-hour country-style lunch in Évora, with enough wine to raise our spirits and build up our courage (including that of the pilot.) Then we raced to the vineyard, with its beautiful old country house begging to be restored. When the light of day was beginning to fade, we were ready to fly back to Porto. Our pilot asked us to remind him to put out the landing gear; it clearly made him nervous that the plane had no autopilot controls, landing lights, or even enough light to read the manual; a summer storm was building up. We landed safely—with the landing gear out—just as the last bit of daylight died. However, it was the wrong landing strip, and quite a long distance from Porto. In the end, we loved the opportunity, but felt that the estate was too small for us to become serious winemakers. We did not like the Alentejo wines well enough to risk our lives for them. Using my Che Guevara yardstick to measure investments, we rejected Herdade do Vau on grounds of it being something to live for but not something we were willing to die for.

The next country on our list was Argentina, I have for many years had a love-hate relationship with this country and its intriguing culture.

> *Argentina's like a novel, he said, a lie, or make-believe at best. Buenos Aires is full of crooks and loudmouths, a hellish place, with nothing to recommend it except the women, and some of the writers, but only a few. Ah, but the pampas—the pampas are eternal. A limitless cemetery, that's what they're like.*[104]

> **—Roberto Bolano, *The Insufferable Gaucho***

---

[104]   Bolano, Roberto. *The Insufferable Gaucho,* translated by Chris Andrews, New York, Penguin Books Canada, 2010.

Argentina has a remarkably eclectic collection of heroes, who, like my Argentinian friends, all share a great sense of drama. There are famous soccer players like Lionel Messi, five-time winner of the Ballon d'Or for best soccer player in the world, and Diego Maradona, who has images of Fidel Castro and Che Guevara tattooed on his body and who swore that God once helped him to score a decisive goal. There are Ernesto Che Guevara, Evita Perón, Jorge Borges, and Pope Francis. There are also some interesting imaginary heroes, like La Difunta Correa, and Gauchito Gil. During the civil wars of the 1840s, La Difunta (Deolinda) Correa tried to follow her husband into the desert, after he was forcefully recruited into a band of Montoneros (partisans); she died of hunger and thirst when her supplies ran out. Her baby miraculously survived, drinking milk from her dead body's ever-flowing breasts, until a band of *gauchos* found it a few days later. Nowadays, her spirit protects road travelers. Everywhere in Northern and Western Argentina there are small shrines, decorated with large quantities of plastic water bottles, to quench her eternal thirst, where people commemorate her history and pray for a successful journey.

Gauchito Gil, a soldier in the Paraguayan War, became an honorable bandit like Robin Hood. When he finally got caught, he told the police sergeant who was about to execute him:

You are going to kill me now, but you will arrive in Mercedes (the town, not the car) tonight at the same time as a letter of my pardon. In the letter they will also tell you that your son is dying of a strange illness. If you pray and beg me to save your child, I promise you that he will live. If not, he will die.[105]

The sergeant was not impressed by these famous last words. Saying simply, "I don't care," he killed Gauchito Gil by slitting his throat. I still wonder whether this comment inspired Che Guevara, whose famous last words were, "Shoot, coward, you are only going to kill a man."

Of course, when the sergeant returned to Mercedes that evening, he indeed found a soldier there with a letter of pardon for Gauchito Gil. The letter also said that the sergeant's son was very ill with a strange disease, on the verge of dying. Frightened, the sergeant prayed to Gauchito Gil to save his son. The next day, his son was inexplicably cured, and all those present believed that

---

[105] *Francesca Fiorentini (2010-02-19).* "O Beloved Gauchito Gil: Worshipping a Homegrown Saint". *The Argentina Independent. Retrieved 2013-03-16.*

Gauchito Gil had saved him. Scared and grateful, the sergeant gave Gil's body a proper burial and built him a shrine in the shape of a red cross; this shrine was linked to lots of miracles. News of the miracle spread and Gauchito Gil became a folk hero. All over the interior of Argentina, you will pass small roadside shrines, often very well-kept, with red flags (not unlike the prayer flags of the Himalayas) and thank-you notes for miraculous recoveries.

We had a carefully selected list of small wineries in the Mendoza region to look at, but, over the course of a few days, became ever more enthusiastic and greedy. We abandoned the idea of buying a tiny old-growth vineyard and winery already in production from an old farmer and traditional winemaker, and, pushed by Jorge Carneiro, decided to go for a much bigger piece of virgin land, where we could shape all of our ideas from scratch, rather than building on the work of others. As Paulo Coelho says, "when you want something, all the universe conspires in helping you to achieve it." Fate guided us to a place that wasn't on our list, did not meet any of our carefully formulated criteria, and had nothing built or developed on it, in an area that—before the blessings of global warming—was considered too cold to plant grapes. These 85 hectares, which we bought out of a bankruptcy, lay pressed against the Andes Mountains, like the bodies of lovers fitting together. It was in the higher reaches of the Uco Valley, at 1,200 to 1,400 meters, close to Tupungato (in the Quechua language, "the place from which to gaze at the stars.")

We rented horses from nearby *gauchos* (in Manzana Histórico) and did our first *recorrido* through the dust of what soon was to become our property. It felt wonderful to survey land that nobody ever walked on, and we were all quickly sold.

In the background rose the snow-clad Andes Mountains. Rabbits fled in front of our horses, a fox or two crossed our path, and at some stage my horse disappeared halfway into a rabbit hole, or maybe it fell through all the way and I ended up at the other end, like Alice, in Wonderland. It did not matter. As Alice says, there's no point going back to yesterday, because "I was a different person then." We had passed the point of no return and were on our path to becoming high quality, organic winemakers.

Soon, we found out why we had got such a bargain. There was no running water on the property. There was an old well, but it was not deep enough; we could choose between making a significant donation to the local party in power, or starting a long and arduous fight against the Departamento General de Irrigación (which we soon renamed the Departamento General de Irritación) to obtain permission to dig a well deep enough to irrigate the vineyard all year long. This book is not thick enough to describe all the tribulations we went through to obtain the license for the well. After two years of pushing and pulling, we decided to make a short movie about how INSEAD inspired us to start this project. We explained the problem of the well from within the walls of the Departamento. Our camera was rudely pushed away during interviews, making for great footage. Luckily, we did not have to push the issue to its logical extreme as our CEO and lawyer found a loophole in the law. We managed to make the old well work for long enough to get the permit we needed to dig a deeper one.

In retrospect, this saga became a great story to tell. Gabriel García Márquez once said: "What matters in life is not what happens to you but what you remember and how you remember it."[106] Until the water was flowing and the first vines planted, the vineyard had no soul—it didn't feel like a real vineyard. Similarly, in the Mapesu Private Game Reserve, there was no real reserve until the first elephants came off their truck and started to break trees.

Our next challenge was to put together the team. We quickly found the always smiling and energetic Gaby Soto to run the project as its CEO and to sell shares and later wine. We then chose Guillermo Cacciaguerra to be our agronomist,

---

[106] Vanessa Thorpe "Magical realism... and fakery: the ailing Nobel Laureate is writing the definitive account of his life", *The Observer,* January21, 2001

take care of the vineyard, and manage the lodge. The selection of the winemaker was probably the most crucial choice and we were lucky enough to find Karim Mussi, an Argentine with a great nose, of Chilean and Lebanese ancestry, and a representative of a new way of making new world wines. At the time, he was not yet famous, but his enthusiasm convinced us. Lesser key functions were outsourced. So, after the first few years of working together, Guillermo now does all the hard work of plowing and fertilizing the soil and growing the vines organically. I monitor the business side and try to keep us close to economic reality; Karim works his magic and somehow each time makes better wine than ever before; and Gaby adds love, making the wine and project intoxicating for all involved. The camaraderie between our group of investors made it gel—I had a new group of friends.

Alma y pasión, soul and passion, became our motto. By the end of 2012, only two years into the project, we finished our first wines. We did not yet have our own grapes, due to a small well problem, so we bought grapes and later rootstock from our neighbors. The largest of them is Clos de Los Siete, for which Michel Rolland is the key winemaker. I had a wonderful day when we went to introduce ourselves over lunch to the neighbors and ended up rolling out of the wine cellars of the famous winemaker at close to midnight, having tasted literally every barrel in their extensive cellar.

We spent many lazy afternoons, sitting at long tables in the shade of some olive or walnut trees or under a pergola with vines, tasting wines, comparing notes and making plans. The classic combination of wine, food and creativity enhance your life whenever applied. We had tough discussions about whether to use a screw cap or a cork bottle stopper but, as our group has some Portuguese members, it could not be other than cork. We also chose bottles. Our logo is a fingerprint. The use of fingerprints to identify people is an Argentine invention dating back to 1891, somewhat crudely applied in 1967, when Ernesto "Che" Guevarra's hands were cut off and sent for identification in Buenos Aires. On our top-class wines, the fingerprints of all of our investors appear. As we are attracting more and more investors, we now take turns. The fingerprint emphasizes that all we do is up-close and personal and that we all have our say and can all have our fingers in the project. The label has become a hit, and we apply it to everything, including a section of our vineyard that is planted in the shape of a fingerprint and visible from Google Earth. Every investor and importer got his or her own rows of vines within the project.

Our first wines were a smooth Malbec, oaked for ten months in first-use French barrels, and a wonderful Private Selection, a more European-style wine that tastes like a first kiss: soft, sweet and with a very long after-taste. It has been unceremoniously classified as, and named, "Old School." This second one is still my favorite blend, the most iconic wine we have made so far.

We forbade anyone to cut corners and accepted that, at every step of the way, we would accept ONLY the very best. This led sometimes to disbelief and opposition from the Argentines, but in the end, it worked. We have an organic vineyard; we use real first-to-third use French oak barrels; we follow best practice to the letter and try to do everything at the highest possible level of quality. As a result, given the skills of our agronomist and winemaker, most of our reviews ended up being excellent; we got 90 points from *Robert Parker* for our wine, 91 from *Wine Enthusiast*, and 95 plus from *Decanter*. Our Private Selection received a silver medal as one of the best wines of Argentina; we were awarded the Trip Advisor Certificate of Excellence for our lodge, several years in a row. Even our entry level WhataboutMe? wine received 88 points from *Decanter*. I am proud that we make a high-quality product. Everyone can make a wine, but you feel a lot more pride and satisfaction when you make something of high quality. I would never want to make a mediocre wine, or a mediocre anything, for that matter.

Within three years, Gaby signed up importers in 15 countries, mostly where the shareholders live, who in turn pressured their favorite restaurants and bars to put our wine on their wine list. Of course, everyone likes to point out their fingerprints on the bottles and to tell the story of the wine to their friends. So far, we have been able to sell all the wine we've been able to make. As volumes grow, we will have to keep that momentum going.

We got a couple of the investors together and planted our own first vines. In 2017, we will harvest ourselves the first grapes from our own vineyard and by 2018, we will have our first significant harvest. By 2019, Alpasión Wines should be profitable as well, almost exactly on schedule and pretty close to budget, as per our initial plans when we set out in 2010.

We originally wanted to build a simple block hut to stay in while visiting, but after many discussions, it grew and grew until it became a much bigger cozy lodge for the shareholders to gather in. Rooms can be rented out when we aren't there. The famous architectural firm of Bórmida y Yanzón designed it, and it turned out to be very nice. In the morning, you can see from your bedroom how the Andes Mountains turn pink, purple, blue, green, and several other colors, in the few minutes before the sun comes up. I have seen that sight many times now, but I always make sure not to miss it when in Valle de Uco. A little restaurant for day-visitors, featuring healthy local food with our wine, was constructed next to the lodge. The first phase of our own winery is under construction. We are getting there! The nature all around is silent and impressive, not just the towering mountains or cold streams full of trout, but also the gullies running through the terrain and the clusters of bushes, containing many different type of herbs and plants, hardly used for any purpose. My fingers are aching to find an opportunity to use the local lavender and sage in cosmetics or other localized products. I guess that will have to wait until I retire or otherwise free up some time. It is strange how easily people who live in the midst of abundant nature take it so much for granted that they no longer see it as bountiful and full of ideas.

We organized some tango classes. The tango is a wonderful dance. Having both African and Southern European origins, like the tambó (in Cuba) and the tambú (in Curaçao), it's so tantric—when two people come together in their yin and yang and make a whole, they are perfectly complimentary. For the duration of a pulsating song, two people create a sublime experience, and then part, and then do it with someone else. It's very sensual and I think it's beautiful.

The roles of the leader and the follower in the tango are very different. The moves are mirror images of each other, but what underlies each gesture is its exact opposite. The leader focuses on directing the encounter; the follower must be extremely attuned to the lead to be able to follow. The combination of the two is what makes it exquisite to watch.

Some people feel that it is somehow lesser to be in the role of the follower, that because it is more "feminine," it must somehow be passive and weak. Actually, it is more difficult to follow someone very closely unless you are totally attuned—especially when the leader is passionate and imaginative. "Masculine" qualities are thus equally important. In the traditional view, women's essence is to be yin on the outside and yang on the inside, whereas men's is to be yang on the outside and yin on the inside. This makes us equal but not the same. Were we the same, the world would be boring. Just as men and women are equal but not the same, cultures are equal but not the same, and religions are equal but not the same. Political convictions are equal but not the same. It is the dynamic tension between male and female energies that keeps a relationship strong. It is the differences between cultures that makes travel such a valuable way of understanding your own life and circumstances.

We structured the project into a Mutual Fund, and the original eight shareholders each invited some of their friends. Over time, our group of investors grew to more than 50 individuals. Some are very active, while others just lean back and enjoy the wine; many have become great friends. According to Pope John Paul II: "Men are like wine—some turn to vinegar, but the best improve with age."

We organized many wonderful events. One week we did a *cabalgata*. We got on horseback, dressed up as *gauchos*, and spent the days riding into the Andes Mountains, until we reached an altitude of over 4,000 meters. In the evenings, we took our saddles from the horses and used them as pillows. The *gauchos* lit a fire, and we ate roasted sheep from the spit, or a full rack of lamb cooked over an open fire—accompanied by a couple of bottles of our own wine as "a dinner without wine is like a day without sunshine" (Robert Mondavi).

It gets cold at night, high in the mountains. Even in the midst of summer, frost forms on my sleeping bag, and I can see literally millions of stars and the Milky Way dripping with surplus light. Those millions of stars together form a single galaxy, one of billions of galaxies in a universe that we can't see the end of. We don't know how many planets it contains or whether any extraterrestrials on any of those other planets make a good or even a passable wine. It makes me wonder how important any of us is to the universe. The view and the feel of space beats that of any hotel with only five stars—until you have to get out of your comfortable sleeping bag to find a place to pee, of course, and run into a wandering horse, or worse, step into what it left behind. During the day, we could see the barren silent emptiness of the mountains, crowned by the snowcapped peaks, guanacos, and even huge condors circling high above us, looking for rabbits and hares.

As the days passed, our group became more and more quiet; each of us deep in thought and closely connected with the horses, the mountain, and the endless silent space.

On that horse, I've forgotten its name, but I called it "La Poderosa" (after a famous motorcycle), I pondered some Gordian decisions and chewed on the words of Gabriel García Márquez (*Love in the Time of Cholera*):

He allowed himself to be swayed by his conviction that human beings are not born once and for all on the day their mothers give birth to them, but that life obliges them over and over again to give birth to themselves.[107]

Yes, I definitely need to spend less time shuffling paper and more time creating something tangible, sustainable and durable.

On another occasion, we went with a group of Norwegian friends to pay our respects at the site of the remains of el *Avión de los Uruguayos*; a plane with an Uruguayan rugby team on board that crashed in 1972 in the Andes, not far (less than 40 kilometers, as the condor flies) from our lodge. We went there again mostly on horseback, accompanied by a lively group of gauchos, strong, independence-loving people, who guided (and at times herded) us there safely. One of the older ones had been present when the survivors of the plane crash first went back to the plane wreck, where they had spent over two months, twenty years after their ordeal. That was a moving story about lack of experience (they crashed only hours from rescue, had they known where to look for it) and team spirit (those who survived the plane crash also survived the months

---

[107]   Márquez, Gabriel García. *Love in the Time of Cholera,* translated by Edith Grossman, London: Penguin Books, 2007.

isolated in the snow by eating the frozen bodies of their comrades). The initial search was cancelled after eight days. The survivors of the crash had found a small transistor radio on the aircraft and they first heard the news that the search had been called off on the 11th of what ultimately would become 72 days on the mountain. Piers Paul Read's *Alive: The Story of the Andes Survivors* described the moments after this discovery:

The others who had clustered around Roy, upon hearing the news, began to sob and pray, all except Parrado, who looked calmly up at the mountains which rose to the west. Gustavo [Coco] Nicolich came out of the aircraft and, seeing their faces, knew what they had heard... [Nicolich] climbed through the hole in the wall of suitcases and rugby shirts, crouched at the mouth of the dim tunnel, and looked at the mournful faces which were turned towards him. Hey boys, he shouted, there's some good news! We just heard on the radio. They've called off the search. Inside the crowded aircraft there was silence. As the hopelessness of their predicament enveloped them, they wept. Why the hell is that good news? Paez shouted angrily at Nicolich. Because it means, [Nicolich] said, that we're going to get out of here on our own. The courage of this one boy prevented a flood of total despair.[108]

It was getting late in the season and some 20 degrees below zero at night. The gauchos kept themselves warm around the wind-swept fire, by drinking copious quantities of our best wine straight from the bottle and singing out loud throughout the night. I stared at the full moon, wondering how much courage I would need to eat the meat of someone I knew. And would my friends all taste the same?

---

[108] Read, Piers Paul. *Alive: The Story of the Andes Survivors*. New York: Avon Books; Reissue edition, 2002.

When the sun came up, we were ready to go up to the peak and see the plane. We ended up enjoying a copious picnic, celebrating life, right next to the place where 44 years before, the survivors had been eating the corpses of the victims. We debated whether it was right to have such a sumptuous lunch in such a place. In the end, we agreed that, had we been there, the survivors would have joined us. We shared our banquet with all climbers who made it up that mountain that day, and still ahd food left.

It is important for us to continue adding like-minded people to the group, people who are authentic and share our vision and passion for life. As this is a long-term project, it is important to have fun and enjoy each step of the way—at some stage, we will bring in the next generation. I hope that in 50 years the children of my children will go to the Alpasión Lodge and have a few drinks with the children of the children of some of the other investors, and reminisce about the unremarkable or stupid things their grandparents might have done with their lives. But this project will grow, develop, mature with age, and will remain great fun. I love the notion that it will be here long after we are gone. Elsewhere, in Curaçao, I planted cork oaks (Quercus Suber), that in 25 years will produce cork, which can then be used as stoppers for our bottles. Most people I describe my experiment to say, "why bother? By then you will be old." For me, that's a reason to speed up planting. Those trees live up to a few hundreds of years. I will not. In a hundred years, someone may remember who planted them.

One of our investors, Andrés Villasmil, (El Rey del Pollo Frito) lives in Santo Domingo, where he got to know the Kelner family, in the cigar making business. Hendrik Kelner is a third-generation cigar maker, from a family in Kampen, the Netherlands. Being of Dutch origin, he only smokes the rejects from the cigar making process, the ones with color deviations and impurities in the leaves. His business became very successful and people come from all over the world to select or design cigars. He showed us around the factory, explaining every step of the process of hand-making great cigars. He proudly showed us a small framed note hanging on the wall of his office, signed by Bill Clinton, when he was President. It was a thank-you note; "Thank you for the cigars, I really enjoyed them," it says. Hendrik Kelner added, "You see, he never said he actually smoked them." To the displeasure of his son, Mr. Kelner sold the factory to Davidoff. And so, the junior Kelner founded his own specialty cigar factory, with some advice from his father. There the father, son, and Andres worked on creating the Alpasión Robustos as well as the Coronas, packaged in the most beautifully designed cigar boxes I have ever seen. The tobacco leaves used in our cigars come from the same plantations as the Davidoff ones. And the Cotui wrapper used in our cigars is unique: only Kelner's wife's family has access to it.

I am not really a smoker; my father died at a young age of heart disease caused by smoking, but I love to (once in a while) light one of our cigars. Our logo, the fingerprint, appears on the cigar rings and on the black lacquer box. It looks beautiful, and the combination of the wine and cigars tastes great.

Over time, we hope to add more products to our collection of, currently seven, wines, most of them based on Malbec. During our very first trip to Argentina, Bill Fisher, one of the larger investors, said he was interested in the project as someday he wanted us to distill a grappa. Grappa is a digestive made out of the most (the remains after the juice is pressed out) of the grape skins. We found a grappa maker near Mendoza, who twice won a world championship in grappa making. We took our most and designed a soft and fruity grappa, in a traditional apothecary's bottle with a light blue label and our hallmark fingerprint. When we met for our annual INSEAD reunion, in Marrakech, we tried the first few bottles of Grappa Don Bill, by Alpasión. They tasted wonderfully soft.

Next up will be Alpasión gin. Gin evolved in England from Dutch *jenever*, after the Dutch conquest of England in 1688. From there, it made it to Argentina and became a well-known, locally produced spirit. We intend to make a gin using Argentine junipers and local wild herbs.

The Alpasión project has a profound and purifying influence on all of us. I never felt so proud as on the day we were making preparations for the next reunion of the INSEAD group. One of us had booked us initially into a very expensive place; others had to stay in a much more modest place nearby. In the end, we had quite a few defectors, choosing to stay at the more modest place, as it felt like the right thing to do.

I travel a lot, and after all those years on the road still love the freedom and the ever-changing perspectives of life on the move. One recent night, I left Singapore, which was hot and humid. Engulfed by all the sweet and damp smells of the tropics, and the hustle-bustle of East Asia, I fell asleep in the plane and, in the morning, I got off in Moscow. Suddenly, the palm trees had given way to birch trees, squirrels were running like mad in the city parks to finish their work during the last days of autumn and the first snowflakes silently melted on the still green grass. I really enjoy Moscow. I feel it is one of the most intriguing and characterful cities in Europe, and definitely one of my personal favorites. A city chockfull of 800 years of bizarre history, generations of old buildings like open-air storybooks, and everywhere statues of interesting writers, interesting people.

If Cuba is held together by salsa dancing and *guajira* singing, Russia is held together by science and literature. Almost every Russian I meet has a significant and serious side interest: knowledge, books, lectures, science, culture; they seem like an antidote against a political and economic system that is highly autocratic, isolationistic, and corrupt, producing little that people can identify with or be proud of. Most people have little interest in politics and shun political comment, although ratings for Putin as a strongman remain high. For those who cannot hope to beat the system by resisting, pursuing knowledge-based interests and being part of the global culture is comparable to trying to grow a garden in the middle of hell. On the way from the Domodedovo airport to the city, I remember that Fyodor Dostoyevsky once said:

To study the meaning of man and of life—I am making significant progress here. I have faith in myself. Man is a mystery: if you spend your entire life trying to puzzle it out, then do not say that you have wasted your time. I occupy myself with this mystery, because I want to be a man.[109]

I have been to Moscow many times and have seen the city change from a poor, dark, potholed place, devoid of any service or comfort—mysterious and slightly threatening—to a bright, modern, prosperous, and very self-aware city in just 25 years. The economic progress is clearly there, and there is now a large and prosperous middle class for whom the Soviet Union is at best a distant memory. The personal freedom, shared ethics, and relative fairness of a chaotic democracy to go with it, are, however, still lacking. On this trip, a group of us visited the construction site of a new stadium being built for the Dynamo Moscow sports club. It will be ready in time for the 2018 FIFA soccer

---

[109] Mochulsky, Konstantin. Translated by Michael A. Minihan, *Dostoevsky: His Life and Work by Konstantin Mochulsky*, USA: Princeton University Press, 1967.

championships, to be held in Moscow. The organizing committee intends to honor its most well-known player, Lev Yashin, who was the best goalkeeper of the 1960s (or ever) and won the Ballon d'or for being the best soccer player of the year in 1963, as only goalkeeper ever. On one famous tour, the Soviet National Team went to Chile, Brazil, Uruguay, and Argentina. Lev Yashin, all dressed in black, earned everyone's respect as well as the nickname Araña Negra (the black spider). People came from all over Argentina to see him play in the Club Atlético River Plate Stadium. The crowd allegedly included the former owner of the land on which the Alpasión vineyard grows, a recent immigrant of Soviet (Ukrainian) origin, and the grandfather of Nacho (Juan Ignacio) Groisman, a good friend and the organizer of some of our *cabalgatas*. Someone connected us with Dynamo Moscow and came up with the idea of producing a wine in Argentina to commemorate this legendary tour, remember the famous goalkeeper, and strengthen the ties of friendship between Russia and Argentina. The link was made. Lev Yashin himself is long dead, but his widow and his daughter embraced the idea and Alpasión is proudly making Lev Yashin limited edition Malbec for the opening of the Dynamo Moscow stadium in 2017. I ended up in a group photo with his widow and the remaining members of the famous team of 1961— my first soccer photo since high school. I stand between famous soccer players in their late seventies and eighties, still passionate and proud of their accomplishment, and a team of young actors trying to pick up the atmosphere and memories of the old men while it is still possible. They are working on a movie about the life of Lev Yashin, which will be released when the stadium is ready. As Lev Yashin himself, once said in an interview:

What kind of a goalkeeper is one who is not tormented by the goal he has allowed? He must be tormented! And if he is calm, that means the end. No matter what he had in the past, he has no future.[110]

For Alpasión, producing this special edition presents a great opportunity. Not only is Russia a good market for Argentine wine, but the project also gives us, and especially Nacho, an intimate connection with really interesting people on the other side of the world. We are looking forward to the official opening and tournament. Of course, a night at Tchaikovsky's Swan Lake, the actual Swan Lake, is a really great experience. It is wonderful to walk around Red Square to the mausoleum of Lenin and then on to Café Pushkin or the Bolshoy Restaurant—but it is better to do something together with people in another

---

[110]   http://www.nationalpubliclibrary.net/articles/Lev_Yashin

country that creates a basis for enduring friendship and a true understanding and appreciation of each other's cultures and ways of thinking. I think most problems between countries and ideologies, as well as within companies, could be avoided if their leaders would just take time to walk a mile each other's moccasins and look at issues from the other side.

Why do I mention the story of the COL Wine Fund Ltd. (its official name, COL, stands for Challenge of Leadership) here? The Fund serves no social purpose, it is not really saving anyone from poverty or any other predicament. It occupies 85 hectares of previously pristine nature that has now become cultivated, albeit in an organic fashion. Without global warming, even ten years ago, its location was considered too cold for planting vines. There are plenty of vineyards in the world, and wine, however enjoyable, is not a necessity of life. Although we expect the land to increase in value over time—and both the lodge and the winery to make money—there was no compelling economic reason to invest in this agricultural project.

I got involved because I longed for friendship. Here were (initially 10, later many more) people I was getting to know really well. Apart from the two professors, the other eight were successful top managers and business people. When we take pictures at the dinner table, we take pictures of our friends, not just of the food. Although we ALWAYS compete in everything else we do (from running, to karaoke, to horseback riding) we NEVER have to compete in business, as we are all from very different businesses. That created a solid basis for friendship—a feeling that the others were in a similar (cold and lonely at the top) situation and ultimately, deep within, sharing the same insecurities, dreams, and needs. Now I feel part of a great and loving web that spans the globe. Alpasión is what connects the spiders in that web.

Investing in friendship:

1)   Having friends is an essential need in life. It has been proven that people with a good group of friends (not the same as a large group of friends) live four to five years longer than people who do not maintain friendships. Friendship creates escape valves for frustration, remorse, sadness, loss, bereavement, and disappointments. A group of friends gives color to your life, adds to your happiness and challenges body, mind, soul, and spirit.

2) Friendship builds a social network that can help to overcome economic setbacks and make one feel more secure and moderate in one's opinions, as well as more team-spirited.

3) Friends provide an audience to share successes with, they celebrate the victories in life, and the little successes. Friends provide encouragement and support, helping you to undertake difficult tasks and not give up.

4) Together we can achieve much more than we could alone. Doing something together with friends makes the work seem effortless and the rewards more fulfilling—and the celebrations more fun.

Investing in the Alpasión project provides me with a plethora of returns. Those returns always come at unexpected moments. They come when we have a chance meeting and drink a bottle at a rainy airport when delayed, or when we organize a horseback riding trip on a beautiful day or a week in the Andes. One week, we went on snowmobiles onto the ice of Spitsbergen, got a shot of vodka in Barentzburg, and camped out on the ice. They came when a couple of us ended up climbing pole-pole (slowly) into the snows of Mount Kilimanjaro, and—at the top—were too exhausted or nauseated to open the bottle of Alpasión we had carried all the way up for the occasion. They come in the revelations of a dream seminar we organized at the lodge, seeing people come out with secrets hidden for years. They come when I see friends master their first tango ever, on the roof of the lodge under a starry sky. They come in the tears in the eyes of our friend Don Bill, when we presented him with the first bottle of grappa. And in the pride on the faces of investors all over the world when they recognize their own signature on the label, or see someone ordering a bottle of Alpasión from the wine list in their favorite restaurant. I will never again in my life have to decide what to take to a dinner party—the bottle with the fingerprint gives me both a personalized present and an excuse to talk for hours about what I love and what makes me proud.

We still need to raise some money to finish the project, but we are close to break-even. We have decided not to take out any loans, but to time the project to match the speed of fundraising and selling shares. We can still add another 20 or 30 friends to our family. So far, we have investors from about 20 different countries; all have their stories, all are unique personalities, and all share our passion for Alpasión. One of the best Argentine writers ever, José Hernández, writes in *El Gaucho Martín Fierro:*

Los hermanos sean unidos porque esa es la ley primera; tengan unión verdadera en cualquier tiempo que sea, porque si entre ellos pelean los devoran los de afuera. Brothers should stand by each other, because this is the first law; keep a true bond between you always, at all times —because if you fight among yourselves, you'll be devoured by those outside. [111]

It is the friendship between the investors that makes Alpasión strong. Friendship is a huge return on investment.

I think that every day we need to show up for life, live it to the fullest, with guts and grit, and share it with the best. Or, in the words of Paulo Coelho:

Accept what life offers you and try to drink from every cup. All wines should be tasted; some should only be sipped, but with others, drink the whole bottle. [112]

---

[111]   Hernández, José. *El Gaucho Martín Fierro*, translated by C.E. Ward, New York: State University of New York Press, 1967.

[112]   Coelho, Paulo. *Brida*, translated by Margaret Jull Costa, London: Harper Collins, 2008.

Afterword

Understand that you can have in your writing no qualities which you do not honestly entertain in yourself. Understand that you cannot keep out of your writing the indication of the shallowness and evil you entertain in yourself. If you love to have a servant stand behind your chair at dinner, it will appear in your writing. Or if you possess a vile opinion of women, or if you grudge anything, or doubt immortality—these will appear by what you leave unsaid, more than by what you say.[113]

—Walt Whitman

There is something invigorating about writing a book. It feels very much like stripping in public. However comfortable you are with your own body, there remains the difficult choice between revealing too little, too slowly, and not getting the senses aroused and the intended emotion across, or revealing too much, too quickly, and not managing to trigger the viewer's (or reader's) fantasy. With either approach, at the end of the effort one stands exposed, with all one has to offer in the eye of the beholder. Vulnerable, but sincere and denuded of all but your bare essentials.

I actually would love to be a full-time author, a true merchant of meaning, as nothing clears my mind better than committing my thoughts, ideas, and dreams to paper, leaving a mental void into which, afterwards, I can pour new thoughts, new ideas, and new dreams. Yet that is unlikely to happen, as to write sincerely I need to live an intense real life to generate those thoughts, ideas, and dreams or I would—like so many writers—be condemned to rewrite the same book over and over again. In conversations with the first readers of this book, it is clear that much remains to be said or written, and that (reading between the lines) much still warrants further investigation.

The purpose of this book is to inspire anyone who has been lucky enough in life to have acquired or obtained either more assets (money) or more skills than needed for the regular maintenance of his or her own existence at a decent

---

[113] Whitman, Walt. *Complete Writings of Walt Whitman* (New York – London, 1902), Vol. VI, p.39.

but modest level. Of course, individuals and families must assess their own needs themselves.

My parents were never wealthy or lucky by any measure; they owned a small farm in the Netherlands containing an orchard, some breeding cattle, pigs, and chickens. On the side, my father made money as an agricultural contractor, using his farm equipment to work on other people's farms. It was a tough and pretty meager existence, and my parents were constantly struggling to make ends meet. The profit for the year might or might not be enough to buy a washing machine for my mother. A TV-set, shower, and flush toilet did not enter our house until many years after most people in the Netherlands already had one. Nevertheless, it was not a big deal, as many of the farmers in our area lived in much the same circumstances. The farm provided many of our basic needs, producing vegetables, potatoes, meat, and fruit. Milk and honey could be exchanged with neighbors; the weekly delivery from the local supermarket easily fitted into one small carton box, containing matches, detergent, coffee, tea, and flour. Disaster struck when my father, at the age of 50, suffered a heart attack and had to spend many weeks in hospital having open heart surgery. As he did not have proper health insurance, this crisis meant the end of the farm. The animals, tractors, farm equipment, and land were all sold. All that remained was the actual farmhouse, big and empty. At times, the financial situation was really tight.

Analyzing this situation, I subconsciously set myself a target: to become financially independent as quickly as possible. From when I was eight years old, I have always been working—buying and selling stuff, and covering at least my own spending money. From the day I left for college, my father never had to give me a penny.

Many years later, when my own business finally started to take off and I had surplus money for the first time, it did not feel right to spend it on luxuries or put it in a bank. My parents died young, without leaving us much of material value. My brother and sister are not wealthy. Most of my friends are not wealthy either. Showing off to them does not feel like the right thing to do.

The trip I made on the hippy trail to India and beyond at age 20/21, to satisfy my nascent interest in Hindu and Buddhist philosophies, taught me that the deprivation I knew as a child completely paled in comparison with the way most people in India lived. I saw up close how people struggled and died of hunger and misery. When I returned from the trip, I adopted an Indian Fosters Parents Plan child and knew, in the back of my mind, that one day I would do something meaningful for India. For no other reason than because it felt like the right thing to do.

When a good regular income started to produce regular surplus money, I sponsored small charity projects; as they increased in number and size, they became corporate social responsibility projects and later, social enterprises. The social enterprises tended to focus on agriculture. I guess I felt somehow compelled to finish the work my father was given no time to complete.

I never wanted to convert the money my good fortune gave me into big cars, an impressive house, or a yacht. My wife does not crave branded handbags or jewels. And we are totally OK with not leaving much financial wealth to our children. We are satisfied that the projects we support and work on will continue to grow in Argentina, Indonesia, and South Africa.

Children will never grow up the way you tell them to grow up; by definition, they will not listen to your words, but they do end up copying what you do. I am proud of my son, who puts his life and youthful energy on the line to save endangered animal species in South Africa, and my daughter in Australia, studying war crimes to help bring war criminals to justice. I hope that the projects my wife and I have undertaken will rub off on them, and that they will at least consider dedicating a part of their lives to helping change the world for the better.

They have had a good start in life, with a good education. They grew up in three very different parts of the world, have seen many different countries, both rich and poor, and understand what their efforts can achieve. I think that realizing that everyone can make a difference (if s/he wants to make that difference) is priceless. I know that is not how our education system works.

It is difficult to find happiness within oneself, but it is impossible to find it anywhere else.

—Arthur Schopenhauer

When we ourselves were kids, we experienced the world as big and full of wonders. Anything could be a toy; everything was fun. Then we were taught that some objects were not ours to play with, as they belonged to our siblings or friends. That birthday cakes were small and the biggest piece had to be fought over. At school, we were tricked into competing with our classmates, and we ended up being classified as good or not good at a particular subject, judged through the eyes and criteria of teachers and the School Board.

The smarter kids won more accolades and higher marks; the ones born early in the year won most of the sports prizes and awards. We learned that winning was not only the most important thing, but also the only thing—that ending up in second place was being the first loser. Winning always seemed to happen at the expense of others.

All that instilled in us a scarcity mentality: believing that it was important to win ahead, or even at the expense of, others, and that it was important to have the most because there wasn't enough for all of us to enjoy and share. We believed that we would have to fight to get a fair piece of the small pie. Of course, none of these misconceptions were true; solutions are constantly being created and scarcity is constantly being overcome. The world is full of abundance and it's up to us to tap into its full potential and boundless energy. Twelve thousand years ago, the world was full of hunter-gatherers and could not feed more than 6–8 million humans. Now it feeds close to 8 billion humans, somehow managing to keep all of us alive, albeit at the expense of other species. It would, of course, be much better if there were fewer of us, and eco-diversity could survive, but we can cope. We will also cope when, in another 20–30 years, there are ten billion of us. In the meantime, we have all it takes to overcome not just malnutrition, but also poverty: making it possible for the first time since the agricultural revolution to secure a decent living for ALL people on earth.

The best way to benefit from everything there is in the world is to give abundantly. If you want a happy child, you give it something to play with and a smile or a hug. If you want a happy spouse, you spend time with him or her. To have a happy employee, you show appreciation for his or her efforts and provide challenges that put his or her talents to work. If you want a successful business relationship, you extend benefits, so that both parties profit from the business.

If both parties benefit from the relationship, they will not only come back for more, but will also tell their friends and partners.

This is called "abundance mentality" and it works in any relationship. The world is huge and has endless resources and satisfaction to offer, if you are able to tap into its potential. You can tap into the potential of the whole world or even universe by appreciating that it is a single interconnected and inter-dependent system, of which you are not only the center, but also the master. You are connected to all other parts, and everything exists within you. What you put in, you will get back—where and when you need it most. Anything you give, the universe will give back in multiples. However, if you only take from it, it will soon stop giving.

A business needs to create win-win situations with its different stakeholders. To its clients and suppliers, it offers fair business terms and perfect personal service. To its shareholders, it offers a fair return on investment. For its employees, it must provide fair wages, a chance to expand their skills and knowledge, challenging tasks, and appreciation for a job well done. To contribute to society, it must help the weak and provide examples of corporate social responsibility. And to the environment, it must show respect, at least replenishing what it depletes.

Success will automatically come to you when you find win-win situations in all four of these aspects, because you will receive back more than you have given. In win-win situations, you will always win. Start by being generous and success will flow your way. All dots in life connect; make every day meaningful and success and happiness will flow. This is an undeniable law of nature, called the "Law of Attraction." Oprah Winfrey advises us to "be thankful for what you have, and you'll end up having more. If you concentrate on what you don't have, you will never ever have enough."

If we contemplate long and hard, we will sooner or later realize that we are one with the universe and all of the universe at the same time, and that the loss of even one species on earth, or the loss of one human being, or the loss of one ecosystem, is everyone's loss. However, we each have the power and the imagination to influence the universe, pushing it in the direction we want it to go.

In the Sanskrit language, this concept is called *Tat Tvam Asi*. It was first developed as a Hindu concept some 5,000 years ago and is usually translated as "Thou art that," or "That you are." It is one of the Mahāvākyas (Grand Pronouncements) in Vedantic Dharma. To realize that we have the power to change the universe, which is present in its entirety inside us, is a thousands-of-years-old principle that remains true today.

The god went home, and at last found that he was the Self, beyond all thought, one without birth or death, whom the sword cannot pierce or the fire burn, whom the air cannot dry or the water melt, the beginningless and endless, the immovable, the intangible, the omniscient, the omnipotent Being; that it was neither the body nor the mind, but beyond them all.[114]

The statement "that thou art" ultimately conveys an overriding experience of oneness which is beyond our body, mind, soul, and spirit as well as beyond our ego. When we realize this oneness and our tantric connection with everything and everyone around us, we may start to feel that our role and importance go beyond the transience of embodied beings. Our sensations, body, mind, spirit, and soul are for now our present reality; it is up to us to make this the best possible reality for as long as this round lasts. It takes only a second to choose a great attitude and make this a perfect life.

> *I have my own peculiar yardstick for measuring a man: Does he have the courage to cry in a moment of grief? Does he have the compassion not to hunt an animal? In his relationship with a woman, is he gentle? Real manliness is nurtured in kindness and gentleness, which I associate with intelligence, comprehension, tolerance, justice, education, and high morality. If only men realized how easy it is to open a woman's heart with kindness, and how many women close their hearts to the assaults of the Don Juans.*

> **—Sophia Loren**

We are one with all and all is us. Having been endowed with unique skills, with health, with energy, with our imagination and intelligence, we must apply our best efforts, all the resources at our disposal, and everything around us will

---

[114] Vivekanda, Swami. (2016). *Raja Yoga: Conquering the Internal Nature.* India: The Adhyaksha, Advaita Ashrama.

flourish. The closer we come, the greater the return on our investment will be. There are no excuses; our ego will by definition be extinguished someday, but the positive energies we radiate and our good deeds will remain forever. It is completely within our power and potential to change some important aspect of our world for the better.

As I have not worried to be born, I do not worry to die.[115]

—Federico García Lorca

I invite you to send your questions, your comments and your constructive criticism to t.knipping@amicorp.com:

---

[115] Quoted in "Diálogos de un caricaturista salvaje," interview with Luis Bagaría, *El Sol*, Madrid (1936-06-10)

Toine Knipping is involved in managing or coordinating several sustainable business activities. He is the Chairman of the Amicorp Group, where he is responsible for strategic development. As a co-founder, he is closely connected and involved with the ongoing global development of new tax-compliant and efficient investment solutions, as well as the development of new markets and opportunities.

He has been instrumental in convincing multiple High Net Worth Individuals to structure their wealth in ways that not only serve their family's needs for financial security, but also create common endeavors that reflect a common mission and common values which help to keep the family's members, business, wealth, and ideals together for more than just one or two generations. Toine regularly speaks at universities, conferences, and seminars on developments in international taxation and financial structuring.

In addition, he is involved in a variety of often agricultural business ventures that serve to demonstrate the impact small investments can have. He strongly believes that all relevant change in the world ever has come from small groups, with a razor-sharp focus. If enough people simultaneously make impact investments, however small, or organize sustainable efforts, we will jointly change the world. One of the companies he invests in has been instrumental in developing new applications for aloe vera-based supplements and health drinks. Some of those supplements and creams are based on ancient recipes.

In 2012, Toine authored *Mind Your Business,* a book that links one's spiritual life with advice on how to run a business. It encourages everyone to truly believe in themselves and to passionately dedicate their talents to meaningful efforts, in order to be happy and successful in life.

Toine loves the outdoors. He has been hiking, scuba diving and skydiving in many parts of the world. He particularly enjoys Bali, the Himalayas, the African Wild and the Southern Cone of Latin America. He strongly promotes the protection of endangered species, such as rhinoceros and elephants, in Southern Africa.

Toine lives between Singapore and South Africa, with his wife Paula.

Some of the ventures mentioned in this book would like to receive your help and earn your support. If you feel like contacting them with questions or to offer some support (not a pre-requisite to asking them for help or information), please feel free to do so:

Amicorp Community Foundation / AmiForestadora

Email: csr@amicorp.com

This foundation is constantly searching for contacts who want to offset their CO2 production, and contacts who want to set up their own or contribute to an existing CSR or a philanthropic project. It can help with advice and practical solutions.

Desa Les Community Center

Email: info@desalescommunitycenter.org
Website: www.desalescommunitycenter.org

This entity is searching for help with the development of a training center in Bali for people seeking a career in the hospitality business. It needs donations, internships for its students and sponsors helping to build its presence, its reputation and its quality.

Tuma Mi Man Daycare Center

Contact person: Derk Scheltema
Email: info@tumamiman.com
Website: www.tumamiman.com

TMM is looking for sponsors, for people willing to contribute to schooling and development on the island of Curaçao.

Shared Universe Ventures Ltd / Shared Universe Foundation

Contact person: Quinten Knipping
Email: contact@shareduniverseafrica.com
Website: www.shareduniverseafrica.com
                      www.shareduniversefoundation.org

Shared Universe is on the lookout for people who are interested in the conservation of African wildlife, who want to make a real contribution to the preservation of endangered species, including elephants, rhinos, cheetahs, and wild dogs—or who want to invest in the conservation of nature for future generations.

African Caribbean Aloe Products

Contact person: Piet Viljoen
Email: info@aloe-acap.com
Website: www.aloe-acap.com

ACAP is producing and distributing aloe vera based products and using part of the proceeds to help people in need.

Alpasión Wines

Contact person: Maria Gabriela Soto
Email: info@alpasion.com
Website: www.alpasion.com

This friendship project is constantly searching for additional distributors in new markets as well as additional friends to be joining in building this company to a global brand.

And Amicorp, as a company providing trust and assurance services, can help you to analyze your own situation, and (based on your own values and preferences) to select sustainable projects, ventures, or dreams to invest in. We can manage them with you or for you and provide you with support in many different ways.

Amicorp Private Clients Unit:

Contact person: Geralda Buckley
Email: amicorp@amicorp.com
Website: www.amicorp.com

Glossary

Abhayadānam: Sanskrit word meaning the protection of life.

Adat: Sanskrit and Bahasa Indonesian word for customary law, or habit, as opposed to religious law.

Adharma: Sanskrit for individual disharmony with the nature of things; chaos, and disorder; connotations of wrong, evil, immorality and vice; antonym of dharma in the Indian religions of Jainism, Hinduism and Buddhism.

Ahimsa: Sanskrit "non-injury," nonviolence, non-injury or absence of desire to harm any life forms.

Alang-alang: Reeds, weeds or weeds (Imperata cylindrica Raeusch) This is a type of sharp leaved grass, which often become a weed in farmland and is frequently used for constructing thatch roofs.

Alentejo: A geographical, historical and cultural region of south-central and southern Portugal. Literally, in Portuguese it means "beyond the Tagus."

Allahabad: Also known as Prayag, this is a city in the Indian state of Uttar Pradesh and the administrative headquarters of Allahabad District at the confluence of the Ganges and Yamuna rivers, the most populous district in a state of more than 4,900,000 inhabitants.

Aloe vera: (Aloe barbadensis Miller) a plant species of the genus Aloe. It grows wild in tropical climates around the world and is cultivated for agricultural and medicinal uses.

Aloverose: (also known as acemannan) is a polysaccharide with the peculiarity of the acetylated form. It is a D-isomer mucopolysaccharide in aloe vera leaves. This compound has been known to have immunostimulant, antiviral, antineoplastic, and gastrointestinal properties.

Alowijn: Aloe vera in Afrikaans.

266

Alpasión: Brand of wine from Mendoza, Argentina merged from the word "alma" (soul) and pasión (passion) in Spanish.

Aparigraha: Sanskrit word meaning the concept of non-possessiveness, non-grasping or non-greediness. It refers to desiring only those possessions that are necessary or important, depending on one's life stage and context.

Apartheid: This was as a system of institutionalized racial segregation and discrimination in South Africa between 1948 and 1991, when it was abolished.

Araña Negra: A Spanish nickname given to famous Russian football goalkeeper Lev Yashin, meaning the "black spider," in reference to the dark colors he wore and the impression he gave of having eight arms to catch the ball.

Arawaks: A group of indigenous peoples of South America, Florida, and historically of the Caribbean.

Armillaria ostoyae: Sometimes called Amrmillaria solidipes or honey mushroom or honey fungus, a species of plant pathogenic fungus in the hysalacriaceae family and the yellow-capped and sweet fruiting bodies they produce. Found throughout the U.S. and Canada. In Oregon State, an area of 965 hectares of soil in the Blue Mountains is believed to be home to the largest known organism.

Artha: A Sanskrit word for one of the four aims of human life in Indian philosophy, meaning: sense, goal, purpose or essence.

Ashram: Sometimes also ashrama or ashramam, traditionally a spiritual hermitage or monastery in Indian religions.

Autobahns: (German) The federally controlled-access highway system in Germany.

Avant la lettre: French for "before the letter," i.e., before the (specified) word or concept existed.

Ayurveda: Sanskrit, translated "life-knowledge:" is a science of life (Ayur = life, Veda = science or knowledge).

Ayurvedic Medicine: A system of medicine with historical roots in the Indian subcontinent, based on the belief that health and wellness depend on a delicate balance between the mind, body, and spirit.

Azkhenazi kibbutzniks: Eastern European descended Jewish community jointly conducting agriculture on socialist principles.

Babi guling: Famous Indonesian roasted or suckling pig dish.

Babi pangang: A variety of recipes for Indonesian grilled pork, 'babi' meaning pig or pork, and 'panggang' meaning grilled or roasted in the Malay and Bahasa Indonesian languages.

Ballon d'Or: Directly translated as the "Golden Ball" in French, this is an annual award given to the best-performing football player from around the world, as voted for by football journalists.

Barentzburg: The second-largest settlement on Svalbard, with about 500 inhabitants, almost entirely Russians and Ukrainians.

Batig saldo: Net Return on Investment Policy. A Dutch term meaning balance, profit balance, or surplus balance—used as an explanation and justification for the 19th century colonization policy in Indonesia.

Beit She'an: A city in the Northern District of Israel which has played an historically important role, due to its geographical location, at the junction of the Jordan River Valley and the Jezreel Valley.

Bhagavad Gita: (Sanskrit) Often referred to as simply the Gita, this is a 700-verse Hindu scripture in Sanskrit that is part of the Hindu epic *Mahabharata*. It is considered an important work in the Hindu tradition, as both literature and philosophy.

Big five: In Africa, the big five game animals are the African lion, African elephant, Cape buffalo, African leopard, and rhinoceros. The term "big five game" (usually capitalized or quoted as "Big Five") was coined by big-game hunters and refers to the five most difficult animals in Africa to hunt on foot.

Bill and Melinda Gates Foundation: A private foundation launched in 2000 by Bill and Melinda Gates and said to be the largest transparently operated private foundation in the world. It aims to enhance healthcare and reduce extreme poverty globally, and, in America, to expand educational opportunities and access to information technology.

Biochar: Charcoal produced from plant matter and stored in the soil as a means of removing carbon dioxide from the atmosphere. It is a 2,000-year-old practice, which converts agricultural waste into a soil enhancer that can hold carbon, boost food security, increase soil biodiversity, and discourage deforestation. The process creates a fine-grained, highly porous charcoal that helps soils retain nutrients and water.

Boma: Also known as a kraal, this is a traditional African enclosure, stockade, or fort used to secure and protect livestock. The enclosure is usually made of thorn bushes, wood or steel fencing, for protection from marauders. It is also used in the tourism industry to describe a place where people gather in the enclosure for outdoor dining and lounging.

Brahmacharya: In one context, this is the first of four ashrama (age-based stages) of a human life, with grihastha (householder), vanaprastha (forest dweller), and sannyasa (renunciation) being the other three asramas. The brahmacharya (bachelor student) stage of one's life, up to twenty-five years of age, focused on education and included the practice of celibacy.

Brexit: A term for the potential departure of the United Kingdom from the European Union.

British Raj: (From rāj, literally, "rule" in Hindustani) was the rule by the British Crown of the Indian subcontinent between 1858 and 1947.

Burocrazy: Slang for bureaucracy and crazy unified. "Bureaucracy" is an idiom that refers to excessive regulation or rigid conformity to formal rules considered redundant or bureaucratic that hinder or prevent action or decision-making.

Bushmen: A collective term use to describe the hundreds, probably thousands, of tribes, which were the only inhabitants of southern Africa until the arrival of more numerous and more centrally organized Bantu peoples from further north.

Bush-packing: A method of fighting soil erosion by packing branches into strategic locations to act as a barrier to water runoff, reducing its velocity, and encouraging sedimentation.

Cabalgata: A multi-day horseback ride.

Chai and Pie: A chain of "pie and chai shops" selling sweet Nepali tea and cakes.

Compañeros: Spanish for "companions" or "comrades." In many Spanish-speaking countries, the word "compañero" is used to refer to someone of equal status, such as a coworker or classmate.

Compay Segundo: Máximo Francisco Repilado Muñoz Telles (November 18, 1907–July 13, 2003), known professionally as "Compay Segundo," was a Cuban trova guitarist, singer, and composer. The Buena Vista Social Club may be my favorite singing group.

Cotuí: A city in the Dominican Republic that is one of the oldest cities of the New World. It is the capital of Sánchez Ramírez Province in the Cibao.

Das Kapital: (German: Capital [3 vol., 1867, 1885, 1894]) one of the major works of the 19th-century economist and philosopher Karl Marx (1818–83), in which he expounded his theory of the capitalist system, its dynamism, and its tendencies toward self-destruction. He described his purpose as laying bare "the economic law of motion of modern society."

Departamento General de Irrigación: Spanish for General Department of Irrigation

Desa: Indonesian word for village community in Java, Bali, or Madura (formerly relatively independent).

Dewi Sri: Or Shridevi (Dewi literally means goddess) (Javanese), Nyai Pohaci Sanghyang Asri (Sundanese) is the Javanese, Sundanese, and Balinese pre-Hindu and pre-Islamic era goddess of rice and fertility, still widely worshipped on the islands of Bali and Java.

Dhana: Or Dāna is a Sanskrit and Pali word that connotes the virtue of generosity, charity, or giving of alms in Indian philosophies.

Dharma: In Hinduism, dharma signifies behaviors that are considered to be in accord with Ṛta (natural order), the order that makes life and universe possible, and that includes duties, rights, laws, conduct, virtues and the "right way of living."

Dizengoff: A business area in the center of Tel Aviv, Israel.

Djarason: Wednesday in Papiamento.

Doms: Keepers of the torch that lights funeral pyres. They stem from the lowest sub-caste, the Harijan, once known as "the untouchables" but later changed by Gandhi, who bestowed the new name, Harijans, which means "people of God."

Dongola Wildlife Sanctuary: Starting in 1918, General Jan Smuts (later Prime Minister of South Africa) and Pol Evans (a botanist), both believers in a holistic approach, were instrumental in purchasing government land to create the Dongola Botanical Reserve. Later, the Dongola Wildlife Sanctuary Act initiated a proposal for a trans-frontier park in 1944 in which 124 farms, 86 of which were privately owned in the northern-most region of Limpopo Province, South Africa, would be converted. The proposal was opposed and debated for years; this "Battle of Dongola" at first approved a trans-frontier park in 1947 but later with a change in government, returned the land to its original owners and abolished the park in 1949. At a later time, this area was partially unified and handed over to the South African National Parks. It later became what is now known as Mapungubwe National Park.

Dusuns: Malay slang for parts of villages and the people who dwell there in rural or mountainous areas.

Dynamo Moscow: Russian football club based in Khimki, Moscow Oblast.

Dzongs (monastery fortresses): A distinctive type of fortress found mainly in Bhutan and the former Tibet.

Ego: A person's sense of self-esteem or self-importance.

El Che: Nickname for Ernesto Guevara Ruiz, an Argentine/Irish Marxist revolutionary, physician, author, guerrilla leader, diplomat, and military theorist. A major figure in Cuba, his stylized visage has become a ubiquitous countercultural symbol of rebellion and a global insignia in popular culture.

El Comandante: Nickname for Fidel Castro, the Cuban revolutionary and politician who governed the Republic of Cuba as Prime Minister from 1959 to 1976 and then as President from 1976 to 2008.

Entebbe: A major town on a peninsula in Lake Victoria, in central Uganda.

Évora: is the capital of Portugal's south-central Alentejo region.

Fever trees: Vachellia xanthophloea is a tree in the Fabaceae family that is native to eastern and southern Africa. The characteristic bark is smooth, powdery, and greenish yellow, although new twigs are purple, flaking later to reveal the characteristic yellow bark.

Freak Street: A small street located at the south of Kathmandu Durbar Square. Freak Street was the epicenter of the "Hippie trail" from the early 1960s to the late 1970s. During that time, the main attraction drawing tourists to Freak Street was the government-run hashish shops. Hippies from different parts of the world traveled to Freak Street (Basantapur) in search of legal cannabis.

Fuku: Word used in Latin America to mean bad luck or a voodoo curse.

Funchi: A Caribbean cornmeal mash similar to grits from the U.S.A., polenta from Italy, or pap from South Africa.

Gabion: A cage, cylinder, or box filled with rocks, concrete, or sometimes sand and soil for use in civil engineering, road building, military applications, and landscaping.

Galungan festival: This is a Balinese holiday celebrating the victory of dharma over adharma. It marks the time when ancestral spirits visit the Earth. The last day of the celebration is Kuningan, when they return. The date is calculated according to the 210-day Balinese calendar. It is similar to Diwali, celebrated by Hindus in other parts of the world.

Gamelan music: The traditional ensemble music of Java and Bali in Indonesia, made up predominantly of percussion instruments.

Gangkhar Puensum: The highest mountain in Bhutan and a strong candidate for the highest unclimbed mountain in the world, with an elevation of 7,570 meters (24,836 ft).

Ganesha (also known as Ganapati and Vinayaka) is one of the best-known and most worshipped deities in the Hindu pantheon.

Gauchitos: A diminutive of gaucho.

Gaucho: Spanish and Portuguese word for a migratory or stationed horseman, a country person, experienced in traditional livestock farming

Gautama Buddha (also known as Siddhārtha Gautama, Shakyamuni Buddha, or simply the Buddha, after the title of Buddha) was an ascetic and philosopher, on whose teachings Buddhism was founded. He is believed to have lived and taught mostly in the eastern part of ancient India sometime between the sixth and fourth centuries BCE.

Gede Aria: Noble name given to Charles Jacobs upon his conversion to Hinduism.

Ghats: A series of steps leading down to a body of water, particularly a holy river.

Gowri Ganesha Festivals: Prominent festivals of Southern India, celebrated with pomp and glory. Also known as Swarna Gowri Vratam, this is an important festival that coincides with the famous Ganesh Chaturthi festival in Karnataka and some parts of Andhra Pradesh. It is observed on the third and fourth day of the Kannada Bhadrapada month; the festival is also known as Gowri Habba.

Grappa Don Bill: Grappa is an alcoholic beverage, a fragrant, grape-based pomace brandy of Italian origin that contains 35–60 percent alcohol by volume. This variation has been named after an active participant in the founding of the Alpasión wine, lodge, and vineyard.

Great Zimbabwe Kingdom: (c. 1220–1450) was a medieval kingdom located in modern-day Zimbabwe.

Greater Mapungubwe Transfrontier Conservation: Known for its dramatic scenery, abundant wildlife, and rich cultural heritage, the area currently being developed as the Greater Mapungubwe Transfrontier Conservation area (5,909km2), brings together three countries (South Africa, Botswana and Zimbabwe) and offers a wide range of attractions.

Green company: A company that claims to acts in a way that minimizes damage to the environment, community, or economy,

Grihastha: This literally means, "being in and occupied with home, family" or "householder." It refers to the second phase of an individual's life in the four age-based stages of the Hindu ashram system.

Gringo or Gringa (female): A term used mainly in Spanish-speaking and Portuguese-speaking countries, to refer to foreigners. The word was originally used in Spain to denote foreign, non-native speakers of Spanish.

Grumeti River: A well-known river that runs through the migration path of ungulates in the Serengeti Reserve.

Guajira (the term means "peasant") is a music genre about peasant topics, derived from the Punto Cuba, the Eastern region of Cuba.

Guantanamera: ("The girl from Guantanamo" in Spanish) is perhaps the best-known Cuban song and the country's most noted patriotic song. A poem by the Cuban poet José Martí inspired the lyrics.

Guayabera: A man's shirt typically distinguished by two vertical rows of closely sewn pleats that run the length of the front and back of the shirt. This shirt is typically worn untucked. Guayaberas are popular in the Caribbean regions of Colombia, Mexico, Ecuador, Venezuela, Central America, the Caribbean, Southeast Asia, and throughout Africa. It is also known as a "Wedding Shirt."

Guerilleros: Referring to members of a guerrilla group in which a small group of combatants such as paramilitary personnel, armed civilians, or irregulars use military tactics including ambushes, sabotage, raids, petty warfare, hit-and-run tactics, and mobility to fight a larger and less-mobile traditional military force.

Gunung Batur: An active volcano located at the center of two concentric calderas north-west of Mount Agung on the island of Bali, Indonesia.

Guru: A Sanskrit term that connotes a "teacher, guide, expert, or master" of a particular field of knowledge.

Habaneros: A variety of chili pepper. Unripe habaneros are green; they change color as they mature. The most common color variants are orange and red, but white, brown, yellow, green, and purple are also seen.

Harijans: ("Person of Hari/Vishnu") is a term popularized by Indian revolutionary leader Mahatma Gandhi, referring to the Dalits, who were traditionally considered Untouchable. The euphemism is now regarded as condescending by many, with some Dalit activists calling it insulting. As a result, the Government of India and several state governments forbid or discourage its use for official purposes.

Harishchandra Ghat: A cremation ghat—smaller and secondary in importance to Manikarnika, but one of the oldest ghats in Varanasi, where Hindus cremate their dead.

Hasta la Victoria, Siempre: ("Ever onward, till victory/until victory, always") : Ché Guevara's famous quote, a rallying cry to encourage people to struggle on to victory and never give up

Hasta Siempre: ("Until always"), farewell.

Hasta Siempre, Comandante (or simply, "Hasta Siempre") is a 1965 song by Cuban composer Carlos Puebla. The song's lyrics are a reply to revolutionary Che Guevara's farewell letter when he left Cuba, aiming to foster revolution in the Congo and later Bolivia, where he was captured and killed. Hasta Siempre literally meaning until always but refers to a way of saying goodbye or farewell. Comadante meaning commander.

Hatha yoga: A branch of yoga that uses physical exercises to master the body along with mind exercises to withdraw it from external objects.

Holistic: The tendency in nature to form wholes that are greater than the sum of the parts through creative evolution; characterized by the belief that the parts of something are intimately interconnected and explicable only by reference to the whole.

Ho'oponopono: An ancient Hawaiian practice of reconciliation and forgiveness. Similar forgiveness practices were performed on islands throughout the South Pacific, including Samoa, Tahiti, and New Zealand.

Hominin: A taxonomical tribe of the subfamily Homininae; it comprises three subtribes: Hominina, with its one genus Homo; Australopithecina, comprising at least three extinct genera; and Panina, with its one genus Pan, the chimpanzees.

Homo Sapiens (Latin: "wise man") is the binomial nomenclature (also known as the scientific name) for the only extant human species.

Hoompah band: Oom-pah, Oompah, or Umpapa is the rhythmical sound of a deep brass instrument in a band, a form of background ostinato.

Hora dancing: also knonw as horo or oro, an Israeli circle dance typically danced to the music of Hava Nagila. It is traditionally danced at Jewish weddings and other joyous occasions in the Jewish community.

Ikan Bumbu Bali: A traditional Balinese spicy fish dish.

Il dolce far niente: Italian for "sweet doing nothing" or "sweet idleness," being lazy.

Indies or East Indies: The islands of Southeast Asia, especially the Malay Archipelago; Dutch-held colonies in the area were known for about 300 years as the Dutch East Indies, before Indonesian independence, while Spanish-held colonies were known as the Spanish East Indies, before the US conquest and later independence of the Philippines.

Ivrit: The Hebrew word for the Hebrew language.

Jainism: Traditionally known as Jain Dharma, this is an ancient Indian religion belonging to the Śramaṇa tradition. The central tenet is non-violence and respect towards all living beings.

Jenever: Also known as genièvre, genever, and peket, this is the juniper-flavored national and traditional liquor of the Netherlands and Belgium, from which gin evolved.

Kalahari TV: Slang for watching a fire for entertainment; when fire-watching and conversation replace TV.

Kama: "Desire, wish, or longing" in Indian literature. Kama often connotes sexual desire and longing in contemporary literature, but the concept refers more broadly to any desire, wish, passion, longing, pleasure of the senses, aesthetic enjoyment of life, affection, or love, with or without sexual connotations.

Kamar Mandi: The Indonesian term for bathroom, combining a toilet with a bathing facility.

Kaoxa Rock Art Shelter: An archeological site in Northern Limpopo in which a rock shelter houses over 190 paintings that contain over 16 different animals from the Khoisan people, also known as Bushmen, dating back over 3,000 years.

Katib: A term used to describe the position of writer, scribe, or secretary in the Arabic-speaking world, Persian World, and other Islamic areas as far as India.

Kepala Desa: A mayor or village manager in Bali.

KhoiSan: People of the Northern Cape are descended from two different tribes. An amalgam of the original San hunter-gatherers and the later-arriving KhoiKhoi, they were virtually annihilated by subsequent settlers. But the Khoisan culture lives on through some of the most compelling rock art on Earth.

KhoKhoi: ("People people" or "real people") or Khoi, spelled Khoekhoe in standardized Khoekhoe/Nama orthography, are a group of Khoisan people native to southwestern Africa. Unlike the neighboring hunter-gatherer San people, the Khoikhoi traditionally practiced nomadic pastoral agriculture.

Khunuseti: Constellations in South Africa, the Stars of Spring, (these coincide with the Pleiades), were the daughters of Tsui (the God of the Dawn and Sky).

Kibbutz: A collective community in Israel that was traditionally based on agriculture.

Kibbutzim: Kibbutz in plural, collective communities in Israel that were traditionally based on agriculture.

Kibbutzniks: members of a kibbutz.

Koppie: Afrikaans for a small hill in a generally flat area.

Kruger Transfrontier: One of the largest game reserves in Africa. It covers an area of 19,485 square kilometres in Limpopo and Mpumalanga provinces in northeastern South Africa.

Kumbha Mela: A mass Hindu pilgrimage of faith in which Hindus gather to bathe in a sacred or holy river. It is considered to be the "world's largest congregation of religious pilgrims."

Kundalini: A Sanskrit term meaning "coiled one." In the concept of Dharma, this refers to a form of primal energy (or shakti) said to be located at the base of the spine.

Kundalini yoga: This school of yoga (also known as laya yoga) is influenced by the Shaktism and Tantra schools of Hinduism. It derives its name from its focus on awakening kundalini energy through the regular practice of meditation, pranayama, chanting mantras, and yoga asana.

Kuningan: A day that marks the end of the Gaungan holiday; it is celebrated every 210 days, ten days after Galungan. The Balinese believe that Kuningan day is when their ancestors return to heaven after visiting the earth during the Galungan celebration.

La Difunta (also known as La Difunta Correa, Deolinda Correa or Dalinda Antonia Correa) is the diseased, semi-pagan mythical figure of Argentina, toward which many people from Argentina, Chile, and Uruguay feel devotion. There is a shrine dedicated to her in the town of Vallecito, in the Argentine province of San Juan, where thousands of believers visit to pay their respects and where miracles are said to have occurred.

La Historia me absolverá: A Spanish sentence meaning "history will absolve me."

Latifundistas: (Latin: lātus, "spacious" + fundus, "farm, estate") A very extensive parcel of privately owned land, or major landlords.

Law of Attraction: The belief that by focusing on positive or negative thoughts, a person brings positive or negative experiences into his or her life.

Lebensraum: German for the territory which a group, state, or nation believes is needed for its natural development; also, Germany from the 1890s to the 1940s. The most extreme form of this ideology was supported by the Nazi Party (NSDAP) during the Third Reich, until the end of World War II.

Liberté égalité fraternité: French for "liberty, equality, fraternity;" this is the national motto of France and the Republic of Haiti, and is an example of a tripartite motto.

London Declaration: An international declaration signed by 46 countries including China, France, Russia, Vietnam, and South Africa, which are committed to tackling illegal wildlife trade and crime.

Lucerne: (also called alfalfa or Medicago sativa) is a perennial flowering plant in the pea family Fabaceae, cultivated as an important forage crop in many countries around the world. It is used for grazing, hay, and silage, and as a green manure and cover crop.

Lucy: The common name of AL 288:1, several hundred pieces of bone fossils representing 40 percent of the skeleton of a female of the hominin species Australopithecus afarensis.

Mahabharata: One of the two major Sanskrit epics of ancient India, the other being the Rāmāyaṇa. The Mahābhārata is an epic narrative of the Kurukṣetra War and the fates of the Kaurava and the Pāṇḍava princes. It also contains philosophical and devotional material, such as a discussion of the four "goals of life" or puruṣārtha (12.161). Among the principal works and stories in the Mahābhārata are the Bhagavadgītā, the story of Damayantī, an abbreviated version of the Rāmāyaṇa, and the story of Ṛṣyasringa, often considered as works in their own right.

Mahāvākyas: (literally, "great sentences") are the "Great Sayings" of the Upanishads, characterized by the Advaita school of Vedanta.

Mahout: An elephant rider, trainer, or keeper.

Makamba: The local equivalent of "gringo" in Curaçao.

Malbec: A purple grape variety used in making red wine.

Manikarnika Ghat: One of the ghats in Varanasi, India; it is known for being a place of Hindu cremation.

Mantra: A sacred utterance, numinous sound, syllable, word, phonemes, or group of words in Sanskrit believed by practitioners to have psychological and spiritual powers. A mantra may or may not have syntactic structure or literal meaning.

Manzana Histórico: An Argentinean town located in the district of Los Chacayes, Tunuyán Department, Province of Mendoza, known for a historic speech given by Jose de San Martin.

Mapesu Private Game Reserve: A 72-square-kilometer private game farm in the northern-most region of Limpopo Province, South Africa. The reserve adjoins the Mapungubwe National Park and World Heritage Site, with which it shares a 12.5 km northern border.

Mapungubwe National Park: A national park in Limpopo Province, South Africa. It is located by the Kolope River, south of the confluence of the Limpopo and Shashe rivers and about 15 km to the northeast of the Venetia Diamond

Mine. It sits on the border with Botswana and Zimbabwe, and forms part of the Greater Mapungubwe Transfrontier Conservation Area. It was established in 1995 and covers an area of over 28 000 hectares.

Mara River: A river in Mara Region, Tanzania and Narok County, Kenya; it lies across the migration path of ungulates in the Serengeti/Masai Mara game reserves.

Maslow pyramid (also known as the Maslow hierarchy of needs): A theory in psychology proposed by Abraham Maslow in his 1943 paper "A Theory of Human Motivation" in *Psychological Review*. His motivational theory in psychology comprises a five-tier model of human needs, often depicted as hierarchical levels within a pyramid, using the terms "physiological," "safety," "belonging" and "love," "esteem," "self-actualization," and "self-transcendence" to describe the pattern that human motivations generally move through.

Masse de manoeuvre: Mass of maneuver in French or operating mass.

Médecins Sans Frontières: (also known as Doctors Without Borders) is an international humanitarian non-governmental organization (NGO) best known for its projects in war-torn regions and developing countries affected by endemic disease.

Mentalidad di cangrew: Papiameno for the mentality of a crab, "Crab mentality," sometimes called "cubo de congrejos" or "crab crate" or in Spanish mentalidad de cangrejo, describes a way of thinking that is best described as follows: "if I cannot, then you cannot either." The metaphor refers to a bucket or crate of crabs. Individually, each crab could easily escape from the bucket. In a group, they hold a futile competition to see who can climb on top of the rest, which makes them unable to escape and ensures their collective death. The analogy with human behavior is that members of a group attempt to deny or diminish the importance of any member who achieves success beyond the rest, through feelings of envy, conspiracy, or competition.

Modus operandi: Referring to someone's habits of working, particularly in the context of business, as well as more generally. It is a Latin phrase, loosely translated as method or mode of operation.

Moksha: A Sanskrit term (also vimoksha, vimukti and mukti/mukhti) in Hinduism and Hindu philosophy that refers to various forms of emancipation, liberation, and release. In its soteriological and eschatological senses, it refers to freedom from saṃsāra, the cycle of death and rebirth.

Moncada attack (also known as the Moncada Barracks): A military barracks in Santiago de Cuba, named after General Guillermón Moncada, a hero of the War of Independence. On July 26, 1953, this barracks was the site of an armed attack by a small group of revolutionaries led by Fidel Castro. The armed attack is widely accepted as the beginning of the Cuban Revolution. The date on which the attack took place, July 26th, was adopted by Castro as the name for his revolutionary movement (Movimiento 26 Julio or M 26:7) which eventually toppled the dictatorship of Fulgencio Batista in 1959.

Mopane tree: Commonly called mopane, mophane, mopani, balsam tree, butterfly tree, or turpentine tree, the mopane is a tree in the legume family (Fabaceae), which grows in hot, dry, low-lying areas, 200 to 1,150 meters (660 to 3,770 ft) in elevation, in the far northern parts of southern Africa. The tree only occurs in Africa and is the only species in genus Colophospermum. Its distinctive, butterfly-shaped (bifoliate) leaves and thin seed pods make it easy to identify. In terms of human use, it is, together with camel thorn and leadwood, one of the three regionally important firewood trees. Mopane twigs have traditionally been used as toothbrushes, the bark to make twine and for tanning, and the leaves for healing wounds. The wood is also used to make charcoal and for braai wood. The tree is a major food source for the mopane worm, the caterpillar of the moth Gonimbrasia belina. These caterpillars are rich in protein and eaten by people.

Mount Agung (or Gunung Agung) is a volcano in Bali, Indonesia.

Mount Kilimanjaro: With its three volcanic cones, "Kibo," "Mawenzi," and "Shira," Kilimanjaro is a dormant volcano in Tanzania. It is the highest mountain in Africa, rising approximately 4,900 m (16,000 ft) from its base to 5,895 metres (19,341 ft) above sea level.

Mrs. Ples: (Australopithecus Africanus), is the popular nickname for the most complete skull of an Australopithecus Africanus ever found in South Africa.

Mujahedin (variants include Mujahedeen, Mujahideen, Mudjahidin, and Mogahidin)" The plural of mujahed. The root word comes from the same Arabic triliteral root as jihad ("struggle"). Mujahedin or Mujahedeen are terms used to describe Muslims who struggle on the path of Allah. In recent years, Mujahideen have been most closely associated by the West with radical Islam, encompassing several militant jihadist groups and struggles.

Muktha: or mukta, a sanscrit word referring to release, liberation and freed. Mukta often refers to spiritual liberation.

Museum Kurá Hulanda: Located on the island of Curaçao is a 19th-century merchant house and slave quarters that has been converted into a museum documenting the brutal history of slavery in the New World, including the slave trade, slave culture and abolition. "Kurá" meaning garden or courtyard and "Hulanda" meaning Holland in Papiamento.

Mycorrhizal networks: A collaborative connection between a plant and a fungus, which exchange photo-synthetically derived carbon for scarce resources, including nitrogen and phosphorus.

Nirvana (in Buddhism): a transcendent state in which there is neither suffering, desire, nor sense of self, and the subject is released from the effects of karma and the cycle of death and rebirth. It represents the final goal of Buddhism. In Indian religions, nirvana is synonymous with moksha and mukti. All Indian religions assert it to be a state of perfect quietude, freedom, and highest happiness. It also represents liberation from samsara, the repeating cycle of birth, life, and death.

Northern Sotho: Sesotho sa Leboa (also known by the name of its standardized dialect as Sepedi or Pedi) is a Bantu language spoken primarily in South Africa, where it is one of 11 official languages.

Nos mes por: Papiamento for "Yes we can."

Num: Trance-like state that converts a person into a spiritually potent animal in the spiritual world in which the KhoiSan people reach spiritual awakening.

Nyepi: A public holiday in Indonesia. It is a day of silence, fasting, and meditation for the Balinese, originating from Hinduism. It is commemorated every Isakawarsa (Saka New Year) according to the Balinese calendar. The Balinese saka calendar is one of two calendars used on the Indonesian island of Bali. Unlike the 210-day pawukon calendar, it is based on the phases of the moon, and is approximately the same length as the Gregorian year.

Ogoh-ogoh: Statues built for the Ngrupuk parade, which takes place on the eve of Nyepi day in Bali, Indonesia. Ogoh-ogoh usually represent mythological beings, mostly demons. As with many creative endeavours based on Balinese Hinduism, the creation of ogoh-ogoh reflects spiritual aims inspired by Hindu philosophy.

Old Transvaal: An independent Boer Republic until 1902. In 1910, it combined with three British colonies to form the Union of South Africa. Half a century later, in 1961, the union ceased to be part of the Commonwealth of Nations and became the Republic of South Africa. The PWV (Pretoria-Witwatersrand-Vereeniging) conurbation in the Transvaal, centered on Pretoria and Johannesburg, became South Africa's economic powerhouse, a position it still holds today as Gauteng province.

Operation Litani: In retaliation for the PLO terrorist attack four days earlier, on March 11, 1978, Israel launched Operation Litani and invaded Lebanon with a force of 25,000 men. The purpose of the operation was to push PLO positions away from the border and to bolster the power of the South Lebanon Army. The Israel Defense Forces first seized a security belt about ten kilometers deep, and then pushed north and captured all of Lebanon south of the Litani River, inflicting thousands of casualties.

Padmasambhava (also known as Guru Rinpoche) was an 8th-century Indian Buddhist master. Although there was a historical Padmasambhava, nothing is known of him apart from the fact that he participated in the construction of the first Buddhist monastery in Tibet at Samye, at the behest of Trisong Detsen, and shortly thereafter left Tibet due to court intrigues.

Pagara: A Curaçao New Year's Eve celebration with fireworks. The aim is to chase away the the fuku (bad luck) from the year before.

Paladar: A term that, in Spanish, translates literally as "palatal" and used to convey that meaning in the Spanish-speaking world. However, in Cuba it is used exclusively to describe restaurants run by self-employed people.

Pampas: A South American grassland biome. These are flat, fertile plains that cover an area of 777,000 square kilometers, from the Atlantic Ocean to the Andes Mountains.

Pap: A South African cornmeal mash similar to grits from the U.S.A., polenta from Italy, or funchi from the Caribbean.

Papiamento (or Papiamentu) is the most widely-spoken language on Aruba, Curaçao, and Bonaire, having official status in Aruba and Curaçao. The language is also recognized on Bonaire by the Dutch government.

Parikrma Foundation: A non-profit organization located in Bangalore, India, which addresses the growing gap in urban India between those benefitting from economic liberalization and those who are not; only a minority of children in India can afford access to private schools offering high quality education in English.

Partisipashon di morto: A daily television program announcing who has died and where funerals will be held in Curaçao.

Pastechi: An Antillean meat turnover pastry.

Pauschalbesteuerung: Concessionary flat rate taxation (Swiss German).

Pemangku: A Balinese priest, guardian, overseer, or priest—the person responsible for meeting the needs of a temple and its congregation.

Penyors: Beautifully decorated symbolic bamboo poles placed in front of houses, roads, and alters in Bali.

Pepuun: Balinese for a shrine.

Ploppers: A Dutch nickname given to Indonesians who fought for independence from the Netherlands in the 1940s.

Pole-Pole: Swahili for slowly, gently, softly, quietly: be calm, take it easy.

Pranayama: The formal practice of controlling the breath, which is the source of our prana, or vital life force.

Pujas (or Poojan): a prayer ritual performed by Hindus to host, honor, and worship one or more deities, or to spiritually celebrate an event.

Puputan: A Balinese term for mass ritual suicide when faced with humiliation or surrender.

Pura Dalem: A temple associated with sacrificing to the dead and to the land. Temple of death.

Pura Puseh (or "navel temple"): A temple associated with the ultimate origin of the village, with land, and with harvest rituals. A typically Balinese village has three village temples that symbolize life. The origin is associated with with the pura puseh (navel temple), where the guardians of the village and the creators are worshipped.

Purusartha: Four aims of life. This is a key concept in Hinduism; it refers to the four proper goals or aims of a human life. The four puruṣārthas are Dharma (righteousness, moral values), Artha (prosperity, economic values), Kāma (pleasure, love, psychological values), and Mokṣa (liberation, spiritual values).

Quechua language: An Amerind language spoken by about 8 million people in Bolivia, Peru, Ecuador, Colombia, and Argentina. Quechua was the language of the Inca Empire, which was destroyed by the Spanish in the 16th century.

Raid on Entebbe: A 1976 movie based on a real Israeli commando assault on the Entebbe Airport in Uganda to free hostages of a terrorist hijacking.

Ram naam satya hai: "The name of Rama is the truth;" in Hindi, this prayer is chanted during a funeral procession to the cremation site.

Recorrida: To travel, visit, or tour in Spanish.

Respekt: Papiamento for respect.

Rhizomorphs: An interconnected, underground, fungal root system, like a filament system.

Riksha (rickshaw): A light two- or three-wheeled passenger vehicle drawn by one or more people, chiefly used in Asian countries.

Robustos: Cigars with the following dimensions: 5x50 centimeters

Rondavels: A round native hut of southern Africa usually made of mud and having a thatched roof of grass.

Sadhana: A Sanskrit word for a spiritual practice or discipline leading to a goal.

Sadhu: A Sankrit word for holy man.

Safari: An expedition to observe or hunt animals in their natural habitat, especially in Africa.

Sannyasa: The life stage of renunciation within the Hindu philosophy of four age-based life stages known as ashramas, with the first three being Brahmacharya (bachelor student), Grihastha (householder) and Vanaprastha (forest dweller, retired).

Sanskrit: An Indo-European, Indic language, in use since c. 1200 BCE as the religious and classical literary language of India.

Satyagraha: A Sanskrit word loosely translated as "insistence on truth", "loyalty ot the truth" or "devotion to truth," remaining firm on the truth and resisting untruth actively but nonviolently.

Saudade: (in Portuguese folk culture) a deep emotional state of melancholic longing for a person or thing that is absent

Sawahs: A wet or irrigated rice field in Indonesia.

Shabbat: Also known as "Shabbos" or the "Sabbath," this is the Hebrew day of rest and celebration that begins on Friday at sunset and ends on the following evening after nightfall.

Shamshaan: A Hindu cremation ground.

Shamshaan ghat: The steps of a Hindu cremation ground.

Shoah: The Second World War Holocaust.

Shons: A Papiamento word for slave owners.

Sicarii: A splinter group of Jewish Zealots who, in the decades preceding Jerusalem's destruction in 70 CE, heavily opposed the Roman occupation of Judea and attempted to expel the Romans and their sympathizers from the area.

Sneks: An outdoor bar serving snack foods, meals, and drinks in Curaçao.

Soto Ayam: A popular yellow spicy chicken dumpling soup with vermicelli or egg noodles, commonly found in Indonesia, Singapore, Malaysia, and Suriname.

Spitsbergen: The largest and only permanently populated island of the Svalbard archipelago in northern Norway.

Sundowner: In colloquial British English, an alcoholic drink taken after completing the day's work, usually at sundown.

Syncerus caffer: The African buffalo or Cape buffalo is a large African bovine.

Tambú: (also tambbú), is a drum, music genre and dance form, found on the islands of Aruba, Bonaire, and Curaçao; it is a major feature of Dutch Antillean music.

Tango: A partner dance that originated in the 1880s along the River Plate, the natural border between Argentina and Uruguay, and soon spread to the rest of the world.

Tantra: A Sanskrit word meaning the warp of a loom or the strands of a braid; it is related to the concept of weaving and expansion. It derives from "tan," meaning to expand, spin out, and weave; to stretch or to continue without a break.

Tat Tvam Asi: A Sanskrit phrase, translated variously as "Thou art that," (That thou art, That art thou, You are that, That you are, or You're it). It is one of the Mahāvākyas (Grand Pronouncements) in Vedantic Sanatana Dharma.

Thirstlands: A large arid area.

Tiger's Nest: Also known as Paro Taktsang or Taktsang Palphug Monastery; it is a prominent Himalayan Buddhist sacred site. The temple complex is located in the cliffside of the upper Paro valley in Bhutan.

Tsa-tsas: A form of sacred art sculptures found in all of the various lineages of Himalayan Buddhism. They are small reliquaries containing ashes of the dead, placed in caves or other sacred places.

Tuma Mi Man (also known as Fundashon (Foundation) Tuma mi Man, created in 2008): An Amicorp effort to give something back to society and to provide affordable, qualitative daycare to the children of Curaçao.

Vanaprastha: Part of the Vedic ashram system, which starts when a person hands over household responsibilities to the next generation, takes an advisory role, and gradually withdraws from the world, The stage of being retired, a coach, teacher, or helper, who helps others become successful.

Vedantic Dharma: The Vedas are a large body of knowledge texts originating in the ancient Indian subcontinent. Composed in Vedic Sanskrit, the texts constitute the oldest layer of Sanskrit literature and the oldest scriptures of Hinduism.

Vegas Robaina: Vegas Robaina is the name of a premium cigar brand, produced on the island of Cuba for Habanos SA, the Cuban state-owned tobacco company. It is the second of two new lines introduced by Habanos S.A. in the 1990s. This line was officially launched in Spain, in the spring of 1997. Vegas Robaina is named after D. Alejandro Robaina, who is famed for growing the finest wrappers in the Vuelta Abajo, (Pinar del Rio), region of Cuba for more than fifty years. The cigars are made from the best tobacco in Cuba, and feature wrappers grown on Sr. Robaina's farms. They are described as a medium-strong blend, characterized by an excellent aroma, wonderful presentation, and a fine burn.

Wega di number: A TV show in Curaçao in which lottery numbers are drawn.

Wildebeest (also called gnu) is a genus of antelopes, with the scientific name, Connochaetes. They belong to the family Bovidae, which includes antelopes, cattle, goats, sheep, and other even-toed horned ungulates. The Wildebeest Migration is one of the "Seven New Wonders of the World" and is also known as The World Cup of Wildlife.

Wuku: A Balinese year. Bali has two calendars, the wuku or pawukon, which was used by the Bali Aga, and the saka calendar, which was imported from India during the Majapahit Empire. The wuku calendar has a 210-day cycle and is based on the cycles of the moon.

Yad Vashem: Israel's official memorial to the victims of the Holocaust.

Yagnas: Literally, "sacrifice, devotion, worship, offering." In Hinduism to any ritual done in front of a sacred fire, often with mantras.

Yeh Mampeh: "Flying water" in Balinese, the name for one of Bali's highest waterfalls (40m) in the northern part of Bali.

Yogi: (sometimes spelled jogi), a practitioner of yoga.

Yu d'i Kòrsou: The literal translation is "Child of Curaçao," but the term refers to someone born on Curaçao in Papiamento.

Zakah: One of the five pillars of Islamic belief, based on the notion that all wealth belongs to Allah and we merely act as his trustees. It is almsgiving, the obligatory contribution of a certain portion of one's wealth in support of the poor or needy or for other charitable purposes, considered as one of the duties of Islamic religious practice.

Bibliography

Albion, M. (2006). True to yourself: *Leading a Values-based Business*. San Francisco, CA, USA: Berrett-Koehler Publishers, Inc.

Axelrod, A. (2010). Gandhi, CEO, *14 principles to guide and inspire modern leaders*. New York: Sterling Publishing Co., Inc.

Baggini, J. (2004). *What's it all about?* Philosophy and the Meaning of Life. London, UK: Oxford University Press.

Baghai, M., and Quigley, J. (2011). *As one, Individual Action Collective Power*. London, UK: Penguin Books, Inc.

Buffett, Howard G. (2013). *Forty Chances: Finding Hope in a Hungry World*. New York, NY, USA: Simon and Schuster.

Covey, S. R. (2006). *The Speed of Trust: the One Thing that Changes Everything*. New York, NY, USA: Simon and Schuster.

Crosbie, A. (2004). *Don't leave it to the children: Starting, building, and sustaining a Family Business*. Mumbai, India: Corpus Collossum Learning.

Cutteridge, Lee. (2008). *The Bushveld, a South African Field Guide*. Pinetown, Republic of South Africa: 30 degrees South Publishers (Pty) Ltd.

Debroy, B. (2011). *The Mahabharata*. New Delhi, India: Penguin Books.

Dreher, D. (2000). *The Tao of Inner Peace*. London, UK: Penguin Books.

Dyer, W. W. (2009). *Excuses Begone: How to Change Lifelong, Self-Defeating Thinking Habits*. Carlsbad, CA, USA: Hay House, Inc.

Eastwood, Edward and Catelijne (2006). *Capturing the Spoor: An exploration of southern African rock art*. Cape Town, Republic of South Africa: New Africa Books (Pty) Ltd.

Forssman, Tim and Gutteridge, Lee. (2012). *Bushman Rock Art: An interpretative Guide*. Pinetown, Republic of South Africa: 30 degrees South Publishers (Pty) Ltd.

Friedman, T. L. (2007). *The World is Flat: A Brief History of the 21st Century*. New York, NY, USA: Picador, USA.

Gladwell, M. (2008). Outliers, *The Story of Success*. London, UK: Penguin Books.

Glassman, S. A. (2010). *It's about more than the money: Investment Wisdom for Building a Better Life*. Upper Saddle River, NJ, USA: Pearson Education, Inc.

Godin, S. (2008). *Tribes, We need YOU to lead us*. New York, NY, USA: Penguin Group.

Guevara, Che (2003). *The Motorcycle Diaries, Notes on a Latin American journey*. North Melbourne, Australia: Ocean Press.

Hagstrom, R. G. (1994). *The Warren Buffett Way: Investment Strategies of the World's Greatest Investor*. New York, NY, USA: John Wiley and Sons, Inc.

Haidt, J. (2006). *The Happiness Hypothesis: Finding Modern Truth in Ancient Wisdom*. Cambridge, MA, USA: Perseus Books Group.

Harari, Yuval Noah. (2015). Sapiens: *A brief history of humankind*. New York, NY. USA: HarperCollins Publishers.

Henshilwood, Christopher S. and d'Errico, Francesco. (2011). *Homo Symbolicus: The dawn of language, imagination and spirituality*. Amsterdam, the Netherlands: John Benjamins B.V.

Kakar, S. (2011). *The essential Sudhir Kakar*. New Delhi, India: Oxford University Press.

Kalanithi, Paul (2016). *When breath becomes air*. London, UK: Penguin Random House UK.

Kets de Vries, M. F. (2009). *Sex, Money, Happiness, and Death: the quest for authenticity.* London, UK: Palgrave Macmillan.

Kets de Vries, M. F. (2011). *Reflections on Groups and Organizations.* Chichester, UK: John Wiley and Sons, Ltd.

Kets de Vries, Manfred. (2016). *You will meet a tall, dark stranger: Executive coaching challenges.* London, UK: Palgrave MacMillan.

Kim, W. C., and Mauborgne, R. (2005). *Blue Ocean Strategy: How to Create Uncontested Market Space and Make the Competition Irrelevant.* Boston, MA, USA: Harvard Business School Publishing Corporation.

Lama, T. D. (2009). *Becoming Enlightened.* London, UK: Random House Group Limited.

Levy, Patrick (2010). *Sadhus: Going beyond the Dreadlocks.* India: Prakash Books India Pvt. Ltd.

Lipton, B. H. (2005). *The Biology of Belief: Unleashing the Power of Consciousness, Matter and Miracles.* USA: Hay House Inc.

Logan, D., and King, J. (2008). *Tribal Leadership: Leveraging Natural Groups to Build a Thriving Organization.* New York, NY, USA: Harper Business.

Mashruwala, Gaurav. (2015). *Yogic Wealth: The wealth that gives Bliss!* Mumbai, India: TV 18 Broadcast Ltd.

Millman, D. (2006). *Wisdom of the Peaceful Warrior: A companion to the book that changes lives.* Tiburon, CA, USA: New World Library.

Mutwa, Vusamazulu Credo. (1964). *Indaba, My children, African Tribal History, Legends, Customs and Religious Beliefs.* Cape Town, Republic of South Africa: Blue Crane Books.

Norbeerg-Hodge, H. (2009). *Ancient Futures: Lessons from Ladakh for a globalizing world.* San Francisco, CA, USA: Sierra Club Books.

Obama, B. (1995). *Dreams from My Father*. New York, NY, USA: Three Rivers Press.

Osho. (2001). *Zen: the path of paradox*. New York, NY, USA: St. Martin's Griffin.

Peirce, Richard. (2013). *The Poacher's Moon: A true story of life, death, love and survival in Africa*. Cape Town, Republic of South Africa: random House Struik (Pty) Ltd.

Pfeffer, Jeffrey (1998). *The Human Equation: Building Profits by putting people first*. Boston, Massachusetts, USA: Harvard Business School Press.

Rothschild, B. (2000). *The Body Remembers: The Psychophysiology of Trauma and Trauma Treatment*. Los Angeles, CA, USA: W.W. Norton and Company.

Ruiz, D. M. (1997). *The Four Agreements: A Toltec Wisdom Book*. San Rafael, CA, USA: Amber-Allen Publishing.

Safina, Carl. (2015). Beyond Words: *What Animals Think and Feel*. New York, NY, USA: Henry Holt and Company, LLC.

Sanyal, Sanjeev. (2013). *Land of the Seven Rivers: A Brief History of India's Geography*. Gurgaon, India: Penguin Random House.

Siegel, Daniel J. (2017). *Mind: A journey to the heart of being human*. New York, NY, USA: W.W. Norton and Company, Inc.

Smith, H. W. (2000). *What Matters Most: The Power of Living Your Values*. New York, NY, USA: Simon and Schuster, Inc.

Stengel, R. (2010). *Mandela's Way: Lessons on Life*. London, UK: Random House Inc.

Stoute, Kees, (2015), *Help, I'm Rich: your compass to a value-adding private banking experience,* Singapore, John Wiley and Sons Pte. Ltd.

Swass, Joachim. (2011). *Wise Wealth, Creating it—the Entrepreneur, Managing it—the Family Business, Preserving it—The family Office*. London, UK: Palgrave MacMillan.

Tolle, Eckhart. (2005). *A new Earth: Create a better Life*. London, UK: Penguin Books Ltd.

Tutu, D. (2011). *God is not a Christian*. Chatham, UK: Random House Group Limited.

Van As, Jo (2012). *The Story of Life and the Environment: an African perspective*. Cape Town, South Africa: Random House Struik (Pty) Ltd.

Walker, Clive and Anton. (2012). *The Rhino Keepers: Struggle for Survival*. Auckland Park, Republic of South Africa: Jacana Media (Pty) Ltd.

Wucker, Michele. (2016). *The Gray Rhino, How to recognize and act on obvious dangers we ignore*. New York, NY, USA: St. Martin's Press.

Wynn, Thomas and Coolidge, Frederick L. (2012). *How to Think like a Neandertal*. New York, NY, USA: Oxford University press, Inc.

Yunus, M. (2010). *Building Social Business: The new kind of capitalism that serves Humanity's most pressing needs*. Philadelphia, PA, USA: Public Affairs.

Printed in the United States
By Bookmasters